Edinburgh German Yearbook

Edinburgh German Yearbook

General Editor: Peter Davies

Edinburgh German Yearbook

Volume 11

Love, Eros, and Desire in Contemporary German-Language Literature and Culture

Edited by
Helmut Schmitz and Peter Davies

CAMDEN HOUSE
Rochester, New York

First published 2017
by Camden House

Camden House is an imprint of Boydell & Brewer Inc.
668 Mt. Hope Avenue, Rochester, NY 14620, USA
www.camden-house.com
and of Boydell & Brewer Limited
PO Box 9, Woodbridge, Suffolk IP12 3DF, UK
www.boydellandbrewer.com

ISSN: 1937-0857
ISBN-13: 978-1-57113-978-8
ISBN-10: 1-57113-978-8

This publication is printed on acid-free paper.
Printed in the United States of America.

Edinburgh German Yearbook appears annually.
Please send orders and inquiries to Boydell & Brewer at the above address.

Edinburgh German Yearbook does not accept unsolicited submissions: a
Call for Papers for each volume is circulated widely in advance of publication.
For editorial correspondence, please contact either the General Editor,
Professor Peter Davies, or the editor(s) of individual volumes, by post at:

Edinburgh German Yearbook
German Section
Division of European Languages and Cultures
59 George Square, Edinburgh, EH8 3JX
United Kingdom

or by email at: egyb@ed.ac.uk.

Contents

Introduction: Love, Literature, (Post-)Modernity: On the Re-Emergence of Love in Contemporary German Literature

Helmut Schmitz, University of Warwick

> *I've looked at love from both sides now*
> *From give and take*
> *And still somehow*
> *It's love's illusions I recall*
> *I really don't know love at all*
>
> —Joni Mitchell

IN HIS ESSAY "On Some Motifs in Baudelaire," Walter Benjamin comments on the concept of experience in Bergson's *Matière et Memoire* that the reader "is bound to conclude that only a poet can be the adequate subject of such an experience."[1] One is tempted to make a similar claim with respect to the phenomenon of love. While it would be foolish to claim that only a poet might be an adequate subject for the experience of love, it is certainly possible to say that s/he might be the adequate subject to give voice to this experience. In other words, it is poetry, or literature in general, that is perceived as the "adequate" form of expression of love's qualities. From the Middle Ages to the middle of the nineteenth century, literature is the dominant medium through which ideas and experiences of love find expression, at first through poetry, and, in the bourgeois age over the last two centuries, increasingly through fiction. Niels Werber points to the historically shared semantics between the terms "love" and "novel": "Der Roman handelt also von der Liebe, aber auch umgekehrt bezeichnet man Liebesabenteuer als 'Roman.' Gattung und Sujet sind derart verknüpft, dass der Begriff 'Roman' beide zu bezeichnen vermag."[2] Describing literary representations and literature on love as a "model" for lovers in society, Elke Reinhardt-Becker claims that love is the favorite topic of literature.[3] Matthias Luserke-Jacqui comments at the end of his *Kleine Literaturgeschichte der großen Liebe*: "Liebe braucht Literatur."[4]

The historical, literary, and social field of love is too vast to be adequately summarized here; this introduction will therefore cast a light on a number of issues addressed by the chapters in this volume without attempting to be exhaustive. In the first instance, it is worth noting that the fields of literature, culture, and social theory are closely intertwined when it comes to the phenomenon of love, as a number of sociotheoretical studies either take their cue entirely from literary works or closely refer to literary or cultural models for their formation of central concepts. Secondly, and despite the fact that over the past fifty years social developments have vastly changed the way intimate emotions are both represented and discursified, the contemporary landscape of love and desire would not be understandable without a historical context, as images of love both in high and popular culture feed off historic and historically variable models of romance. As literature and love are, historically speaking, coterminous, a brief historical outlook is also necessary to contextualize contemporary problems. In what follows, I therefore will first outline a brief overview of the sociohistorical role of love in Western discourse as conceptualized by the major historical and social theories of the last forty years, before moving to the field of literature proper. What will emerge is a series of paradoxes with respect to the position of love both in modernity and postmodernity, as well as in literature and its relation to the problems of modernity.

Love, Romance, Desire: The Socio-Historical Picture

Love is as central to the culture of modernity as technology, rationalization, and industrialization. Indeed, it is only in relation to the rationalizing processes of modernity and their influence on the individual that love acquires its central importance for the individual in Western culture. Both social theory and literary studies largely agree on the emergence of the social and literary codes of modern romantic passion at the end of the eighteenth century as a result of the increasing differentiation and fragmentation of social roles in the transformation from a feudal to a bourgeois society.[5] This transformation results in an increasing dislocation of the subject, which is split into a diversity of social roles and responsibilities. In this insecure environment in which the subject's relation to the world is no longer given, and where the subject increasingly has to constitute his/her own world out of his/her biography, romantic love acquires a compensatory function insofar as it promises affirmation and recognition of the whole social person in an exclusive interpersonal relationship: "Our insecurities are healed, our importance guaranteed, only when we become the object of love."[6] As a result of these changes, ideas of romantic love in the nineteenth century influence the development of a conception of marriage that combines love and sexuality, as well as the idea of equality between partners due to the romantic ideal of free object choice:[7] "The complex of ideas associated with romantic love for the first time associated love with freedom, both being seen as normatively desirable states. . . . Ideals of romantic love . . . inserted themselves directly into the emergent ties between freedom and self-realisation."[8] Romantic love is thus an essentially "modern" phenomenon, insofar as the idea of love becomes essential to the biographical narrative of the modern subject; the "process of the capturing of the heart of the other" in romantic love is "in fact a process of the creation of a mutual narrative biography."[9]

In his influential study *Love as Passion*, Niklas Luhmann analyzes love as a medium of communication that encourages the formation of intimate emotions for the reproduction of intimacy.[10] For Luhmann, love is less an emotion than a symbolic code with the purpose of making an otherwise unlikely form of communication—the intimate understanding between two subjects with exclusive communicative expectations towards one another—successful. Distinguishing between two mutually exclusive codes, the French "amour passion" and the English model of love as "companionship" (for which Jane Austen's novels are seen as the prime exponent), it is the first that becomes dominant in modernity because only "amour passion" is capable of integrating the enhanced status of sexuality that romantic love encompasses.[11]

The problem that arises for Luhmann out of this constellation, however, is that both the individual person and the semantic code of love are increasingly overburdened over the course of the development of modern society. Because each modern individual is essentially looking for affirmation in relation to his/her own difference to society, the romantic other is burdened with the task of featuring in the world of the subject as someone who affirms that subjective world. This creates the paradox that each subject is pushed by the other into the role of "affirmer of a particular world."[12] To put it more simply, each subject is required to play in the world of the other the role of object. The codes of love thus create a "two-world-problem" where each partner is animated by the question: "is your partner acting in a way which is based on your (and not his) world?" The chance of a successful lovers' communication is thus a "quite normal improbability."[13]

A number of social theorists follow Luhmann's assessment of the overburdening of romantic discourse as a result of the functional diversification of society and the ensuing pressures on the subject. Werber argues that the sociological research of the last two hundred years is dominated by ascertaining the "kompensatorische, dialektische oder therapeutische Funktion der Liebessemantik für die Modernisierung der Gesellschaft."[14] Ulrich Beck and Elisabeth Beck-Gernsheim, Mary Evans, and, most recently, Eva Illouz all testify to the increasing improbability of a suc-cessful romantic relationship in modernity in general and in the contem-porary in particular.[15] As a response to the differentiation of society in modernity, love, in these theories, is increasingly bound up with failure, unhappiness, and dissatisfaction, due to the impossibility of realizing its promises in the everyday.

Moreover, in the first half of the twentieth century, and with the development of mass media and mass entertainment, the discourse of love, romance, and fulfillment undergoes a commercialization and com-modification. Illouz has described romantic love as an ideology that reinforces central ideological aspects of industrial capitalism such as indi-vidualism, privacy, and the nuclear family. The "romanticization of com-modities and the commodification of romance" creates an intersection of romance and capitalism in which "the experience of romantic love was translated into economic practices and . . ., in turn, economic practices were translated into a structure of feeling." As a result, "the meaning of romance became enmeshed with that of consumption."[16] In the increas-ing secularization of modern society, love and romance become glorified as "supreme value" and acquire a quasi-religious, utopian status.[17]

While love, and particularly romance, enters the discourses of adver-tisement, Hollywood entertainment, and mass literature in the form of "romances," it plays a lesser and lesser role in serious literature. The more modern high culture represents the negative or critical aspects of love, the more its ideal aspects are pushed into popular and trivial culture and into the culture industry, the Hollywood film, pop music, and cheap literature of the "Mills and Boon" kind.[18] In the lower depths of the culture indus-try the ideal aspects of love wholly deteriorate into ideology.

In the second half of the twentieth century, Western culture under-goes an unparalleled liberalization of the social structures of intimacy. The last forty years have seen a "radicalization of freedom and equality within the romantic bond," from the uncoupling of love and sexuality, to the development of different models of cohabitation, to the increasing social and cultural acceptance of non-heteronormative forms of intimacy and sexuality, homosexuality, and LGBTQA.[19] In contrast to the nine-teenth century, where a combination of love and sexuality is central to the development of romantic love and marriage, the second half of the twentieth century sees an increasing de-coupling of love and sexuality. Anthony Giddens notes an "extended variety of sexual activities in which most people either engage or deem it appropriate for others to participate in."[20] Giddens coins the term "plastic sexuality" to denote an increasing sexual freedom and tolerance, a liberation from male sexual experience in which sexuality is "made accessible to the development of a variety of life-styles."[21] Noting that pressures of female emancipation and auton-omy have fragmented ideals of romantic love, he argues that romantic love is giving way to what he calls "confluent love": confluent love "is active, contingent love, and therefore jars with the 'for-ever,' 'one-and-only' qualities of the romantic love complex."[22] The contemporary era is thus characterized by a democratization of both the private sphere and of personal life; this causes a transformation of the ideals of romance into "pure relationships" where relationships are becoming fundamentally contractual: "social relation is entered for its own sake, for what can be derived by each person from a sustained association with another; and which is continued only insofar as it is thought by both parties to deliver enough satisfactions for each individual to stay within it."[23] This liberalization of forms of intimacy results in relationships acquiring an increasingly contractual status where partners negotiate the conditions of their relationship for their mutual benefit. In addition, Evans, following Judith Butler, stresses the essentially performative nature of codes of love and desire both with respect to gender, sexuality, and sexual identity.[24] While models of romantic love continue to exist, the founding of intimate relationships on "contractual assumptions," together with the commercialization of images of intimacy over the past decades makes ideas of romance appear increasingly both outdated, unrealistic, and risible. One result of this is that, in a field where freedom with respect to partner choice leads to an increasing arbitrariness, the romantic notion of a "special" partner becomes difficult to maintain. The continued existence of this romantic paradigm, however, in the absence of its social viability leads to an increasing sense of irony towards romantic models in the post-modern era. One reason for the increasingly ironic stance of our era towards romantic models of love is their deconstruction by the leading discourses of modernity.

Love and the Discourses of Modernity

Whereas modern literature increasingly either exits from the representation of love and intimacy or represents its failure, and the mass media, identifying love exclusively with romance, turn romance into a capitalist consumerist utopia, the leading discourses of modernity—philosophy, psychoanalysis, science, and social theory—subject love to an increasing rationalization. With respect to the leading discourses of modernity, Roland Barthes notes already in 1977 that the lover's discourse is "spoken, perhaps, by thousands of subjects . . . but defended by no one, it is completely forsaken by the surrounding languages: ignored, disparaged, or derided by them."[25] This position is complemented by Illouz's 2012 study *Why Love Hurts*, which argues that the rationalist discourses of twentieth-century hypermodernity have all but emptied out the semantic codes of romance that have been a central aspect of bourgeois modernity since the late eighteenth century. One of the main reasons for this is that, deemed a fundamentally irrational emotion, romantic love falls prey to the Enlightenment project of disenchantment which looks upon it as a mere illusion.

For social theory, psychoanalysis, and classical philosophy love essentially arises out of lack. For Plato, the hapless coupling of heterosexual humans is a desperate attempt to restore the primeval spherical shape out of which man and woman were created. For psychoanalytical theory, particularly Freudian and Lacanian thought, love and desire of the other signify that which is lacking in the self. For modern social theory, finally, love is a social code for the expression of emotions that seeks to compensate for the increasing diversification and fragmentation of social roles. Contemporary social theory, frequently following Foucault, is predominantly interested in the normative discursification of social codes of emotions. From the perspective of Foucauldian social theory, the inflation of sexual discourses is little more than an increasingly refined apparatus to (heteronormatively) regulate the expression of sexuality and emotions.

In modern philosophy, with the exception of Kierkegaard, love plays virtually no role at all. Nietzsche's definition of love, "die einzige die eines Philosophen würdig ist, . . . —in ihren Mitteln der Krieg, in ihrem Grunde der Todhass der Geschlechter," is as embittered as it is misanthropic.[26] Freudian psychoanalysis, with its ideal of subjective autonomy, turns love, passion, and romantic suffering into an "unacceptable and unjustifiable symptom, emanating from insufficiently mature psyches."[27] In their investigation of figurations of love in Western, Middle Eastern, and Indian cultures, psychoanalysts Sudhir Kakar and John Ross describe love as "a form of insanity, as Freud himself acknowledged. . . . All lovers must be fools, crazed in some transcendent, even mystical sense."[28] Irvin D. Yalom, professor emeritus of psychoanalysis at Stanford University, maintains that love and psychoanalysis are "im Grunde unvereinbar . . . Ein guter Therapeut kämpft gegen die Dunkelheit und sucht Erleuchtung, während die romantische Liebe im Mysterium Nahrung findet und bei näherer Prüfung in sich zusammenfällt."[29] For contemporary biology and evolutionary anthropology romantic love is either a purely chemical reaction with Serotonin-effects that liken it to a compulsive disorder,[30] or an evolutionary principle designed to solve the problem of self-interest in the primeval horde.[31] Thomas Lewis, Fari Amini, and Richard Lannon declare in their neurobiological study *A General Theory of Love* that love "has to be lawful," that it behaves according to fundamentally discoverable and intelligible principles.[32]

Feminist and gender theory treats the discourse of love (not without justification) either as an ideology that compensates and prepares for the real social enslavement of women and thus as a dangerous illusion, or as an "asymmetrical" discourse that encodes a dominant masculine perspective. Arguing from a Foucauldian perspective, Stefan Neuhaus asserts that the social discourse on love and sexuality predominantly regulates the "correct" use of sexuality and speaks of a "Diskursivierung und Allgegenwart von—weitgehend normierter—Sexualität" in public discourse (if not in social praxis).[33] Regarding romantic love as the "cement with which the edifice of male domination has been built,"[34] feminism questions the relationship between the idealization of femininity in romance and the real social status of women. The cult of romantic chivalry created a cultural system that transfigured and cemented both the subjection of women and male power.[35] The tradition of romantic love thus appears inextricably connected to a heteronormative system of gender relations that is ideologically involved in the subjection of women through their apparent elevation and transfiguration as objects of (male) desire. Consequently, both Evans and Wendy Langford take issue with Giddens's theory of a democratization of love, and argue that "the issue of power remains problematic," not least because the democratization of intimacy in the twentieth century was accompanied by a history of sexual liberation that both commercialized desire and favored masculine sexual fantasies of availability without intimacy.[36]

In contrast to and as an alternative to romantic love, Evans thus re-invokes Jane Austen's "sober" love, the model that, according to Luhmann, was superseded by romantic love: "The proposal, therefore, is that just as love was part of a process of modernisation, so our understanding of love demands—and deserves—retrieval from those careless and irrational spheres to which it has been assigned. . . . Rather than regarding the rational as the cold and uncaring enemy of love, we might well regard it as its only true defender in a social world awash with deadly cocktails of romance, hedonism, and personal entertainment."[37] However, as Illouz notes, feminist theory tends to overlook the "egalitarian strain contained in the ideology of love."[38] Barbara Sichtermann asserts, in contrast to approaches that stress the inequality of love relationships from a gender perspective, that love is ideally a field for the practice of an equality based on difference: "dass Liebe eines der wenigen Felder ist, auf denen Männer und Frauen sozusagen von Natur aus alle Bereitschaft mitbringen, einander ihre Wünsche . . . ganz und gar zu erfüllen."[39] To reduce (romantic) love to mere false consciousness is both reductive and depends on an assumption of the primacy of social discourses over structures of desire and emotion, that is, a unidirectional relationship between images of love and human desire.

Be that as it may, the result of all these deconstructions and rationalizations of romantic love is, according to Illouz, a loss of the "cultural pathos" of love. Whether we take Giddens's model of contractual relationships, Evans's re-invocation of Jane Austen's "sober" love, or the tendency towards a self-reflexively performative attitude towards desire, love in the present appears thoroughly disillusioned and disenchanted, commercialized and commodified. Illouz notes a "de-structuration of the romantic will" and a "de-structuring of romantic desire" in the age of internet dating and dating apps.[40] The progressive rationalization of emotions together with the destabilization of clear gender roles in the latter half of the twentieth century have resulted in uncertainty and irony towards love relationships. Irony as a consequence of growing insecurity is, according to Illouz, the dominant rhetorical form in the contemporary discourse about love: "The process of rationalization of love is at the heart of the new ironic structure of romantic feeling which marks the move from an 'enchanted' to a disenchanted cultural definition of love."[41] The discourse of love, however, is fundamentally tied to a belief in subjective authenticity; as Manfred Schneider has asserted, the lovers' discourse is the model of a "truthful" language that appears "suited to authenticate emotions."[42] Irony, the dominant mode of postmodernity, however, is a mode of existence of disappointed romantics and incompatible with both authenticity and passion. The TV-series *Sex in the City* is the paradigm of this mode of existence in the early 2000s, as testified to by its global success.[43]

The consequence of these rationalizations and the ensuing loss of clarity regarding gender roles is, according to Illouz, "that uncertainty and irony dominate the cultural climate of romantic relationships."[44] At the beginning of the twenty-first century, according to Illouz, (heterosexual) romantic love appears to find itself in a state of exhausted paralysis: "Because, historically, sexual desire has been coded through male and female inequality, the situation we face in the early twenty-first century is precisely one in which the traditional rituals of sexual interaction and dynamic of sexual desire are disrupted."[45] As Maureen Dowd has noted: "[C]ulturally, emotionally the whole idea of romance is gone, gone, gone."[46] The consequence is "disappointment as a cultural practice."[47]

Love and Modern Literature: An Enlightenment Paradox

(Modern) literature reflects (on) many of the issues outlined above. European literature knows mainly unhappy unfulfilled, and fatal love stories from the medieval *Minne* via Dante and Beatrice, Petrarch and Laura, to Shakespeare's Romeo and Juliet: in the high literary tradition of Europe between the Middle Ages and the Renaissance, love, suffering, and frequently death belong closely together.

In the modern novel there is likewise no luck in love, probably because the idea of fulfilled love plays such a central role in the spiritual structure of the modern subject, and modern literature, with the exception of Romanticism, understands itself as predominantly socially critical. When it comes to love and intimate relationships, the modern novel essentially explores love's failure and the contradiction between romantic fantasy and reality. Whether for reasons of social history or narrative logic which seems to demand conflict and insurmountable obstacles, what the modern novel finds worthy of narration is predominantly unhappiness and love's failure: "Unless the course of love is being hindered there is no 'romance.'"[48]

In the onset of bourgeois modernity, it is thus literature that for Luhmann occupies a particular role in the codification of love, romance, and passion. However, it would be too simple to argue that literature predominantly reflects love's unhappiness in a literary response to the sociohistorical tensions to which the modern individual is subject. While that is certainly part of the issue, it is first worth noting a curious paradox in relation to literature's role in the social semantics of love. This paradox is expressed as a methodological conundrum in Luhmann's *Love as Passion*. Luhmann claims that the semantic code of love exists prior to literature, that is, literary texts do not add to it and literary characters behave according to a pre-established code. On the other hand, he ascribes to literature an orienting function, that is, the role of example.[49] Literature is thus ascribed a dual role, as both reflector of this overburdening of the romantic code and as its co-generator. It is worth noting in this context that all major sociotheoretical approaches to the problem of love—Luhmann, Evans, Illouz, and Giddens—take their cue from literature, which is treated as a model that both reflects and influences the social codification of love.[50] Far from being just a methodological aporia, this chicken-and-egg-situation, the question whether literature reflects emotions or creates them, in which romance literature is both read as instruction and criticized for evoking "false," that is, fictional emotions, is as old as European literature on love itself. Love, literature, and reading are inextricably connected since at least Ovid's *Ars Amatoria*, which implores the reader to take the poem as a lesson in order to become a master of the art of love.[51] According to Walter Haug, this constellation takes a sharp development towards self-reflexivity in the Middle Ages, which discover, together with the fictionality of literature, also love's unhappiness. According to Haug, Gottfried von Straßburg's *Tristan und Isolde* represents the discovery of fictionality in European literature, simultaneously with the discovery of love as both personal and physical experience. Before *Tristan und Isolde*, says Haug, there is no discussion of love as "Erfahrung spezifischer Art."[52] This engenders the problem of literary love's relationship to the extratextual world, particularly the problem that love stories are taken as a model, begetting and enhancing unrealistic ideas of love outside of fictional representations. Since *Tristan und Isolde*, a central aspect of literary representations of love is a reflection of their own fictionality in contradistinction to the world outside the text. A few examples shall suffice here: in *Tristan und Isolde*, the two illicit lovers tell each other classic love stories that reflect their own situation while staying in the lovers' grotto, an unreal place removed from courtly reality. In Dante's *Commedia* the illicit lovers Paolo and Francesca are confined to the fifth circle of hell after being seduced into adultery by their reading of the Lancelot novel. In Goethe's *Die Leiden des jungen Werthers* (*The Sorrows of Young Werther*, 1774), Werther and Lotte's emotions are spurred on both by their reading of Ossian and by their common reference to Klopstock's poetry. Moreover, Goethe's novel entails a critical revision of Petrarchian motifs as obsolete literary tropes.[53] The period of *Empfindsamkeit* is characterized by a prolonged debate about the negative influence of reading (romance) novels on the mental capacities of their readers.[54] Flaubert's *Madame Bovary* (1856) is essentially an ironic critique of the incompatibility of sentimentalist ideas about love with the realities of provincial life in France in the middle of the nineteenth century. Finally, moving into contemporary literature, Elfriede Jelinek's *Die Liebhaberinnen* (1974) is a satirical feminist deconstruction of the structures of trash romance stories that put false and delusional ideas in the head of one of the protagonists.[55] What is frequently reflected in literary texts about love, then, is the problem of misunderstanding literature's fictional nature and mistaking it as an instruction or education for life outside the text. Haug comments on the Paolo and Francesca episode in Dante: "Wer die Fiktionalität der neuen erotischen Literatur in ihrer experimentellen Bedeutung nicht erfasst und sie als Lebensanweisung missinterpretiert, kommt in die Hölle."[56]

This notwithstanding, the literary subject of love, like few others, tempts us to transfer literary motifs into our subjective experience, not least because of the inseparable connection between experience of love and experience of self in the formation of the precarious subject of European modernity since Petrarch.[57] Jörn Steigerwald notes, "dass jedes Wissen um die Liebe an die Darstellung der Liebe gebunden ist, da nur diese, sei sie sprachlicher oder piktoraler Natur, ein Wissen von der Liebe produziert. Daraus resultiert wiederum, dass jede Liebesdarstellung indes selbst zu einem Akt des Begehrens wird, da sie eine Form des Verstehenwollens kennzeichnet."[58] A case in point is the trans-European phenomenon of the reception of *Werther*, a novel that combines its unhappy love story with the troubles of subjectivity in an administered society where love appears to Werther as the only promise of a solution to the conflicts of bourgeois society.

Both as a literary subject and as a social phenomenon, love, like poetry and religion, is in conflict with Enlightenment rationality and defies transcription into a rationalist discourse. Love, poetry, and religion are all of magical origin and part of mystic experience—recognizable by the fact that love is the main topic of European poetry and is imbued with quasi-religious significance in the Middle Ages, and again at the threshold to early modernity. The concept of mystery and enchantment is central to all three, the experience of love is bound up with aspects of the experience of the sacred: the uniqueness of the object, the experience of being overwhelmed, the suspension of the division between subject and object, the ineffability of the experience.[59] The skeptical light of Enlightenment destroys, together with religion, progressively also poetry and (romantic) love.

Heinrich Heine captured this contradiction two hundred years ago in his poem "Gespräch auf der Paderborner Heide" (1821). The poem is a staged confrontation between two voices, one a romantic and the other a realist. The romantic voice reacts to sense impressions from his environment with recourse to stock images from idyllic and romantic poetry. The realist voice in turn uncovers the romantic impressions as illusions and reduces the idyllic images to a mundane and frequently crude reality:

> Hörst du nicht die fernen Töne,
> Wie von Brummbaß und von Geigen?
> Dorten tanzt wohl manche Schöne
> Den geflügelt leichten Reigen.

> "Ei, mein Freund, das nenn ich irren,
> Von den Geigen hör ich keine,
> Nur die Ferklein hör ich quirren,
> Grunzen nur hör ich die Schweine."

Over the course of the poem the entire catalogue of romantic transfigurations of nature is called up and given the treatment of disillusion, from the hunter's horn and the shepherd's chalumeau that turn out to be the sounds of the swineherd and his pigs, to the vision of the beautiful beloved which is uncovered to be an old hag on crutches. While Heine's poem thus satirically mocks the image repertoire of romantic and idyllic poetry which by his own time had descended into a series of empty clichés, the sting is, as is often the case in Heine's poems, in the tail:

> Nun, mein Freund, so magst du lachen
> Über des Phantasten Frage!
> Wirst du auch zur Täuschung machen,
> Was ich fest im Busen trage?[60]

Heine's poem addresses the question of the status of our emotions in relation to the (socially mediated) images and ideas that trigger and capture them. If the images of romance are nothing but an empty mediated construct, does this mean that our feelings are also an illusion? In this context it is worth pointing out that the romantic has the last word in Heine's poem and that, while he refers to himself as a fantasizer, he insists on the individual certainty of his feelings which he carries "fest im Busen." Heine's poem thus expresses the paradox between love as an emotion experienced by individuals and society as a whole as a repository of socially codified images and imaginations. Love, while on the one hand the most intimate form of communication, is simultaneously conspicuously public. Like pain, love is a radically individualizing experience; unlike pain, it can be shared, and relies on intersubjective communication and thus on a socially codified semantics.

A further paradox lies in the fact that the modern conception of love as "enchanted" is as much the product of the onward march of rationalized modernity as it is incompatible with it. While on the one hand it is only within modernity that (romantic) love acquires its all-encompassing meaning for the Western subject, the discourses of enlightened modernity are profoundly hostile to its non-rational essence. Seen dialectically, love is, together with art, one of the refuges of enchantment in a modernity that destroys the experience of enchantment. Ultimately, all theory proceeds by discursification, conceptualization, and generalization, whereas the experience of love, despite the "Geschwätzigkeit" of the lovers' discourse, is essentially non-discursive, individualizing, and non-rational. The paradox that Adorno and Horkheimer identified with respect to Enlightenment rationality in their *Dialectic of Enlightenment,* that one cannot think without concepts and that concepts by their very nature as generalizing operations violate the particular by subsuming it under a generalizing framework, applies to love as it applies to art.[61] To return to the opening statement about literature being the most adequate expression of the ambivalences and emotional realities of love, all discursive and conceptualizing thought about love must ultimately miss its object. The conceptualizations of love in the discourses of social theory, psychoanalysis, and feminism are thus fundamentally reductive. This is nowhere more obvious than when they refer to literature or other aesthetic products that they treat as instantiations and examples of a discourse, as a number of social-theory models of love do, from Luhmann and Evans to Illouz. Literary texts, however, as Rainer Warning has argued, are not discourses in the Foucauldian sense. Discourses are "systems of statements that arise from certain institutional practices (e.g., medicine, biology, jurisprudence, etc.), and are characterised by clarity, transparency and a regulative function." While literary texts are always embedded in a discursive field, their "knowledge" cannot be reduced to this field, especially as literary texts are predominantly interested in "denseness, opacity, and excess."[62] With respect to the literary representation of love, sexuality, and eroticism, Stefan Neuhaus asserts that literature not only analyzes the social discourse about sexuality and love, but "sie bereichert die analytische um eine weitere Perspektive, die als Gegen-Moral bezeichnet werden kann."[63] Due to its "openness," both on a semantic level and on the level of reception, literature lacks the normative moral power that characterizes discourses.

Literary Studies approaches to love in literature—and here it is worth noting that in the Germanic tradition the Humanities are classified as sciences—thus face the double paradox of having to adequately describe their object in a "scientific" theoretical discourse that is in danger of both missing its object (literature) and its object's object (love). Andrea Egger-Riedmüller, for example, notes that the affirmations of the failure of love in literary studies focus on lovers in the literary texts predominantly as paradigms or embodiment of social tensions, not as individuals or humans.[64] Literary Studies, particularly in its contemporary form, thus participate in the modern discourse of disenchantment. In her 2008 study *Uses of Literature*, Rita Felski criticizes that Literary Studies partakes of the (self-appointed) Enlightenment task of demystifying its object, insofar as "[e]nchantment is a term with precious little currency in literary theory." Literature, however, functions as a reminder "of the persistence of the mysterious, wondrous, and perplexing in a rationalized and at least partly secularized world."[65]

Love in (Contemporary) German Literature

Love, as Egger-Riedmüller notes in 2004, is experiencing a "revival" in German literature.[66] In contrast to the scarcity of literature on love in the postwar period up to the 1990s, since unification, and even more so since the turn of the millennium, German literature has seen a steady rise of literary texts that take intimate relationships as their central topic. Over the past decade a number of German authors of all generations have written novels about love, for example Monika Maron, Navid Kermani, Uwe Timm, Bodo Kirchoff, Hanns-Josef Ortheil, Hans-Ulrich Treichel, Feridun Zaimoglu, Dagmar Leupold, Wolf Haas, Ulrich Woelk, Wilhelm Genazino, Judith Hermann, Martin Walser, Helmut Krausser, Günter Ohnemus, just to name a few.[67] This "revival" is unparalleled in the period of German literature since the end of the Second World War and represents the largest engagement with the topic of intimate relationships since the Weimar period. A brief sketch of the major developments in modern German literature with respect to the representation of love shall illustrate this.

Modern German literature more or less begins with a novel about the failed love of an increasingly isolated young man which acquires the status of a trans-European "model" for the tribulations of modern subjectivity in relation to unhappy love: Goethe's *Die Leiden des jungen Werthers*.[68] German Romanticism, in critique of Goethe's negative model in *Werther*, sought to turn this negative model around in the stipulation of a utopian model of love as a "Seelenbund," a union of souls that was supposed to "heal" all the fragmentations that modernity had caused in the subject: "Traditionell wurde die Liebe in der Literatur mit Krankheit, Wahnsinn,

Raserei oder Blindheit gleichgesetzt . . . In der Romantik verändert sich diese Auffassung von der Liebe radikal. Der romantische Mensch gesundet durch die Liebe, er überwindet eine schwere Krankheit, unter der er bis dahin gelitten hat."[69] The romantic model, especially Friedrich Schlegel's *Lucinde*, replaced the *Werther* model of failed, unhappy love with a model of successful mutual understanding which is based on a theory of "metaphysical" mutual understanding that distinguishes love from all other forms of communication.[70]

This model, however, which even in its literary formulation depends on the removal of the social environment from the love relationship, was not followed and did not break the paradigm of love foundering on modern social problems.[71] On the contrary, in the early part of the twentieth century, love in German literature already underwent the "disenchantment" that Illouz notes as a defining moment of contemporary attitudes to love. The period of "Neue Sachlichkeit" saw a literary development of the romantic model of a "Seelenbund," a union of souls, into a model of sober "Partnerschaft" as a "radical countermodel" to romantic love. The "sachliche" model of partnership regards romanticism as a mere "Störfaktor." Reinhardt-Becker explicitly connects this "sobering" and "cooling down" of the romantic model to the processes of the individual's emotional adaptation to the cold, rationalized, and mechanized world that surrounds it. This adaptation is representative of a "new anthropology" which, in accordance with modern science, looks at humans in analogy to machines: "Diese neue Anthropologie . . . befreit die Liebe von ihrer romantischen Funktion der Individualitätskonstruktion . . . Sachliche Liebe offenbart weder den Sinn des Daseins, noch erhellt sie dem Liebenden die Zusammenhänge seines Lebens."[72] This "sobering" of love in the literature of the "Neue Sachlichkeit" may, together with the experience of the Second World War and the burden this placed upon German culture to come to terms with its social and historical traumas, explain the relative absence of the theme of love in postwar German literature. Postwar German literature's self-appointed task of being the "conscience of the nation" and to generally engage with issues of a public and political nature on the whole made it shy away from purely private and personal matters. Frank Michael Schicketanz in his 1995 study *Liebe nach dem Krieg*, until then the only major study of love in postwar German literature, numbers love among the "things lost in the last war" and argues that love in postwar literature undergoes a social transformation, insofar as it "is increasingly used to express things beyond itself and perhaps nothing as much as its own demise."[73] This is to say that the theme of love is primarily used to represent issues of wider social concern.

Whereas the theme of love in German literature of the period around 1800 is widely researched,[74] there are comparatively few studies of love in postwar and contemporary German literature. This scarcity largely reflects the status of the theme of love in the literature of the postwar era up to the 1980s and 1990s. While Niklas Luhmann opens his *Love as Passion* with the declaration that love is the "subject *par excellence* of novels," by the end of the book he doubts "whether and how the topic can be treated in literature."[75] Schicketanz's *Liebe nach dem Krieg* focuses on a small selection of canonical texts (Koeppen, Mann, Grass, Böll, Handke, and Walser) with just two female authors (Christa Wolf and Karin Struck) and makes scant use of secondary or conceptual literature on the issue. Helmut Schmiedt's historical overview from the eighteenth to the twentieth century *Liebe, Ehe, Ehebruch* (1993) only mentions Arno Schmidt, Martin Walser, and Elfriede Jelinek as postwar authors. Luserke-Jacqui's *Kleine Literaturgeschichte der großen Liebe* mentions works by just two twentieth-century authors, Musil's *Der Mann ohne Eigenschaften* (The Man without Qualities, 1930) and, curiously (given the subject matter of the study), Elfriede Jelinek's *Die Klavierspielerin* (The Piano Teacher, 1983), a novel about (female) sexual perversion, and *Lust* (1989), a novel about the language of pornography. Andrea Egger-Riedmüller's idiosyncratic *Figurationen einer fortgeschrittenen Liebe* (2004) is the conceptually most comprehensive study on the relationship between contemporary literature and (unhappy) love. Egger-Riedmüller's study is a "Suche nach dem lebbaren Lebensglück in der Literatur" and an attempt to deconstruct the modern myth in both theory and literature that happiness is not "literaturtauglich" because it eliminates critique and complexity and swaps the process of time for the standstill of bliss.[76]

Schicketanz, Schmiedt, and Egger-Riedmüller essentially affirm Denis de Rougemont's 1940 assessment of classical literature that "[h]appy love has no history. Romance only comes into existence where love is fatal, frowned upon and doomed by life itself."[77] Relating the theme of love to microsocietal developments over four decades, Schicketanz notes that "Theodor Adorno's dictum regarding the impossibility of poetry after Auschwitz applies as well, or more so, to love as a theme of postwar literature."[78] Schmiedt notes with astonishment "daß nicht ein einziger unserer Texte plausibel von einer Liebe zu berichten weiß, die sich verläßlich gegen alle Widrigkeiten durchsetzt."[79]

Egger-Riedmüller discovers in both the literature of modernity and central theoretical approaches (Adorno and Horkheimer, Foucault, Deconstruction) a structure that assigns to love the status of the Other of modernity's discourse of order. Love, in Egger-Riedmüller's dialectical reading, is the ecstatic product of the order of modernity: order is what is not love; love is what is not order.[80] As the Other of order, passion, love, and romance are also the Other of the everyday. Hence, love and romance are constructed as outside of the ordinary, and thus cannot be integrated into the banality of the everyday. The utopian character of love thus consists in and of the negation of "Alltag."[81] Hence, in both literature and theory, the lovers only have a choice between "lebbare Langeweile oder tödliche Ekstase."[82]

The origin of this construction, suspects Egger-Riedmüller, is Western culture's history of thinking in binary categories of subject and object that assigns to the male the role of subject and to the female the role of object; an object that is constructed by the male subject in relation to himself, a relation that is constructed as devotion ("Hingabe"). Furthermore, Riedmüller's sharp critique of this construction targets predominantly the conception of love as arising out of lack, from Plato's idea of the original spherical being to Freud's and Lacan's conceptions of desire as arising from the split between love's aim and its (lack of) satisfaction. The problem she identifies in the "2000-year-old myth" of the idea of completeness through love is the conception of completeness as the end point of desire itself: "Diese Lücke hat mit der Liebe also nicht mehr zu tun, als daß mit dem (auf der Grundlage der Paradiesfolie konstruierten) Mangel und der (ebenso auf der Grundlage der Paradiesfolie konstruierten) Sehnsucht umgegangen wird. Die Crux allerdings ist die paradiesische Basis: die Setzung und Voraussetzung der Befriedigung."[83] The result of the construction of love out of lack, the desire to return to an imaginary paradise is the constant re-invocation of the Platonic system as the only basis for desire: "Ohnehin wird man durch das aus der Abwesenheit heraus inszenierte Liebessehnen immer wieder auf das platonische System zurückgeworfen."[84]

With respect to literature, and literary representations of love, this construction is fatal, as it results in either unhappy or deadly love stories: "Es scheint ein Grundgesetz zu sein: Die Liebe dauert nicht, lebt nicht, ist flüchtig, berührt nicht, ist nicht glücklich und dauerhaft; weder narrativ noch intertextuell."[85] Looking for a different conception of love in contemporary literary texts that thematizes, instead of the "either-or" structure of love or death, an "in-between," Egger-Riedmüller can only find a handful of texts by minor writers.[86]

Egger-Riedmüller's critique of our conception of love as arising out of lack is so fruitful because it identifies a repeated literary structure that produces either death or unhappiness, a structure that is affirmed by the critical literature which identifies it with the human condition as such: "Die Unstillbarkeit entspricht einer bestimmten 'Struktur' von Liebe, kann aber genausowenig als ihr Wesen festgemacht werden, wie der Mangel als die Conditio humana schlechthin."[87]

The Present Book

The chapters in this edition of the *Edinburgh German Yearbook* all address the aspects discussed above. The first section addresses revisions of literary romance and Romanticism in contemporary literature. Esther K. Bauer's chapter examines a set of novels by Swiss writer Alain Claude Sulzer, all of which reflect on the suitability and adaptability of romantic models in the contemporary period. Trying in vain to emulate romantic heroes and heroines, Sulzer's hetero- and homosexual protagonists frequently founder on their inability to integrate their fictional romantic ideals into their lives. Bauer reads Sulzer's novels as self-reflexive explorations of the fictional nature of romance where characters stylize themselves according to a romantic "script" that frequently leads them into unfulfilled lives.

Hanns-Josef Ortheil's *Die große Liebe* (Great Love) is an unabashedly happy love story which self-reflexively sets itself against the tradition of unhappy love stories in modernity. Set in Germany's traditional favorite holiday destination, Italy, Ortheil's novel is animated by an aesthetic program that references and reviews central aspects of the literary tradition of romance from the Middle Ages via the Renaissance to Goethe's *Werther* and Schlegel's *Lucinde*. Helmut Schmitz's chapter examines the novel's intertextual reference horizon and argues that the novel's anti-modernist focus of love's happiness self-reflexively celebrates love as a purely literary and aesthetic phenomenon.

The second section examines variations of literary conceptions of love in the contemporary. Sven Glawion's chapter on Thomas Brussig's *Helden wie wir* looks at Brussig's satirical critique of the GDR's sexual politics, especially its conception of a heteronormative "healthy" sexuality as expression of a rounded socialist personality. Analyzing the relationship between Brussig's novel and one of its intertexts—Siegfried Schnabl's sexual guide *Mann und Frau intim*—Glawion's chapter reads the sexual history of Brussig's protagonist as a picaresque unmasking of the GDR's idea of a "healthy" socialist personality.

One of the oldest genre forms to represent love and intimacy is the epistolary novel, from Samuel Richardson's *Pamela* (1740) to Goethe's *Die Leiden des jungen Werthers*. Angelika Vybiral's chapter examines a twenty-first-century variation of the epistolary novel, Daniel Glattauer's virtual love story *Gut gegen Nordwind* (Translated as *Love, Virtually*), a novel about the development of an email romance. Analyzing how the technology of emails influences the way of self-expression and the development and expression of intimacy, Vybiral explores Glattauer's concept of virtual love, its potentials, and its limitations.

Maria Roca Lizarazu's chapter on Maxim Biller concludes this section. Roca Lizarazu examines Biller's remediations of sadomasochism in his novella *Im Kopf von Bruno Schulz* (In Bruno Schulz's Head) and the short story *Harlem Holocaust*. She argues that Biller transposes the sadomasochistic relation from the realm of erotic gender relations in Polish-German writer Bruno Schulz's original story to the realm of German-Jewish relations, which involves a polemical re-interpretation of the "German-Jewish symbiosis" and post-Holocaust German-Jewish identity.

The final section looks at love in relation to cultural exclusion. One of the most pressing experiences of social exclusion is unemployment, frequently referred to as "social death." Silke Horstkotte's chapter looks at the condition of love under the pressures of precarity in Thomas Melle's *3000 Euro*, Feridun Zaimoglu's *Isabel*, and Julia Wolf's *Alles ist jetzt* (Everything is Now). Working with Judith Butler's conceptions of precarity and vulnerability, Horstkotte examines the way Melle, Zaimoglu, and Wolf's novels test the durability of traditional literary conceptions of love in confrontation with contemporary conditions of social hardship.

Finally, Sarra Kassem's chapter on Fatih Akin's *Gegen die Wand* (In English: *Head On*) looks at the film's construction of the relationship between its two protagonists Cahit and Sibel. While the two characters initially enter into a marriage of convenience to enable Sibel to live out her idea of free sexuality outside of her family's constraints, the emerging love story between them soon complicates matters and takes the film into a territory that explores sociocultural, ethnic, and gender norms. Kassem examines how the film's representation of the romantic relationship between the two Turkish-Germans asserts the inescapability of certain norms set in place to regulate gender and sexuality. Arguing that the emerging love story between Cahit and Sibel serves as a platform to engage with the social and cultural boundaries that constrain desire in German-Turkish culture, Kassem contends that while Akin deconstructs some of the prominent mythologies upon which representations of love depend, the film ultimately re-enforces a set of normative characteristics about romance.

Notes

[1] Walter Benjamin, "On Some Motifs in Baudelaire," in Benjamin, *Selected Writings*, vol. 4, ed. Howard Eiland and Michael W. Jennings (Cambridge, MA: Belknap Press, 2003), 313–55, here 315.

[2] Niels Werber, *Liebe als Roman: Zur Koevolution intimer und literarischer Kommunikation* (Munich: Fink, 2003), 9.

[3] Elke Reinhardt-Becker, *Seelenbund oder Partnerschaft? Liebessemantiken in der Literatur der Romantik und der Neuen Sachlichkeit* (Frankfurt am Main: Campus, 2005), 14.

[4] Matthias Luserke-Jacqui, *Kleine Literaturgeschichte der großen Liebe* (Darmstadt: Wissenschaftliche Buchgesellschaft, 2011), 160.

[5] See, e.g., Niklas Luhmann, *Love as Passion: The Codification of Intimacy*, trans. Jeremy Gaines and Doris L. Jones (Cambridge: Polity Press, 1986 [first published 1982]), Ulrich Beck and Elisabeth Beck-Gernsheim, *The Normal Chaos of Love*, trans. Mark Ritter and Jane Wiebel (Cambridge: Polity Press, 1995 [first published 1990]). On the literary codification of love see, e.g., Julia Bobsin, *Von*

der Werther-Krise zur Lucinde-Liebe: Studien zur Liebessemantik in der deutschen Erzählliteratur 1770–1800 (Niemeyer: Tübingen, 1994), Werber, *Liebe als Roman*, Elke Reinhardt-Becker, *Seelenbund oder Partnerschaft?*, and *Codierungen von Liebe in der Kunstperiode*, ed. Walter Hinderer (Würzburg: Königshausen & Neumann, 1997).

[6] Ethel Spector Pearson, *Dreams of Love and Fateful Encounters: The Power of Romantic Passion* (New York: Norton Company, 1988), 59.

[7] See Eva Illouz, *Why Love Hurts: A Sociological Explanation* (Cambridge: Polity Press, 2012), 11, with reference to a series of sociological studies.

[8] Anthony Giddens, *The Transformation of Intimacy: Sexuality, Love & Eroticism in Modern Societies* (Cambridge: Polity Press, 1992). References are to the paperback edition, 2003, 40.

[9] Giddens, *The Transformation of Intimacy*, 46.

[10] Luhmann, *Love as Passion*, 15–17.

[11] Luhmann, *Love as Passion*, 10.

[12] Luhmann, *Love as Passion*, 21.

[13] Luhmann, *Love as Passion*, 35 and 11.

[14] Werber, *Liebe als Roman*, 14.

[15] See, e.g., Beck and Beck-Gernsheim, *The Normal Chaos of Love*, introduction. Mary Evans, *Love: An Unromantic Discussion* (Cambridge, Polity Press, 2003), 2. Illouz, *Why Love Hurts*, 12.

[16] Eva Illouz, *Consuming the Romantic Utopia: Love and the Cultural Contradictions of Capitalism* (Berkeley: University of California Press, 1997), 25 and 26.

[17] Illouz, *Consuming the Romantic Utopia*, 28.

[18] See Illouz, *Consuming the Romantic Utopia*, 42.

[19] Illouz, *Why Love Hurts*, 9.

[20] Giddens, *The Transformation of Intimacy*, 11.

[21] Giddens, *The Transformation of Intimacy*, 15.

[22] Giddens, *The Transformation of Intimacy*, 61 and 62.

[23] Giddens, *The Transformation of Intimacy*, 58.

[24] See Evans, *Love: An Unromantic Discussion*, 15. For Butler, see, e.g., *Gender Trouble: Feminism and the Subversion of Identity* (Abingdon: Routledge, 1990), and "Performative Acts and Gender Constitution: An Essay in Phenomenology and Feminist Theory," *Theatre Journal* 40, no. 4 (Dec. 1988): 519–31.

[25] Roland Barthes, *A Lover's Discourse*, trans. Richard Howard (London: Penguin, 1977), 1 (translation modified).

[26] Nietzsche, *Ecce Homo*, in *Werke*, vol. II, ed. Karl Schlechta (Munich: Hanser, 1994), 1106.

[27] Illouz, *Why Love Hurts*, 164 and 165.

[28] Sudhir Kakar and John Ross, *Tales of Love, Sex and Danger* (Oxford: Oxford University Press, 2011), 38.

[29] Interview with Irvin D. Yalom in *Kölner Stadtanzeiger*, accessed January 5, 2015, http://www.ksta.de/kultur/kino--yaloms-anleitung-zum-gluecklichsein--portrait-eines-psychiaters-,15189520,28584312.html.

[30] See Jens Reich, "Sexualität und Fortpflanzung als technisches Konstrukt," in *Next Sex: Sex im Zeitalter seiner reproduktionstechnischen Überflüssigkeit: Katalog der Ars Electronica 2000*, ed. Gerfried Stocker and Christine Schöpf (Vienna: Springer, 2000), 84–89, esp. 84.

[31] See Illouz, *Why Love Hurts*, 167–68.

[32] Thomas Lewis, Fari Amini, and Richard Lannon, *A General Theory of Love* (New York: Vintage, 2001), 5.

[33] Stefan Neuhaus, *Sexualität im Diskurs der Literatur* (Tübingen: Francke, 2002), 46.

[34] Illouz, *Why Love Hurts*, 15.

[35] Illouz, *Why Love Hurts*, 8.

[36] Evans, *Love*, 56–58 and 67. Wendy Langford, *Revolutions of the Heart: Gender, Power and the Delusions of Love* (New York: Routledge, 1999), 21.

[37] Evans, *Love*, 143.

[38] Illouz, *Why Love Hurts*, 5.

[39] Barbara Sichtermann, "Männer, Frauen und die Symmetrie," in *Macht–Geschlechter–Differenz*, ed. Wolfgang Müller-Funk (Vienna: Picus, 1994), 13–29, here 28.

[40] Illouz, *Why Love Hurts*, 196–97.

[41] Illouz, *Why Love Hurts*, 195.

[42] See Manfred Schneider, *Liebe und Betrug: Die Sprachen des Verlangens* (Munich: Hanser, 1992), 148.

[43] See Illouz, *Why Love Hurts*, 57.

[44] Illouz, *Why Love Hurts*, 192.

[45] Illouz, *Why Love Hurts*, 185.

[46] Maureen Dowd, "Tragedy of Comedy," *The New York Times*, August 3, 2010, http://www.nytimes.com/2010/08/04/opinion/04dowd.html. Quoted in Illouz, *Why Love Hurts*, 161.

[47] Illouz, *Why Love Hurts*, 215.

[48] Denis de Rougemont, *Love in the Western World*, trans. Montgomery Belgion (Princeton, NJ: Princeton University Press, 1983 [first published 1940, revised 1956]), 52.

[49] Luhmann, *Love as Passion*, 11.

[50] For a critique of social theory's disregard of the "Eigengesetzlichkeit" of literature, see Bobsin, *Von der Werther-Krise zur Lucinde-Liebe*, 20.

[51] Ovid, *Ars Amatoria*, trans. A. S. Kline, accessed May 20, 2017, http://www.poetryintranslation.com/PITBR/Latin/ArtofLoveBkI.htm.

[52] See Walter Haug, "Tristan und Lancelot. Das Experiment mit der personalen Liebe im 12./13. Jahrhundert," in *Über die Liebe: Ein Symposion*, ed. Heinrich Meier and Gerhard Neumann (Munich: Piper, 2001), 197–233, here 197–98.

[53] See Bobsin, *Von der Werther-Krise zur Lucinde-Liebe*, 92.

[54] See Georg Jäger, *Empfindsamkeit und Roman* (Stuttgart: Kohlhammer, 1969), esp. 57–63.

[55] See Michael Fischer, *Trivialmythen in Elfriede Jelineks Roman "Die Liebhaberinnen"* (St. Ingbert: W. J. Röhrig, 1991).

[56] Haug, "Tristan und Lancelot," 201.

[57] On Petrarch as model for the struggle for subjectivity in love see Michael Bernsen, "Die Herausbildung der europäischen Zivilisation und der Petrarkismus," *Comparatio* (1/2009), 45–58.

[58] Jörn Steigerwald, "Liebes-Geschichten. Von Petrarcas Amorallegorien zu Fontenelles Allegorisierungen der Liebe," *Comparatio* (1/2009): 59–86, here 66–67.

[59] See Illouz, *Why Love Hurts*, 286–93.

[60] Heinrich Heine, "Gespräch auf der Paderborner Heide," in Heine, *Sämtliche Schriften*, ed. Klaus Briegleb (Munich: dtv, 2007), 1:63.

[61] See Max Horkheimer and Theodor W. Adorno, *Dialectic of Enlightenment*, trans. John Cumming (London: Verso, 1979 [first published 1944]), 7–10.

[62] Rainer Warning, *Heterotopien als Räume ästhetischer Erfahrung* (Munich: Fink, 2009), 24 and 25.

[63] Neuhaus, *Sexualität im Diskurs der Literatur*, 191.

[64] Andrea Egger-Riedmüller, *Figurationen einer fortgeschrittenen Liebe: Eine topologische Suche nach dem Glück in Liebesgeschichten der deutschsprachigen Gegenwartsliteratur* (Innsbruck: Universität Innsbruck, 2004), 233.

[65] Rita Felski, *Uses of Literature* (Malden, MA: Blackwell, 2008), 54 and 75.

[66] Egger-Riedmüller, *Figurationen einer fortgeschrittenen Liebe*, 232n545.

[67] Monika Maron, *Animal Triste* (1996), Hanns-Josef Ortheil, *Die große Liebe* (2003), *Das Verlangen nach Liebe* (2007), *Die Liebesnähe* (2011), Martin Walser, *Der Augenblick der Liebe* (2004), Wilhelm Genazino, *Die Liebesblödigkeit* (2005), Helmut Krausser, *Eros* (2006), Dagmar Leupold, *Grüner Engel, blaues Land* (2007), Feridun Zaimoglu, *Liebesbrand* (2008), Bodo Kirchhoff, *Die Liebe in groben Zügen* (2012), Hans-Ulrich Treichel, *Mein Sardinien: Eine Liebesgeschichte* (2012), Wolf Haas, *Verteidigung der Missionarsstellung* (2012), Ulrich Woelk, *Was Liebe ist* (2013), Navid Kermani, *Große Liebe* (2014), Judith Hermann, *Aller Liebe Anfang* (2014), Günter Ohnemus, *Ava, oder die Liebe ist gar nichts* (2014), Uwe Timm, *Vogelweide* (2015).

[68] On the model status of Goethe's *Werther* see, e.g., Gerhard Neumann, "Lektüren der Liebe," in *Über die Liebe: Ein Symposion*, ed. Heinrich Meier and Gerhard Neumann (Munich: Piper, 2001), 9–80, esp. 9, and Bernd Witte, "Casanovas Tochter, Werthers Mutter. Über Liebe und Literatur im achtzehnten Jahrhundert," in *Eros–Liebe–Leidenschaft: Ringvorlesung der Philosophischen Fakultät*

der RWTH Aachen im SS 1987, ed. Kaspar H. Spinner and Frank-Rutger Hausmann, Meisterwerke der Weltliteratur vol. 2 (Bonn: Romanistischer Verlag, 1988), 93–13, esp. 94.

[69] See Reinhardt-Becker, *Seelenbund oder Partnerschaft*, 79.

[70] Reinhardt-Becker, *Seelenbund oder Partnerschaft*, 106. On the specific modernity of this model, see Bobsin, *Von der Werther-Krise zur Lucinde-Liebe*, 190.

[71] See Reinhardt-Becker, *Seelenbund oder Partnerschaft*, 73, and Bobsin, *Von der Werther-Krise zur Lucinde-Liebe*, 173.

[72] Reinhardt-Becker, *Seelenbund oder Partnerschaft*, 205 and 216–17.

[73] Frank Michael Schicketanz, *Liebe nach dem Krieg: The Theme of Love in Post-War German Fiction* (Würzburg: Königshausen & Neumann, 1995), 1 and 3.

[74] See for example Bobsin, *Von der Werther-Krise zur Lucinde-Liebe*, Werber, *Liebe als Roman*, Reinhardt-Becker, *Seelenbund oder Partnerschaft?*, Günter Saße, *Die Ordnung der Gefühle: Das Drama der Liebesheirat im 18. Jahrhundert* (Darmstadt: Wissenschaftliche Buchgesellschaft, 1996), *Codierungen von Liebe in der Kunstperiode*, ed. Walter Hinderer (Würzburg: Königshausen & Neumann, 1997).

[75] Luhmann, *Love as Passion*, 58 and 159.

[76] Egger-Riedmüller, *Figurationen einer fortgeschrittenen Liebe*, 9.

[77] De Rougemont, *Love in the Western World*, 15.

[78] Schicketanz, *Liebe nach dem Krieg*, 1.

[79] Helmut Schmiedt, *Liebe, Ehe, Ehebruch: Ein Spannungsfeld in deutscher Prosa von Christian Fürchtegott Gellert bis Elfriede Jelinek* (Opladen: Westdt. Verleg, 1993), 149–50.

[80] Egger-Riedmüller, *Figurationen einer fortgeschrittenen Liebe*, 21.

[81] Egger-Riedmüller, *Figurationen einer fortgeschrittenen Liebe*, 41.

[82] Egger-Riedmüller, *Figurationen einer fortgeschrittenen Liebe*, 51.

[83] Egger-Riedmüller, *Figurationen einer fortgeschrittenen Liebe*, 64.

[84] Egger-Riedmüller, *Figurationen einer fortgeschrittenen Liebe*, 65.

[85] Egger-Riedmüller, *Figurationen einer fortgeschrittenen Liebe*, 232.

[86] Egger-Riedmüller, *Figurationen einer fortgeschrittenen Liebe*, 247.

[87] Egger-Riedmüller, *Figurationen einer fortgeschrittenen Liebe*, 65.

Revisions of Romantic/
Literary Traditions

Not So Happily Ever After: Romantic Love in Novels by Alain Claude Sulzer

Esther K. Bauer, Virginia Polytechnic Institute and State University

> *[N]o love is original.*
> —Roland Barthes, *A Lover's Discourse*

"D IE EINZIGEN LEBEN, die sich berühren, sind die, die einem Manuskript folgen, das nicht das eigene ist."[1] For contemporary German writer and director René Pollesch, love alone is an inadequate basis for long-term relationships. Since the feeling's initial intensity is impossible to sustain, love relations are destined to become unsatisfying or to end.[2] Only on stage—and, one may add, in literature, film, or art—may audiences witness seemingly eternal passionate love, because the characters' "lives" are limited by the perspectives of the respective works.[3] Arguably, this is most obvious in traditional romantic love stories, or romances, that conclude with the couples' happy unions.

The novels by Swiss writer Alain Claude Sulzer (1953–) evoke the popular romance genre and its ideal of unconditional, never-ending love. However, as Sulzer expands the scope of the typical romance plot beyond the height of the partners' emotional connection and explores the aftermath of infidelity and rejection, readers encounter figures who try to overcome the tensions pinpointed by Pollesch. The protagonists' efforts to preserve their relationships beyond the break-ups are informed by the ideals promoted in literary, operatic, and cinematic romances. Thus, Sulzer's characters try—though in vain—to emulate the heroes and heroines of the well-known genre and go to great length to protect their romantic stylizations of themselves and their lovers against the frustrations of reality. Simultaneously, Sulzer creates a similar experience for his readers, as his works conjure the traditional romance, yet only to subvert the romantic plot and reveal limitations of the romantic paradigm. As a result, his novels emerge as explorations into the ways in which the genre's conventions may shape audiences' expectations of relationships. Read through the lenses of Jean-Paul Sartre's work on subjectivity, Jacques Lacan's concept of desire, and Elke Reinhardt-Becker's comparison of romantic love and "sachliche Liebe,"[4] Sulzer's novels *Ein perfekter Kellner* (A Perfect Waiter, 2006), *Privatstunden* (Private Lessons, 2009), *Zur falschen Zeit* (At the Wrong Time, 2010), and *Postskriptum* (Postscript, 2015) emerge as insightful depictions of the power of socially constituted and endorsed concepts of love and desire and of the difficulties involved in overcoming an all-pervasive, culturally idealized model such as that of romantic love. At the same time, comparing the four works reveals Sulzer's nuanced approach to the romance genre and the different ways in which he uses it to shed light on sexual and gender politics since the 1930s.

Despite Sulzer's success with readers and critics alike, his works have been the subject of few scholarly studies.[5] One reason may be his narrative style and language and tone, which frequently evoke nineteenth-century bourgeois realist novels and hence may seem old-fashioned to some readers. Moreover, at first glance his novels appear to be apolitical love stories that do not fit any of the categories that have dominated recent literary studies, for example, minority literature, works dealing with the effects of the Third Reich and the GDR on German society today, or *Popliteratur*.[6] The main parts of Sulzer's novels discussed here take place during important periods in European history that all saw far-reaching social, political, and cultural changes, namely the interwar years, the 1950s, 1960s, and 1970s, and today. Sulzer evokes these contexts through stereotypical settings and characters, as well as through references to well-known political and (pop) cultural events and figures. Despite the author's great skill in conjuring historical periods, scholars of literature and culture studies interested in these time periods have not turned to Sulzer's works, perhaps because his novels do not offer any new insights into these periods' sociocultural dynamics. His works concentrate on relationships of love and desire, and reviewers have praised the author's sensitive explorations of emotions and romantic disappointment. Given this positive reception together with the recent increased interest in love, and especially romantic love, in a variety of academic fields, including sociology, discourse analysis, and literary studies, scholars' neglect of Sulzer's works appears particularly surprising.[7] Sulzer's novels bespeak the writer's acute awareness of the challenges that have arisen with the prevalence of the model of romantic love as it has developed over the past two hundred years in Western Europe and North America, particularly of the tensions within romantic relationships and between individuals' emotional needs and societies' demands. In fact, his works mirror key findings of current scholarly studies of love and desire, most importantly the existence of a conflict between modernity's functionalization of all areas of life, including intimate relationships, and the expectation to find romantic fulfillment.[8] Nonetheless, the absence of intriguing socio-historical explorations in Sulzer's works may discourage the kind of New Historicist or cultural analysis informing many literary studies, including those focusing on love, today.

Rooted in nineteenth-century bourgeois culture, typical romances revolve around a heterosexual couple's efforts to establish a sexual and love relationship.[9] Most of these works follow one of two plot lines: one depicts lovers, whose mutual attraction is based on great mental, spiritual, moral, and physical compatibility, but who must overcome personal, familial, or social obstacles before they can marry and start a family; the other presents a forbidden, often adulterous, relationship that is at risk of being discovered and may end with the death of one or both partners. Romances rehearse existing forms of relationships and experiment with new ones. At the same time, they offer the vicarious experience of unwavering love and desire and the titillation of proscribed erotic relations. Shifts in cultural norms have affected the genre. Thus, for instance, premarital sex and same-sex relationships now occur frequently, and depictions of lovers' encounters have become more overtly physical. While many romantic love stories reflect the changes in gender roles since the late nineteenth century, traditional notions of femininity and masculinity have continued to inform the genre.

As Reinhardt-Becker shows, since the 1920s, a paradigm of "sober" love that competes with that of romance can be traced in literature. This younger concept is associated with the artistic and literary movement of *Neue Sachlichkeit* and emphasizes sobriety, rationality, and a matter-of-fact perspective on life and relationships. In romances, the partners' union is thought to ensure their mutual completion, and the sexual act is presented as an expression of emotional, mental, and spiritual closeness achievable only with one unique lover. By contrast, "objective" love stories present intimate relationships as arrangements between equal partners entered primarily for one's own benefit. They are often described as comradeships, and unlike romantic lovers, objective partners are not considered unique, exclusive, irreplaceable matches. Consequently, sexual intercourse appears first and foremost as a way of sharing pleasure, and the choice of partners is guided by the economic principle of supply and demand, that is, whether the partners provide each other with what each wants.[10] For the past hundred years, the romantic and objective paradigms have existed side by side, and many of the conflicts in Sulzer's novels result from their incompatibility.

Jacques Lacan's work on desire provides an explanation of the dynamics underlying the impact and durability of the concept of romantic love and of the images of romantic lovers as they have been promulgated through novels, operas, and films. According to Lacan, our desires are not immediate expressions of physical urges, but are driven by socially constructed narratives. These are part of what Lacan calls the "symbolic order," and they offer idealized images of the self and the objects of its desire and of the structures organizing their interactions. Such idealizations shape the fantasies feeding desire, while simultaneously accounting for desire's fragility when confronted with a less than perfect reality. Defining love, Lacan maintains that "it's one's own ego that one loves in love, one's own ego made real on the imaginary level."[11] In other words, love for Lacan is a narcissistic project revolving around the self as opposed to the desired other. Thus, what we really desire is another's desire, as it secures us a place as idealized object in a narrative of desire, and romance has been a particularly pervasive such narrative.

The novels studied here revolve around both adulterous heterosexual and gay relationships—the latter set during times when homosexual acts were still legally and socially prohibited. Although these works concentrate on the effects of betrayals and break-ups, descriptions of the lovers' times together anchor them in the tradition of romances about illicit love—a subgenre where the couple's every encounter is erotically charged, yet intimate moments are limited to spaces removed from society to indicate that their love and desire place them outside the social order.[12] Sulzer evokes key elements of romances: the lovers' coincidental first encounter and immediate attraction, the physical confirmation of their mutual attraction once beauty or agreement, for instance in interests, values, or worldview, has led to their reciprocal idealization, and finally their sexual union as the ultimate expression of unconditional acceptance of one another, that is, love.[13]

Told from the perspective of the waiter Erneste, *Ein perfekter Kellner* seems to follow this pattern most closely. The novel's plot is split between two time periods: the 1930s, when Erneste has an affair with Jakob, and the 1960s, the novel's present, when Erneste receives a letter from his former lover that triggers the memory of their relationship. In the 1930s, the two men work as waiters at the Swiss Grand Hotel Giessbach, and Erneste is instantly smitten with his new colleague and thinks of Jakob as his soulmate. The latter's handsomeness serves as the basis for Erneste's idealization of Jakob's character, an idealization that ignores any flaws. Soon Erneste develops the kind of "passion" that Niklas Luhmann sees at the core of romantic love: an affliction beyond the control of the affected.[14] Jakob confirms that the desire is mutual: he kisses Erneste on a public trail, and when the two make out, they have "das unverschämte Glück, für einige Augenblicke allein auf der Welt zu sein . . . und unbemerkt."[15] Sharing a bedroom under the hotel's roof, they can regularly indulge in each other's bodies without fear of discovery. For Erneste, their sexual compatibility is proof that they are a perfect match not only physically but also mentally and that they are both equally emotionally invested in their relationship.

The beginnings of Emil and André's relationship in *Zur falschen Zeit* show great similarities to that between Erneste and Jakob. Teenagers in the late 1940s, Emil and André meet in the schoolyard and are instantly attracted to each other. Before long, André challenges Emil to a race on the school track, and when they lie in the grass afterwards, he kisses Emil and the two masturbate one another. Again, Sulzer presents a fortunate moment of isolation in a public space: "Die anderen waren weiter entfernt als der Mond. . . . Der Hitzewall, der sich zwischen ihnen und dem Rest der Welt erhob, flirrte und wellte sich und machte sie fast unsichtbar."[16] Unsuspected by their parents, they use regular sleepovers to have sex. For the first time in his life, Emil feels fully accepted, however, their relationship ends when André moves away with his parents a few years later. In the mid 1950s, when Emil is in his twenties, married, and a teacher, he has another homosexual relationship with his colleague Sebastian, who falls for Emil at first sight. On their second encounter, Sebastian uses the privacy of a café's corner to stroke Emil's wrist underneath the watchband, an intimate gesture whose erotic quality matches that of the kisses and embraces in the other relationships and starts their passionate secret affair.

In *Privatstunden*, the liaison between a middle-class mother and wife and a refugee from Eastern Europe is yet another variation on the romantic pattern. Set in the late 1960s, the novel narrates the adulterous affair between the thirty-seven-year-old Martha Grubach and the twenty-two year old Leo Heger whom Martha teaches German at her home. An aid organization matches the two randomly, and initially, the possibility of a romance is suggested very subtly: Leo takes chocolates to the first lesson, yet drops the box accidentally when Martha opens the door. This "mishap" suggests that such conventional gestures have no place between them. Three months later, the two suspend the parts of student and teacher to act on their desires and kiss and embrace. Unprepared to define their relationship within existing structures through language, they connect purely physically in the front yard of Martha's house, where they are shielded from view by trees. Subsequent get-togethers outside of classes involve sex and take place in Leo's small room under the roof of his host family's house, a space as removed from society as is Erneste and Jakob's attic room.

The adulteress is a recurring figure of the romance tradition. Any adultery threatens the bourgeois order, yet well into the twentieth century adulterous women were deemed particularly deviant, as their pursuit of sexual and emotional satisfaction was considered incompatible with the female role of selfless guardian of the family and social norms.[17] Undoubtedly, in Switzerland in the late 1960s, women like Martha were still expected to emulate this traditional female role. Following the romance model, Sulzer ensures that readers will sympathize with Martha despite her "sträfliche Lust, unerlaubtes Verlangen,"[18] because, as did many adulterous heroines before her, she betrays a husband who neglects her, forces himself upon her, and has an affair himself.

Though in *Postskriptum*, Sulzer deviated from the romantic pattern most significantly, readers will easily recognize it nonetheless. As is the case for Emil and Sebastian, one partner is in love sooner than the other, in fact, before the lovers even meet: between the two World Wars, the postal clerk Walter is obsessed with the famous actor Lionel Kupfer, whom he has seen in countless films. Consequently, their first in-person encounter corresponds to the second step in the other relationships discussed here: in 1933, Walter attends an afternoon tea dance at the hotel Waldhaus in Sils Maria, hoping to meet his idol, and their mutual attraction is quickly established, as they deliberately touch knees under the table. As in the other novels, their intimacy goes unnoticed since the hotel guests are too polite to watch the famous actor closely. Continuing the parallels to the earlier works, Walter and Kupfer have sex in the clerk's apartment above the post office (presumably another attic space) or Kupfer's hotel room, and like the other couples, they keep their relationship secret.

Once Sulzer has raised readers' expectations for romances by evoking standard elements of the genre, most of these relationships take an unusual turn and ultimately subvert the romance pattern. The affairs do not end either happily or with a tragic break-up forced upon the lovers from the outside, but by one partner's voluntary decision to terminate the relation. Driven by political or family developments, these figures have to move away, presenting them with two choices: ending the relationships or accepting the commitment entailed in moving together or in waiting for the other. None of the partners leaving considers the second option, and as they had been unfaithful earlier, they merely terminate already tainted relationships.

The couples' ways of coping with the end of their relationships suggest that the partners adhere to conflicting models of relationships. Thus, the ease with which one set of partners break up with their lovers and, in some cases, have multiple affairs, indicates that exclusivity and permanence, two pillars of romance, are not part of their notions of love. Together with their focus on physical pleasure, this suggests instead that they identify more closely with objective love. By contrast, the abandoned figures believe in romantic love and make every effort to "continue" their relationships beyond the break-ups. Ultimately, Sulzer's works endorse the value system of romance, and as the novels show what happens to the partners after the break-ups, the rules of romantic love stories extend beyond the typical romance plot.[19] The "heartbreakers'" fates vary greatly after the affairs, yet the degrees of happiness or success they find seem to reflect the extent to which they adhered to the role of romantic hero earlier, that is, poetic justice is rooted in the romantic order.

Jakob is, arguably, the most ruthless of Sulzer's figures responsible for a break-up and, accordingly, he finds the saddest ending. Erneste and Jakob's affair appears initially as a story about two lovers who fit together perfectly in every regard, but who face great obstacles in a homophobic society. However, Jakob emerges as extremely egoistical, using others to further his career and for physical pleasure. For him, the main purpose of the relationship with Erneste seems to be sexual enjoyment, and thus, Jakob is reluctant to share ideas or emotions with his lover and betrays the latter with ease. While involved with Erneste, Jakob has affairs with the aging writer Julius Klinger, who pays for Jakob's favors, and with Klinger's son Maxi. To escape the draft after the Nazis' rise to power, Jakob accompanies the Klinger family to the United States as Julius's secretary and both Klingers' secret lover. When a few years later Maxi learns of Jakob and his father's affair, he commits suicide; Klinger, who had been unaware of Maxi and Jakob's relationship, evicts Jakob and renounces any further homosexual activities. Thirty years later, the impoverished, mentally disturbed Jakob dies from a brain tumor—an ending that to some readers may signal a kind of poetic justice: he betrayed several men and abused Klinger, but never showed any remorse that might redeem him in readers' eyes. Ensuring that Klinger's adultery does not distract from Jakob's guilt, Sulzer presents the writer as a broken old man who lost his son and whose wife and daughter left him, and who appears eaten up by feelings of guilt and self-hatred. Thus, the novel leaves no doubt that Jakob is the villain.

In Sulzer's other novels, the question of guilt and immorality is more complex than in *Ein perfekter Kellner*. Thus, in *Privatstunden*, Leo appears selfish, yet at the same time he ends a forbidden relationship, which from the point of view of bourgeois morality is laudable. Not only is his affair with Martha adulterous, but their difference in age and Martha's ambiguous gender role between traditional wife and mother, on the one hand, and her active, sexually assertive part in the encounters with Leo, on the other, contribute further to the relationship's impropriety. Leo reminds Martha of her sixteen-year-old son Andreas, which highlights the lovers' age difference while giving her desire an incestuous and hence culturally forbidden undercurrent.[20] Moreover, the power structures characterizing Martha and Leo's affair contradict traditional gendered hierarchies, which define the male partner as active, strong, and dominant and the female partner as passive and weaker—a view still widely held in the 1960s.[21] Although in North America and Western Europe, male and female gender roles have become more equal since then, elements of the traditional role division and stereotypical attitudes can be found to this day.[22] Contrary to these stereotypes, Martha holds a socially more powerful position than Leo: she is in her home country, where she speaks the language, knows the rules and customs, and as a married woman and mother enjoys the respect of her surroundings. By contrast, Leo finds himself in the precarious situation of a refugee, whose abilities to communicate are limited and who depends on the charity of others for his well-being.

Martha's role as Leo's language teacher adds further to this imbalance of power, as it puts her in control of their lessons and hence of his acquisition of communication skills in his host country. As such, the role of language teacher is also related to that of the mother, who is usually instrumental in imparting language to her children. However, a look at Lacan's understanding of language acquisition highlights the "gender trouble" underlying Martha and Leo's lessons. For Lacan, entering into language means entering into the patriarchal symbolic order that informs all social interactions, an order he describes as the "law" of the father or the "name of the father."[23] Developed in the 1960s, Lacan's theory meant that both men and women, mothers and fathers, socialized children into the male-dominated order. In other words, Martha, who, for a woman, finds herself in an unusually strong position vis-à-vis Leo, ultimately supports his entry into the patriarchal order of his temporary home.

Martha and Leo's first sexual encounter provides yet another example of gender fluidity. When traditional male and female social roles developed in the nineteenth century, the sexual act, where men were perceived as playing the active and women the passive, receptive part, often served as the starting point for this definition of gender. Despite the increased equality characterizing erotic relationships today, sexual assertiveness continues to be associated more readily with men than with women, as, for instance, representations in mainstream media confirm.[24] Therefore, even for contemporary readers it is particularly telling that Martha initiates the first intercourse with Leo. His account of the experience evokes the kind of scenario and language typically used in romances to describe from a woman's perspective a man seducing her, in other words, it assigns Leo the female and Martha the male part: "sie (habe) sich kurzentschlossen über ihn gebeugt und ihre Lippen auf die seinen gedrückt. . . . So hatte ihn noch nie jemand geküßt. . . . Ihre Kraft habe ihn mitgerissen."[25] The gender-inverse power dynamics of this scene are underlined by the fact that Leo is lying in bed ill when it occurs and therefore appears particularly vulnerable, that is, in a position very different from that of the manly romantic heroes to whom Martha had mentally compared him earlier.

Leo does not leave Martha because he finds their relationship objectionable, but because he wants to emigrate to Canada. Similarly self-centered, he had not told his former girlfriend Laura about his plans to leave his home country. No longer in love with Laura, he had considered a secret escape an easy way out of a relationship that for him was purely sexual. Such focus on the physical is considered unacceptable both by bourgeois moral standards and within the realm of romance. Thus, Leo's break-ups with Martha and Laura are both ambivalent: he terminates socially and morally unacceptable relationships, yet does so not because he realizes his wrongdoing, but because he puts his own life plans, needs, and desires first. Given these circumstances, romance readers may see a certain "justice" unfold in the course of Leo's life after emigrating. He becomes a well-off dentist, yet marries and divorces two women and ultimately seems limited to short-term relationships. His lack of private fulfillment contrasts with his professional success, and thirty-five years after the affair with Martha, he appears jaded and no longer expecting anything from life.

Despite their unfaithfulness, the characters of André and Lionel appear more positive than Jakob and Leo. Thus, André continues to care for Emil, who, in turn, places great trust in his former lover. André is portrayed as a figure who does not believe in romantic love and is open about his promiscuity. As a teenager, he had already begun exploring his sexuality with other men—with Emil's knowledge—when his family's move to Paris ended their relationship. Despite their diametrically opposed approaches to life in the homophobic societies of the 1950s and 60s—Emil tries to lead a "bürgerliche Existenz"[26] as a teacher, husband, and father in Switzerland; André joins the Parisian gay scene and becomes an erotic photographer—André and Emil stay friends, and André is the only person whom Emil tells about his relationship with Sebastian. Emil's son confirms their bond when he thinks about André's death from AIDS: "Die unheilsame Krankheit, an der er starb, ähnelte in keiner Weise jener, an der mein Vater litt [depression, E.B.], aber es gab einen intimen Zusammenhang, als hätte einer den anderen nicht losgelassen."[27] Unlike Jakob, who betrays others for his own advantage, André makes no secret of his changing partners, and given today's wide acceptance of homosexuality in Western Europe and North America, many readers may find André less morally reprehensible than Jakob.

The Austrian-born actor Lionel Kupfer, the main protagonist of *Postskriptum*, stands out among the figures ending a relationship, as several aspects explain his behavior and secure the readers' sympathy—despite the fact that for Kupfer, the affair with Walter is merely a pleasant distraction, while the young man truly loves him. The breakup follows the Nazis' rise to power. Originally Jewish, Kupfer and his parents were baptized when he was a child; later, "um seine jüdische Herkunft zu tarnen,"[28] the rumor is spread that the actor has Romanian roots. Berlin was the center of German-language cinema and theater during the interwar years, and knowledge of Kupfer's Jewish origins would have resulted in discrimination and harmed his career. However, once the Nazis rule Germany, discovery of Kupfer's background is imminent and he must emigrate to the United States. His long-time lover Eduard delivers this devastating news and simultaneously ends their relationship, fearing that his connection with Kupfer could harm him.[29] However, the actor's feelings for Eduard diminish quickly. In an interview, Sulzer called relationships such as the one between Kupfer and Eduard "kurzfristige Zweckgemeinschaften,"[30] and the term also describes Kupfer's approach to his affair with Walter, "der ihm am letzten Tag ihrer Bekanntschaft genauso fremd und gleichgültig sein würde wie am ersten."[31]

Kupfer's inability (fear?) to commit may go back to his beloved older brother Tobias's death by drowning when Kupfer was six years old. While the accident happened, Kupfer was drawing and "flirting" with Tobias's acquaintance Siegfried, who admired Kupfer's artwork. "Siegfried" was also Tobias's family nickname, suggesting that during this homoerotically tinged exchange, Kupfer shifts feelings from his brother to Siegfried. Kupfer's decision, that very day, to give up drawing indicates that he feels guilty for his brother's death. Six years later, he comes across Goethe's poem "Erlkönig," which provides him with an aesthetic approach to the memory of Tobias's fatal accident. Acting out the ballad's plot, he realizes that he is actually re-enacting his brother's death and the family's discovery of the body. Goethe's poem allows Kupfer to relive the traumatic experience and to find a way to cope with the loss: through acting, he can "embody" Tobias and thus "bring back" his late brother, and he decides to become an actor. For Kupfer, acting, death, eroticism, and guilt belong together, and his choice of profession is an attempt at making amends.

In the United States, Kupfer has to restart his career and must also re-define his self-image and public persona. Before his emigration, he played suave, desirable lovers, and he also emulated this type in public and in his private life: "Er war längst damit eins geworden."[32] In other words, Kupfer identified with the role of romantic lover, and this was the only role he allowed himself to play. Moreover, while living in Austria and Germany, Kupfer kept his Jewish origins secret; Americans, however, take Kupfer to be a Russian or Polish Jew, and initially, he is often cast as a Soviet soldier (less frequently also as a Nazi). During the Second World War, Kupfer's place of birth, the Galician city of Lemberg, which in 1918 had become the Polish Lwów, was occupied by German and Soviet forces, ultimately becoming part of the Soviet Union. Thus, Kupfer's early roles in the United States overlap again with his off-screen and off-stage roles, yet this time linking him to his Eastern European Jewish roots.

Ultimately, the process of re-defining himself as an actor mirrors Kupfer's personal maturing and overcoming of his childhood trauma. A film by Luchino Visconti in which Kupfer plays himself, a once-famous actor, marks the turning point in this development: his scenes are cut from the film, for the actor the "Auslöschung des Schauspielers Lionel Kupfer,"[33] and he falls into a deep depression. Yet similar to a rebirth, three months later, he is ready to move on: he does not play variations of himself as a romantic lover or Soviet soldier anymore, but "ließ sich verunstalten . . . Er spielte so viele Rollen, dass er sie bald nicht mehr aufzählen konnte."[34] No longer acting to embody his dead brother, Tobias, Kupfer is ready to play any role and even to flirt again. This change had been indicated earlier, when on his way to Visconti's film set, he started drawing again, suggesting that he has overcome his feelings of guilt.

The completion of this process is marked by Kupfer's nomination for an Academy Award and his writing of a letter to Walter. Telling Walter about Tobias's death, Kupfer for the first time opens up to another person. He senses that by leaving Walter, he may have missed an opportunity for true love and happiness. Kupfer's struggles, his honesty, and his regrets counterbalance his careless treatment of Walter earlier, and since large portions of the novel are told from Kupfer's perspective, readers are invited to relate to this figure. Moreover, Walter's lack of consideration for his mother, who raised him on her own and who loves him dearly, but of whose working-class background and limited education he seems ashamed, makes him a less positive romantic figure, offsetting further some of Kupfer's guilt.

Although André, Leo, Jakob, and Kupfer are anything but ideal romantic partners, their former lovers all develop images of them as well as of themselves that are informed by romances, and they cling to these stylizations even after the break-ups. Viewed through Lacan's findings on the import of narratives of desire and idealizing images of lovers for relationships, these stylizations emerge as a strategy of coping with abandonment by trying to save the rejected partners' places in the narratives of romantic love and hence their idealization by their lovers. However, their efforts come at the cost of forfeiting the chance of emotional and intellectual development. According to Sartre, besides the limits imposed on us by our corporealities and our histories, we are completely free.[35] This means that we are responsible for our subjectivities, that is, for who we are, how we live our lives, and how we experience the world. By contrast, Sulzer's neglected lovers have decided to live as objects in romantic constellations, even if their reality does not conform to this pattern. In other words, they want others (their lovers) to define them by giving them roles in romances, and when their partners are no longer available to do so, they find ways of "preserving" their roles with the inspiration of romance novels, operas, and films.

These identificatory dynamics are very obvious for the figure of Martha in *Privatstunden*. An avid reader, Martha, who finds her life mundane and unfulfilling, escapes into the worlds of novels. She is fascinated with Leo, because to her, he resembles fictional characters and promises their "Daseinsintensität":[36] "Leo hingegen war widerfahren, was jenen Helden widerfuhr, denen man sonst nur in Büchern begegnete."[37] Martha does not fall for Leo instantly, but only when he tells her about his former girlfriend. Paradoxically, this unhappy love story, which casts a negative light on Leo, serves as the trigger for Martha's stylizations of him and herself as romantic lovers. Thus, she finds it exciting that Leo abandoned Laura, "wie Männer es in den Büchern taten,"[38] and when Martha realizes that her husband is having an affair, she identifies with Laura, who was also "unbemerkt verlassen worden."[39]

Despite the fact that Martha holds the socially stronger position and could dominate their relationship, she embraces the romance narrative and identifies with the traditional female role it offers. Thus, when they first embrace, Martha enters the novel that she fantasizes Leo's life to be and of which he is the author. Indeed, as Leo approaches Martha, he begins telling this story silently: he suspends his student role and maintains that only he can understand the meaning of her gestures, as if she were no longer communicating in the real world, but only with him in his novel. He stylizes her into a typical romantic heroine, that is, a fragile, lonely "damsel in distress" in need of protection, yet simultaneously promising the nurturing care for which Leo longs. As he takes on the masculine role of romantic hero, Leo does not speak the German language Martha is teaching him, but lapses into his native tongue, of which he has full control. Consistent with her new role, Martha refrains from insisting that he use German. Only too willing to fill the part of romantic heroine, she stylizes herself as a passive figure, a cat petted by Leo and a prisoner to be rescued by him: "Leo hatte es in der Hand, sie würde tun, was er von ihr verlangte."[40] Martha the housewife and Martha the lover are like separate individuals, and as she becomes more deeply involved with Leo and his "novel," she finds it increasingly difficult to keep up the appearances of her bourgeois life. For her, Martha the lover represents who she truly is, and she believes that only Leo sees and accepts her.[41]

Though Martha finally understands that her affair is an attempt to do the impossible, namely to live a romance, she is not willing to give up the image of herself as a romantic lover.[42] When she learns that Leo will leave her, she manages the despair by briefly stepping out of their "novel" and looking at the relationship with society's eyes. At that moment, she acknowledges that the age gap and their different backgrounds stand between them. Accordingly, she perceives Leo's room with the furniture of his host family's children for what it really is, "ein Kinderzimmer,"[43] and when she strokes his hair, it is a motherly as opposed to an erotic gesture. Yet after Leo's departure, she returns into her romance, the memory of which she can now control fully. In other words, Martha actively preserves and shapes a love story in which she plays a passive female role. In an effort to protect her romance from any "readings" besides her own, she does not speak about the affair with anyone but her father, who can no longer communicate. She never brings it up with her son Andreas, the only one who knows of it, and she refuses to hear about Andreas's meeting with Leo thirty-five years later. She even keeps it secret that Leo fathered her second son, Bruno, thus protecting her unhappy marriage while keeping her bourgeois life and her affair as separate as possible. Consequently, Martha's desire to sustain her role of romantic heroine acts as a barrier between her and those close to her, including Leo. In fact, she seems so deeply locked into her role that even after her divorce she does not start a new relationship.

For thirty years, Erneste, the protagonist of *Ein perfekter Kellner*, is as unwilling as Martha to leave the past behind, yet, ultimately forced to acknowledge the impossibility of a reunion with Jakob, he begins to define his self-image outside their relationship. Despite Jakob's shortcomings, Erneste has stylized their affair into a traditional romance of two lovers who were separated by life's unpredictability but will be reunited eventually. His favorite aria, "Le Postillon de Lonjumeau" from Adolphe Adam's 1836 opera of the same name, serves as a leitmotif representing his hopes. The opera tells the story of a postilion who leaves his wife on their wedding day to join the Royal Paris Opera. While he is away, she inherits money and a new name, and when after years they meet, he does not recognize her and falls in love again. Upset that he proposes to her despite their earlier marriage, his wife does not unveil her true identity until he is about to be executed for bigamy. In the end the postilion's unfaithfulness emerges as true love, and the couple is happily reunited—presumably what Erneste hopes will happen for him and Jakob.[44] Unlike Martha, who seems afraid that seeing Leo again would jeopardize her fantasy of their relationship, Erneste believes that the relationship with Jakob can continue.

Erneste's fascination with Jakob is based on idealization and identification. Smitten with Jakob at first sight, Erneste strives to make himself and Jakob resemble each other as closely as possible, and the role of the waiter becomes the main vehicle for this project: Erneste aspires to make the two of them equally perfect waiters. On the one hand, this wish for identification suggests that Erneste wants to be desired by Jakob the same way that he desires his lover. On the other hand, their identification means that Erneste can "embody" Jakob and preserve the illusion of their unity beyond their affair. Accordingly, after Jakob's departure, being a waiter is not just a job for Erneste, but an identity—he is nothing but a perfect waiter. This evokes Freud's claim that identification can serve as "Ersatz für eine libidinöse Objektbindung . . ., gleichsam durch Introjektion des Objekts ins Ich."[45] Thus, Erneste maintains, "Jakob schwamm durch ihn hindurch, und er schwamm in Jakob."[46] As the latter image conveys, Erneste cannot imagine separation. As does Martha with Leo, Erneste organizes his life around preserving the images of himself and Jakob that he created when they were together. For Erneste this means avoiding anything that might jeopardize his being a perfect waiter, and thus he leads a highly structured and lonely life. The fact that for years he has not looked at pictures of himself and of Jakob from their time in Giessbach indicates Erneste's fear that a closer look at the past may undermine his romantic idealization.

Only after Jakob's death can Erneste begin to let go of the role connecting him to his former lover. Realizing that their union has become impossible, Erneste is finally able to be a less than perfect waiter, and for the first time ever he takes a break on his way to work to enjoy the view across the foggy lake. He begins experimenting with an existence outside of the romance paradigm, which will allow for development beyond one fixed identity. Likening the time with Jakob to the far side of the lake, Erneste is ready to move on: "Er mußte aber damit rechnen, daß der Nebel sich bald wieder lichtete und die Sicht von neuem freigab. Aber bis dahin wird wieder Zeit vergangen sein."[47] Unlike Martha, Erneste ultimately gives up his fantasy of romance for reality and accepts responsibility for who he is and for the need to develop.

While *Ein perfekter Kellner* and *Privatstunden* both revolve around lovers whose desire for romance is disappointed, the main characters' approaches to their relationships differ in important ways. Swept off his feet by Jakob, the waiter Erneste is a prime example of Roland Barthes's "Intraitable amoureux,"[48] an "incurable" romantic lover who cannot establish the distance necessary to analyze his relationship objectively. By contrast, Martha appears to shape her experience with Leo more deliberately. Though she initially identifies with Leo's former girlfriend, Laura, to create a romantic fantasy that reflects the traditional gender division, Martha breaks out of the passive female role soon after the first embrace. Instead of waiting for Leo to contact her, she visits and seduces him, and when he announces his plans to emigrate, she insists that they carry on their secret affair unchanged until his departure. Considering Leo her one chance at escaping her average bourgeois existence, Martha seems determined to have as perfect a romance as possible—even if this requires her swapping the feminine role of romantic heroine for a more proactive, stereotypically masculine part occasionally. She takes a rational, objective approach to romance: aware that romantic love is an ideal hardly compatible with her middle-class reality, she keeps the two spheres and her roles in each separate—unlike Erneste, for whom being a perfect waiter and being a romantic lover are inseparable.[49] Ultimately, while Erneste is an "incurable" lover *unable* to stop loving Jakob, Martha does not *want* to stop loving Leo.

In *Postskriptum*, allusions to the romance genre are much subtler than in *Privatstunden* and *Ein perfekter Kellner*, and together with the open ending, they leave it to readers to draw connections to the traditional romantic love story. The actor Kupfer usually plays romantic heroes, and Walter's image of him is shaped by these roles. In fact, the young man is not sure whether he is in love with Kupfer's movie figures or with the actor himself, wondering, "ob er sich jene Tage im Engadin . . . nicht bloß eingebildet habe, nachdem er zu viele Lionel-Kupfer-Filme gesehen hatte, . . . ein verwirrend unwirkliches Trugbild, das er aus dem Kinosaal

. . . mitgenommen hatte."[50] The superimposition of the actor's fictional characters informs all their encounters as well as Walter's memories.

When in 1933, Walter walks into the hotel Waldhaus hoping to meet his idol at the afternoon tea, it is as if he steps into one of Kupfer's films. In preparation for the adventure, Walter puts on a "costume" appropriate for the role he hopes to play: his best clothes, including an expensive jacket he stole earlier.[51] The episode is reminiscent of romantic movies from the time, where five o'clock teas at hotels often bring together protagonists from different social spheres. These characters fall in love and, after overcoming many obstacles, get married.[52] Evoking the coincidences typically driving the plots of such cinematic romances, Walter meets Kupfer's only acquaintance at the hotel, who subsequently introduces the two men. Meanwhile, Walter's mother, a low-level hotel employee, watches her son from afar in utter disbelief—not unlike the "little shopping girls" the cultural critic Siegfried Kracauer described as the main audience of romantic movies during the interwar years. Appropriately, Walter's experience of Eduard's arrival on the scene and hence the ending of his affair with Kupfer is conveyed in theatrical or cinematic terms: "Walter spielte nun wieder die Nebenrolle, für die man ihn verpflichtet hatte, Lionel die Hauptrolle. Eduard spielte die zweite Hauptrolle. . . . Licht aus und Vorhang."[53] Not surprisingly, in Walter's dreams, his rival in romance, Eduard, is "ein erhabener Fürst," who combines qualities of an angel and a dancer.[54]

Though his emigration interrupted Kupfer's career, a later encounter between him and Walter once again conjures typical romantic movie scenes. In 1949, the men find themselves on the same Swissair flight, Walter as flight attendant, Kupfer as passenger. By the mid-1900s, airplanes had joined elegant hotels as popular sites in films where couples would meet against social odds. Such chance meetings would typically start relationships or bring separated lovers back together. Although Walter and Kupfer both pretend not to recognize each other, Sulzer's novel evokes these conventional plots. Thus, that evening Walter fantasizes about the actor moving in with him and about visiting Kupfer's grave. In the fantasy, the gravestone displays Kupfer's and another name that is illegible, but is not Walter's and "es war auch kein anderer."[55] This dream reveals Walter's continued hope for a reunion and even for an eternal union in death—a motif that has intrigued writers and audiences since the Middle Ages. Even though he cannot see how such a reunion could ever happen, his feelings for Kupfer are too strong to imagine that the actor might be with someone else. Kupfer flies to a movie shoot, and when later at a screening of the movie the newsreel reports the crash of a Swissair plane, he feels compelled to respond to a letter from Walter. The latter had written on the occasion of the actor's nomination for an Academy Award (again, Kupfer the actor attracted

Walter's attention). It remains open whether Walter died in the crash or is still living and receives Kupfer's letter, in turn, leaving it to readers whether they envision a reunion and happy ending or a story of lost opportunities, that is, a typical romance where the lovers ultimately overcome all impediments or a story about love and desire thwarted by politics and the vagaries of reality.[56]

Despite the novel's allusions to romances, the relationship between Walter and Kupfer does not emulate this model. While both protagonists seem to long for a romantic relationship, their actions hide, even contradict these desires. Instead, their behavior and attitudes evoke aspects of objective love, in particular the tendency to rationalize the choice of partners based on social or economic terms (including intangible assets such as fame).[57] Thus Walter never expects a long-term commitment from Kupfer because of their difference in social status. In turn, Kupfer, who is significantly older and more famous than Walter, perceives himself as superior and in control of their affair, which he initially treats as an interlude between movie shootings. First indications that Kupfer feels closer to Walter than he admits to himself are his urge to hear the postal clerk's voice right before his departure from Sils Maria and the realization that leaving the young man is painful; Walter's sobbing in response to the news of Kupfer's emigration bespeaks his desperation. The two men pretend that their brief liaison is purely sexual, but their emotional involvement is much deeper. Nonetheless, they both seem to move on after Kupfer's departure: over the years, they have other lovers and they do not use their chance encounter on the plane to re-establish contact. However, Walter's fainting after Kupfer disembarks from the plane and his fantasies about a reunion and the actor's repeated musings about a relationship with Walter bespeak their true feelings. Indeed, the two men seem to have internalized the rules of objective love so deeply that they cannot admit to themselves their actual desire for romance, let alone express it.[58]

By contrast, Emil and Sebastian in *Zur falschen Zeit* represent a quintessentially romantic couple, and ultimately, they confirm their relationship in the most radical way—they commit suicide together. This ending is prepared by the operas that Sulzer evokes throughout the novel and that present the *Liebestod* as a final affirmation of love in the face of hopelessly adverse circumstances. When Sebastian's mother threatens to destroy Emil's life by accusing him of seducing her son, Emil's inability to give up his façade of bourgeois propriety becomes fatal. His favorite operas highlight the dangerous tension between forbidden love and social pressure. They weave the possibility of death into the novel's narrative while providing images of ideal lovers with which Emil can identify. Sulzer names explicitly the composers Verdi and Puccini, who are likely to evoke *Aida* and *Tosca*, two operas idealizing lovers who would rather die with their beloved than live without them. Mention of another Puccini opera further characterizes Emil's self-image. As he reads the letter from Sebastian's mother, the aria "Sì, mi chiamano Mimì" from *La Bohème* plays on the radio. When Mimì falls ill with tuberculosis, her poor lover Rodolfo breaks up with her, hoping she will find a wealthy suitor who can pay for her treatment. However, their love is too strong, and eventually Mimì dies in Rodolfo's arms. The allusion to *La Bohème* suggests that Emil may briefly consider leaving Sebastian to protect him, but then embraces a notion of love that cannot bear separation.

Most significant is Emil's fascination with the Italian composer Umberto Giordano and his opera *Andrea Chénier*. Emil comes across Giordano after André's move to Paris, which marks the first time that Emil has experienced the possible ending of love and desire and hence of being the object of idealization. The mental breakdown following André's departure indicates the extent to which the break-up shakes Emil's self-image. In order to retake control of his identity, he tries to liberate himself from bourgeois society's expectations for young men like him. However, these attempts fail and he is sent to a mental institution.[59] He learns that homosexuality cannot be cured and that he will always have to suppress and hide his desires in order to secure social respect and parental love. Giordano's opera seems to offer a solution: set during the French Revolution, it revolves around the love between a poet and a noblewoman, who joins her lover on the scaffold when he is executed as an alleged counterrevolutionary. While André embraces a promiscuous lifestyle, Emil seeks the kind of unconditional love represented by the opera, and the similarity of the names "André" and "Andrea" suggests that Emil fantasizes about dying with André. The importance of Giordano's work for Emil's self-image is confirmed when the opera serves as catalyst for his and Sebastian's suicide: the two listen to love duets from *Andrea Chénier* during their final hours, presumably identifying with the two operatic lovers. Emil and Sebastian's suicide brings their eternal union and marks their voluntary withdrawal from a society that leaves them only the choice between the closet and ostracization: they come out of the closet, yet simultaneously silence this very violation of social norms, thus escaping any repercussions. Whereas Martha in *Privatstunden* permanently withdraws from reality into the world of romances, Emil and Sebastian, for a brief moment, make that world reality—and in both cases, the protagonists elude the social order.

Studied together, Sulzer's four novels emerge as a provocative exploration into the power of the paradigm of romantic love in the twentieth and twenty-first centuries. These works suggest that despite the introduction of the competing paradigm of objective love, the romantic model has persisted as the ideal. It has undergone changes over time, such as the acceptance of same-sex relationships and of sexual encounters outside of committed relationships or marriages—developments Sulzer's works reflect. Nonetheless, romance's central narrative of two lovers who are made for each other and enter into a monogamous, permanent relationship, forming a union that makes each individual whole, has maintained its appeal, and it is also the ideal that drives Sulzer's characters. At the same time, in these works, relationships fail, and most figures are unhappy due to their own or their partners' mentalities and behavior: some act egoistically, others are unable or unwilling to open up emotionally.[60] Romantic relationships, Sulzer's novels show, need more than mutual attraction, namely partners, "die einem Manuskript folgen,"[61] that is, the socially constituted script of romantic love. Sulzer's protagonists are also, themselves, not only readers and spectators of fictional romances, but actors in fictional romantic relationships they have stylized according to literary, cinematic, and operatic models. As we indulge vicariously in these figures' joys and pains, Sulzer's novels challenge us to explore our own expectations regarding love and desire and the extent to which those have been shaped by romances and follow or reject the script of romantic love.

Notes

Epigraph: Roland Barthes, *A Lover's Discourse: Fragments*, trans. by Richard Howard (New York: Hill and Wang, 2001), 136.

[1] René Pollesch, *Fantasma*, in *Kill Your Darlings: Stücke*, ed. Nils Tabert (Reinbek bei Hamburg: Rowohlt, 2014), 15–61, here 29.

[2] Tobias Haberl, "Toleranz ist keine Lösung für Rassismus," *Süddeutsche Zeitung Magazin* 17 (2012), accessed January 17, 2017, http://sz-magazin.suedde-utsche.de/texte/anzeigen/37453.

[3] Pollesch, *Fantasma*, 29.

[4] Elke Reinhardt-Becker, *Seelenbund oder Partnerschaft? Liebessemantiken in der Literatur der Romantik und der Neuen Sachlichkeit* (Frankfurt am Main: Campus, 2005), 3.

[5] Among others, Sulzer received the Einzelwerkpreis der Schweizer Schillerstiftung (2005), the Prix Medicis étranger (2008), the Hermann-Hesse-Preis (2009), and the Literaturpreis des Freien Deutschen Autorenverbands (2014).

[6] See Esther K. Bauer, "Mired in Perfection: Male Images, Forbidden Desire, and 'Bad Faith' in Novels by Alain Claude Sulzer," *German Life and Letters* 69, no.1 (2016): 105–22, here 106.

[7] See, e.g., Niklas Luhmann, *Love as Passion: The Codification of Intimacy*, trans. Jeremy Gaines and Doris L. Jones (Cambridge: Polity Press, 1986, first published Frankfurt am Main: Suhrkamp, 1982); Reinhardt-Becker, *Seelenbund oder Partnerschaft*; Eva Illouz, *Why Love Hurts: A Sociological Explanation* (Cambridge, UK: Polity, 2012); Janice A. Radway, *Reading the Romance: Women, Patriarchy, and Popular Literature* (Chapel Hill: The University of North Carolina Press, 1991); Helga Arend, *Vom "süßen Rausch" zur "stillen Neigung": Zur Entwicklung der romantischen Liebeskonzeption* (Pfaffenweiler: Centaurus, 1993); Jutta Greis,

Drama Liebe: Zur Entstehungsgeschichte der modernen Liebe im Drama des 18. Jahrhunderts (Stuttgart: Metzler, 1991); Marilyn M. Lowery, "The Traditional Romance Formula," in *Gender, Race and Class in Media: A Text-Reader*, ed. Gail Dines and Jean M. Humez (Thousand Oaks, CA: Sage, 1995), 215–22; Pamela Regis, *A Natural History of the Romance Novel* (Philadelphia: University of Pennsylvania Press, 2003).

[8] See the introduction to this volume.

[9] Anthony Giddens, *The Transformation of Intimacy: Sexuality, Love & Eroticism in Modern Societies* (Cambridge: Polity Press, 1992). References are to the paperback edition, 2003, 40; Illouz, *Why Love Hurts*, 10–13.

[10] Reinhardt-Becker, *Seelenbund oder Partnerschaft*, 205–98. On the "economization" of love relationships, see also Illouz, *Why Love Hurts*, 9.

[11] Jacques Lacan, *Freud's Papers on Technique, 1953–1954*, bk. 1 of *The Seminar of Jacques Lacan*, trans. John Forrester, ed. Jacques-Alain Miller (New York: Norton, 1991), 142.

[12] Peter von Matt, *Liebesverrat: Die Treulosen in der Literatur* (Frankfurt am Main: Deutscher Taschenbuch Verlag, 2008), 61–66.

[13] See Regis, *A Natural History*, 30. Since Regis analyzes only romances with happy endings, her list of key elements can serve only as a guideline. However, the three steps outlined here can be found in every romance. See also Reinhardt-Becker, *Seelenbund oder Partnerschaft*, 319–24.

[14] Luhmann, *Love as Passion*, 60–62.

[15] Alain Claude Sulzer, *Ein perfekter Kellner* (Frankfurt am Main: Suhrkamp, 2006), 76.

[16] Alain Claude Sulzer, *Zur falschen Zeit* (Berlin: Galiani, 2010), 133.

[17] Tony Tanner, *Adultery in the Novel: Contract and Transgression* (Baltimore, MD: Johns Hopkins University Press, 1979), 12–13.

[18] Alain Claude Sulzer, *Privatstunden* (Frankfurt am Main: Suhrkamp, 2009), 168.

[19] An earlier example of a novel that continues beyond the romance plot is Theodor Fontane's *Irrungen, Wirrungen* (1888), a harsh critique of the time's class-conscious marriage politics.

[20] Tilman Krause, "Die Loire-Schlösser des Alain Claude Sulzer. Laudatio auf den Hermann-Hesse-Preisträger des Jahres 2009," unpublished manuscript provided by the Stiftung Hermann-Hesse-Literaturpreis Karlsruhe.

[21] Advocates of such strictly separate male and female roles have often promoted an essentialist gender model, maintaining that each sex has both specific physical *and* psychological characteristics, which, in turn, justify a gendered division of labor. Thus, for instance, more women still serve as primary in-home caregivers for children and elderly relatives, often at the price of a successful professional career and social status, while men continue to hold the majority of prestigious leadership positions in business, politics, and the arts; and whereas sexual conquests contribute to men's social standing and hence encourage postponement of commitment, more women seek committed love relationships.

[22] See, e.g., Illouz, *Why Love Hurts*, 59–108, and *Erwerbs- und Sorgearbeit neu gestalten: Gutachten für den Zweiten Gleichstellungsbericht der Bundesregierung*, ed. Sachverständigenkommission zum Zweiten Gleichstellungsbericht der Bundesregierung und Institut für Sozialarbeit und Sozialpädagogik e.V. (2017), accessed June 21, 2017, www.gleichstellungsbericht.de.

[23] Lacan writes: "It is in the *name of the father* that we must recognize the basis of the symbolic function which, since the dawn of historical time, has identified his person with the figure of the law." Jacques Lacan, "The Function and Field of Speech and Language in Psychoanalysis," in *Écrits: The First Complete Edition in English*, trans. Bruce Fink, with Héloïse Fink and Russell Grigg (New York: W. W. Norton, 2006), 197–268, here 230 (italics in original, E.B.).

[24] The following headlines in popular print and online magazines corroborate this observation: "Wollen Männer wirklich immer nur Sex?" (*Freundin*, 18. Juni 2017, http://www.freundin.de/liebe-michael-nast-wollen-maenner-immer-nur-sex-262510.html); "Frauen wollen Blumen, Männer wollen Sex" (*Welt*, June 26, 2013, https://www.welt.de/vermischtes/article117458290/Frauen-wollen-Blumen-Maenner-wollen-Sex.html); "Männer wollen Sex beim ersten Date"; a subheading in this last article emphasizes the difference between men and women: "Frauen beim ersten Date weniger offen für Sex" (*Wunderweib*, September 6, 2012, http://www.wunderweib.de/maenner-wollen-sex-beim-ersten-date-8205.html).

[25] Sulzer, *Privatstunden*, 208.

[26] Sulzer, *Zur falschen Zeit*, 120.

[27] Sulzer, *Zur falschen Zeit*, 125.

[28] Alain Claude Sulzer, *Postskriptum* (Berlin: Galiani, 2015), 25.

[29] Given the value system guiding romances, Eduard's murder by a Jewish man whose detained sister Eduard refuses to help comes as no surprise.

[30] Sulzer in an interview. T. A. Wegberg, "Schreib, so laut du kannst!," accessed October 22, 2016, http://tawegberg.blogspot.com/2015/11/wenns-nicht-tragisch-ist-wei-ich-nicht.html.

[31] Sulzer, *Postskriptum*, 128.

[32] Sulzer, *Postskriptum*, 45.

[33] Sulzer, *Postskriptum*, 237.

[34] Sulzer, *Postskriptum*, 240.

[35] Jean-Paul Sartre, *Being and Nothingness: A Phenomenological Essay on Ontology*, trans. Hazel E. Barnes (New York: Washington Square Press, 1966), 404–45, 557–711.

[36] Tilman Krause, "Die Loire-Schlösser der Literatur," *Die Welt*, January 23, 2010. https://www.welt.de/welt_print/kultur/literatur/article5950877/Die-Loire-Schloesser-der-Literatur.html.

[37] Sulzer, *Privatstunden*, 169.

[38] Sulzer, *Privatstunden*, 136.

[39] Sulzer, *Privatstunden*, 138.

[40] Sulzer, *Privatstunden*, 170.

[41] Reinhardt-Becker defines this kind of acceptance of the whole individual as an important component of romantic love that promises to make the individual more complete. Reinhardt-Becker, *Seelenbund oder Partnerschaft*, 100–118.

[42] Martha's son Andreas recognizes the fiction-like quality of the affair between his mother and Leo: "Das ist doch wie in einem Buch, wie in einem Roman." Sulzer, *Privatstunden*, 210.

[43] Sulzer, *Privatstunden*, 235.

[44] See Walter Krause, "Adolphe Adam, *Le Postillon de Lonjumeau*," *Tamino Klassikforum*, last modified September 3, 2007, accessed December 18, 2016, . http://www.tamino-klassikforum.de/index.php?page=Thread&postID=180880.

[45] Sigmund Freud, "Massenpsychologie und Ich-Analyse," *Studienausgabe*, vol. 9, ed. Alexander Mitscherlich et al. (Frankfurt am Main: Fischer, 2003), 61–134, here 100.

[46] Sulzer, *Ein perfekter Kellner*, 80.

[47] Sulzer, *Ein perfekter Kellner*, 215. For a detailed analysis of the relationship between Erneste and Jakob, see Bauer, "Mired in Perfection," 113–18.

[48] Roland Barthes, *Fragments d'un disours amoureux* (Paris: Seuil, 1977), 29.

[49] For Erneste as a representation of Sartre's concept of "bad faith," see Bauer, "Mired in Perfection," 113–18.

[50] Sulzer, *Postskriptum*, 243.

[51] The motif of the stolen jacket evokes Irmgard Keun's 1932 novel *Das kunstseidene Mädchen*, whose female protagonist steals a fur coat. She views her life as a film and simultaneously hopes the coat will help her gain access to the world of film.

[52] Siegfried Kracauer, "Die kleinen Ladenmädchen gehen ins Kino," in Kracauer, *Das Ornament der Masse* (Frankfurt am Main: Suhrkamp, 1977), 279–94, here 288–89.

[53] Sulzer, *Postskriptum*, 133.

[54] Sulzer, *Postskriptum*, 134–35.

[55] Sulzer, *Postskriptum*, 236.

[56] Although Sulzer maintained in an interview that Walter obviously dies in the plane crash—"Aber das ist doch offensichtlich, dass er umkommt."—the novel itself does not offer a conclusive answer. Karen N. Gerig and Dominque Spirgi, "Alain Claude Sulzer: 'Meine Figuren glauben nicht an die grosse Liebe. Ich schon,'" *Tageswoche*, September 24, 2015. http://www.tageswoche.ch/de/2015_39/kultur/699340/.

[57] Reinhardt-Becker, *Seelenbund oder Partnerschaft*, 230–36.

[58] Kupfer seems emotionally invested in his relationship with Eduard, as is indicated by the secret love note hidden under the stamp on a letter to Eduard and his wife. However, the fact that Kupfer starts an affair with Walter while involved with Eduard, suggests early on that the actor does not adhere to romantic exclusivity.

[59] As a young adult, Emil spends time at a mental institution repeatedly. He and his parents hope he can be "cured" of his homosexuality and his urge to break out of bourgeois structures, which shows, for instance, in his wish to drop out of school and become an artist. While the first stay is forced by his parents, Emil checks in voluntarily several more times. Sulzer, *Zur falschen Zeit*, 86–120.

[60] Tessa Lewis, "*Ein perfekter Kellner*—Der Preis der Gefühle: Alain Claude Sulzers intime Erzählkunst," trans. Katja Meintel, *Viceversa literatur 6: Jahrbuch der Schweizer Literaturen* (Zurich: Limmat, 2012): 145–49, here 145.

[61] Pollesch, *Fantasma*, 29.

Love as Literature: Hanns-Josef Ortheil's *Die große Liebe*

Helmut Schmitz, University of Warwick

"HAPPY LOVE," remarks Denis de Rougemont, "has no history. Romance only comes into existence where love is fatal, frowned upon and doomed by life itself."[1] Noting that the history of love in Western European literature begins in the twelfth century with a story of an adulterous couple—Tristan and Isolde—de Rougemont reminds us that literature knows mainly unhappy and unfulfilled love stories. From the medieval love poetry of the Provencal troubadours via Dante and Beatrice, Petrarch and Laura, to Romeo and Juliet; in the literary tradition of Europe between the medieval period and the Renaissance, love and suffering belong closely together.

In the modern "literary" novel, there is likewise no happiness in love to be found. However, modern love is unhappy for different reasons than pre-modern love. Love in the modern novel is unhappy not (just) as a result of the conflict-ridden structure of desire or because of insurmountable social obstacles but as a reflection of the overburdening of the subject in relation to an increasingly diversified, stratified, and administered society. A number of social theorists comment on the increasing fragmentation of the modern bourgeois subject into to a variety of social roles in the transformation from a feudal to a bourgeois society in the mid to late eighteenth century.[2] This creates a situation where the public role of administrative work and the private, domestic existence of the bourgeois subject can no longer be easily brought into harmony. In this destabilizing social situation, love and intimate relationships become charged with the promise of restoring balance and happiness to the individual in the domestic sphere, promising him/her the recognition the outside world increasingly withholds. With reference to Niklas Luhmann's theory of social stratification, which sees the subject in an increasingly diversified set of social roles, Karin A. Wurst argues that love turns into a compensatory discourse that is supposed to stabilize the bourgeois self within a domestic harmony. The home and the relationship with the designated (female) Other becomes the space where the (male) subject wants to experience his whole persona in the exchange with the partner. According to Wurst, the literature of *Empfindsamkeit* and *Sturm und Drang*, articulating the search for an alternative to bourgeois rationality, is essentially an expression of this overburdening of love with the expectation to "heal" the damaged modern self.[3] However, this search is frequently disappointed, becaue the cult of hypersensual individuality, requiring the reciprocity of intense relationships "decreases the likelihood of finding a suitable 'soul mate' and increases the possibility that the subject desiring the most intimate communication remains without response."[4] Modern literature, from Goethe's *Die Leiden des jungen Werthers* (The Sorrows of Young Werther, 1774) onwards essentially chronicles the failure of this aspiration to find a partner with whom to experience a harmonious unity. Whereas Petrarch's sonnets analyze the antithesis of emotions, creating an "endless debate with himself and within himself . . . because he himself is the theater of a battle between opposing passions,"[5] Werther's unhappy love in Goethe's eponymous novel is not least a symptom of the conditions of the modern subject in conflict with his social environment.[6] Through its heroes and heroines such as Werther, Emma Bovary (from Flaubert's *Madame Bovary*, 1856), and Anna Karenina from Tolstoy's novel of the same name (1873–77), the modern novel explores the irresolvable contradiction between romantic fantasy and reality in the context of the suffocating social norms that entangle the bourgeois subject.

In his overview of the literature of love, *The Double Flame*, poet Octavio Paz refers to the predominantly critical and analytical tendency of modern literature, a characteristic that only intensifies in the twentieth century.[7] Stefan Krankenhagen notes "dass die (westliche) Kunst des 20. Jahrhunderts auf ein nicht gelingendes Leben verweist."[8] With reference to Adorno's idea that modernity with its irresolvable contradictions results in a "damaged life," Krankenhagen argues that the task of modern art is to reflect (upon) this damage: "Wenn also das Einzelne wie das Ganze, Individuum und Gesellschaft nur als beschädigt gedacht werden können, muss sich die Formensprache der Kunst dem beschädigten Leben anverwandeln, um noch 'kritisch und widerständig' zu sein."[9] Whether for reasons of social history or narrative logic which seems to demand conflict and insurmountable obstacles,[10] what the modern novel finds worthy of narration is predominantly unhappiness. Happy love stories are relegated to the fairy tale and the comedy and, in the twentieth century, the trashy romance novel and the Hollywood film. Indeed, it is indicative that the term "romance" that designates the beginnings of Western European narrative literature, today predominantly describes a frowned-upon genre of commercialized trash.[11]

As the introduction to this volume points out, contemporary social theory diagnoses a growing ironization of romantic passion as a result of the "destructuring of romantic desire" in an increasingly rationalized hypermodernity. In her 2012 study *Why Love Hurts*, Eva Illouz describes the discourses of high and hyper-modernity as a program of dis-enchantment and rationalization that ultimately corrodes romantic love as a phenomenon.[12] As early as 1982, Niklas Luhmann made the same observation.[13]

In the face of these diagnoses of the cooling of romantic desire and the overwhelming tradition of unhappy love, and high culture's suspicion towards the romance genre, it may surprise that a contemporary author chose the theme of happy love for a trilogy of novels at the beginning of the twenty-first century. Between 2003 and 2011, Hanns-Josef Ortheil published three novels that all carry the term "Liebe" in the title and that could all be described with the term "Liebesroman," a term originating in *Trivialliteratur*.[14] The titles of the trilogy, *Die große Liebe* (Great Love, 2003), *Das Verlangen nach Liebe* (The Desire for Love, 2007), and *Liebesnähe* (Love's Closeness, 2011), all suggest a proximity to trash romance rather than "high" literature. All three novels tell emphatically blissful and successful love stories; while the first attracted an initially euphoric reception, both in the review pages and among the reading public, the second and third were received with increasing irritation as to their "happy," conflict-free content and topic.[15] Both as individual novels and as a larger project, these texts represent something new in German-language literature, and not just in the contemporary period. They seek to elevate a topic—happy love—that is absent in both postwar German writing and modern European literature and integrate it back into serious literature. This chapter will discuss the first novel of the trilogy, *Die große Liebe*, and position it in relation to the literary tradition of love from the Middle Ages via the periods of *Empfindsamkeit*, *Sturm und Drang*, and early Romanticism to the contemporary period. Without intending to be exhaustive, given the breadth of the subject, I will focus on Ortheil's *reception* of these literary traditions and the way this reception is reflected in *Die große Liebe* through motifs, ideas, and terminology.

Die große Liebe tells the story of the Munich TV editor Johannes, referred to as Giovanni throughout the novel, who travels to San Benedetto del Tronto on the Adriatic Coast of the Italian Marches region to prepare a documentary about the local Institute of Marine Biology. There, he and the head of the institute, Franca, fall in love with each other. Franca, however, is engaged to her colleague and future boss, Dottor Gianni Alberti, who follows the couple to the regional capital Ascoli Piceno, where Giovanni and Franca are spending the night. In Ascoli, Giovanni and Alberti meet at a restaurant after Franca has dis-solved her engagement with Alberti, a scene that Giovanni describes as a "Duell" between two rivals (242). The novel ends with a discussion between Giovanni and Franca's father, who blesses the relationship, and with Franca's decision to visit Giovanni in Munich before they both intend to return to the Marches to finish the documentary.

This short summary of the novel's flimsy, operetta-like plot makes clear that *Die große Liebe* is not interested in the detailed narration of love's pains and obstacles that we are used to from classical love-literature like Goethe's *Die Leiden des jungen Werthers*, obstacles that cause love to grow or to fail. On the contrary, after a short phase of insecurity on the part of Giovanni, and after Franca has taken the initiative sexually during a research outing on the coast, it becomes clear that both partners are in the grip of a mutually reciprocated love; the term "große Liebe" is used several times within a short space (117, 118, 119). On the surface, the novel appears to follow the romance genre with its conventions of immediate attraction, surmounted obstacles, and happy ending.

Die große Liebe as Anti-Werther-Novel

What looks like a clichéd holiday romance in Italy, the country of German desire and longing, however, pursues a designated poetological program that includes a complex intertextual reflection on the literary history of love from the middle ages to modernity and elaborates a poetics of love as an aesthetic project. The name of Giovanni's rival, Alberti, points to Goethe's *Die Leiden des jungen Werthers* as an intertext from which the novel self-consciously distances itself. This ironic critique of Goethe's novel, the "Urtext unserer Moderne"[16] and "Vorbild"[17] of disastrous love stories, both literary and real, is already written into Ortheil's first historical novel *Faustinas Küsse* (Faustina's Kisses, 1998), a novel about Goethe's stay in Rome and his erotic relationship to a local girl. Giovanni Beri, the novel's protagonist, thinks of Werther as "laut, aufdringlich und schwärmerisch . . . er war ein eitler Schwätzer und Redner, der alle mit seinen verdrehten Meinungen bestürmte." Beri can only digest Goethe's novel in small quantities: "er spürte bald, dass von diesem Buch etwas Bitteres ausging, ja, er hatte sofort geahnt, dass es schlimm enden würde." Beri is especially disturbed by the novel's concept of love: "Ach, diese Menschen lebten einfach verdreht! Sie waren nicht füreinander da, sondern standen einander im Wege, jeder trat dem anderen auf die Füße, und das Ganze nannten sie dann 'Schicksal' oder 'Notwendigkeit.'" He would show Goethe "wie man es besser mache . . . denn er hätte aus Werther einen Römer gemacht."[18]

Die große Liebe represents this "improvement" mentioned in *Faustinas Küsse*, a self-reflexive correction of the love represented in Goethe's *Werther*, both with respect to Goethe's protagonist and the tragic relationship between Werther and his environment in Goethe's novel. Julia Eckert's detailed analysis describes *Die große Liebe* as "Umkehrung des Werther'schen Liebeskonzepts" and "Anti-Werther-Roman."[19] Two central motifs in Goethe's novel, frequently noted in critical literature, are the compensatory value of Werther's love to

Lotte, which briefly stabilizes Werther's increasing alienation from society, and his failing attempts to empathize with nature.[20] In the famous letter from 22 May, Werther notes: "Ich kehre in mich selbst zurück und finde eine Welt."[21] Julia Bobsin remarks in this respect that Werther's love for Lotte denotes "die letzte Stufe einer fortschreitenden Verengung des Außenweltkontaktes für Werther."[22] In contrast to Werther's turn towards inwardness, the lovers in *Die große Liebe* carry out a movement outwards, towards the world and towards each other. Through his love to Franca, Giovanni finds a route "zu einer neuen Erkenntnisqualität hinsichtlich seiner Umwelt."[23] At the side of Franca, who guides Giovanni through the landscapes of the Marches region, the world shines with a new light: "es war, als öffneten ihre Hinweise und Worte mir plötzlich auf eine unerhörte Weise die Augen, die Welt war kein Zufall mehr, sie war ein . . . Tempel der Anschauungen, in dem ich mit ihr verschwinden sollte, ganz und gar" (92).

Beyond its reference to Goethe's *Werther* as a novel about "die Unmöglichkeit der Liebe,"[24] the novel's referential horizon ranges from Gottfried von Straßburg's *Tristan und Isolde* (1210) and medieval mysticism via Renaissance Petrarchism and German Romanticism to the contemporary neuro-biological discourses of love as a chemical process with which Giovanni's cameraman wishes to rationalize Giovanni's love: "mehrfach war von Neuropeptiden und emotionalen Systemen die Rede, ich hätte wissen müssen, daß Liebe der Anbahnungszustand der arterhaltenden Partnerwahl war, nichts anderes also als ein vorübergehender biologisch erfaßbarer Zustand . . . Gefühle von großer Nähe, ja sogar von Verschmelzung waren nichts anderes als Ergebnisse eines Hormonüberschwangs" (130). In so doing, *Die große Liebe* self-assuredly counters both the discourses of rationalization in contemporary science and the disillusioning tradition of modern literature with an understanding of love as auto-poetic and self-reflexive literary discourse, as well as a mystery in a secularized Christian-Platonic tradition. It is this line of tradition of medieval mysticism, Petrarchism, and Romanticism that I will now turn to.

Die große Liebe and Medieval Mysticism

Giovanni and Franca's experience of their mutual seduction, their jointly enjoyed ecstatic gaze, and the enjoyment of auratic local dishes recall experiential contexts described by medieval German mystics, particularly female mystics, as "unio mystica," the spiritual union with God. From the outset, the love between Giovanni and Franca is characterized by a quasi-mystic understanding, a devotion and trust. The lovers complement each other in an almost uncanny fashion in a symbiotic, harmonic duality, a *"Zweiheit"* (198, italics original, HS): "noch nie habe ich mich mit jemandem so verbunden gefühlt" (198). The communication between the two produces "Momente puren Verstehens" (213), and a "tiefe Vertrautheit" (196). There is no uncertainty, neither with respect to each other's emotions nor in their relationship to the world: "ich war mir gewiß, daß sie genauso empfand" (243), says Giovanni.

The union between Giovanni and Franca recalls central motifs of the experience of the "unio mystica" as described by Bardo Weiß: "Für die Mystikerinnen dieser Zeit [12th–13th centuries., HS] gehören . . . Ekstase, Liebe und 'unio mystica' eng zusammen. Die 'unio mystica' wird im wesentlichen als Vereinigung des menschlichen Willens mit dem göttlichen geschildert. Zu dieser Einheit kann nur Liebe führen. Diese Liebe zu Gott aber beinhaltet ein Absehen von sich selbst und eine vorbehaltlose und ungeteilte Hingabe an den Geliebten."[25]

Ortheil uses the term "Hingabe" in his discussion of the novel's concept of love as "eine Liebe zweier Menschen ohne Vorbehalte, . . . die von Anfang an von einem starken gegenseitigen Vertrauen und von einer absoluten Hingabe getragen wird."[26] Ortheil's use of the term "Hingabe," evoking religious connotations, demonstrates that the concept of love in *Die große Liebe* is to be distinguished from all the subject-centered and ego-centered concepts of love that dominate the theories of subjectivity in modernity.[27] Love in *Die große Liebe* is not "eine 'Erfahrung des Selbst,'" Ortheil has stated in an interview, but the ecstatic experience of the Other. *Die große Liebe* stages love "als eine Erfahrung von etwas ganz anderem. [Liebe] ist 'selbstlos' im exakten Wortsinne, sie ist eine Aufhebung des sturen Selbst, sie führt zurück zu einem starken 'Weltvertrauen,' ein Vertrauen ins unbefragte Dasein, ins leichte, schwerelose und von Glück getragene Existieren und damit zu jenem Dasein, als das die Schöpfung, folgt man den Erzählungen der Bibel, am Anfang aller Tage einmal geplant war."[28]

Die große Liebe recalls these motifs from medieval mysticism in Giovanni's experience of his union with Franca. These spiritual motifs appear in Otheil's novel transformed into an entirely secular context as "eine Form von säkularisierter Mystik."[29] This transformation, the intersection between spiritual and secular visions of love, is already part of the culture of the middle ages that gives rise to mysticism. Already in medieval *Minne*-literature, as well as later in the period of Romanticism, theological and spiritual motifs mingle with ideas from secular and philosophical literature on love.[30]

Both Weiss and Uta Störmer-Caysa stress that medieval mysticism in its loving devotion to God does not lead mankind away from the world, but "aus seiner Innerlichkeit hinaus nach draußen in die Welt."[31] Giovanni, too, finds the world anew in his love with Franca. He describes his experiences with Franca as a transformation of his self and a discovery of the world: "In der zurückliegenden Woche habe ich ein weites

Terrain erkundet . . . und doch scheint es mir so, als sei die Welt draußen immer mehr zu einem Teil meines Inneren geworden . . . in kaum einer Woche bin ich ein anderer geworden . . . " (270). This formulation is the exact opposite to that of Werther's turn towards inner space in his letter from 22 May: "Ich kehre in mich selbst zurück und finde eine Welt." Whereas Werther's turn towards interiority represents a flight from the world that has to be read in relation to his increasing disappointment with the restrictions of society he experiences as disabling—"[w]enn ich die Einschränkung ansehe, in welcher die tätigen und forschenden Kräfte des Menschen eingesperrt sind"[32]—Ortheil's novel moves its protagonist out of himself into an affirmative investigation of the world as beauty.

Giovanni and Franca's relationship is furthermore characterized by a strong aesthetic element. Like many of Ortheil's protagonists, Giovanni is a habitual writer, his reflective notes are distributed across the entire novel and create a meta-reflexive level of commentary. At the end of the novel, Giovanni's notes are revealed to be the genesis of the novel itself by reference to the novel's opening line, thus creating a cyclical meta-structure that is characteristic of many of Ortheil's novels: "'Plötzlich das Meer, ganz nah'—mit diesem Satz habe ich zu schreiben begonnen" (315). Rather than scientific and analytic, Franca's gaze on the world, too, is synaesthetic and aestheticizing; during her guided tour through the Insitute of Marine Biology, she does not refer to the biological characteristics of the exhibits but exclusively to their aesthetic details: "Es war eine Art Schau, ein begeistertes Sehen . . . eine Verliebtheit in den Anblick von Schönheit, als ginge es hier nicht um Gegenstände der Forschung, sondern um rein ästhetische Reize" (35). Under Franca's guidance through the landscape of the Marches, Giovanni experiences the world as an aesthetic miracle, an ecstatic pleasure of looking: "schauen Sie, ist das nicht wirklich schön, fragte sie immer wieder, als wäre das Universum noch immer der mittelalterliche Kosmos, von Gott geschaffen, den menschlichen Augen zu schmeicheln" (91). This ecstatic gaze transforms all interior and exterior spaces into enchanted auratic spaces: "*Der gesamte Raum um uns herum wird durch unsere Begegnung verändert, er erscheint aufgeladen*" (119, italics original, HS).

Giovanni and Franca's rapturous experiences of looking at the landcape of the Marches are related to what medieval mysticism described as "raptus."[33] Weiß refers to the absence of agency and the experience of being overwhelmed, as well as to the disappearance of "Alltagsbewusstsein"[34] and the "unaniminas voluntatum," the "Einmütigkeit der Willen" in the unity of humans with God as envisioned by Bernhard of Clairvaux and Richard of St.Victor.[35] Weiß writes furthermore of the "Abnahme des eigenen Ichs in der Ekstase" and of "Selbstvergessenheit" as central aspects of the medieval experience of love: "Selbstvergessenheit aber ist sowohl Voraussetzung als auch Folge der Hinwendung zu Gott in der 'unio mystica.'"[36] This self-forgetfulness is not experienced as a reduction of self but as a strengthening of the person: "Bei der Selbstvergessenheit bleibt die eigene Identität gewahrt, ja, sie wird erst ganz verwirklicht."[37]

All of the above elements are characteristic of Ortheil's configuration of Giovanni and Franca's love, transformed into a secular experience. Their communication is characterized by a unanimity of will, "*als käme unser Sprechen und Fühlen aus einem gemeinsamen Zentrum oder Kern*" (120, italics original, HS); their devotion to each other is characterized by a self-forgetfulness that abstracts from obsessive concerns with their selves.

Moerover, Franca and Giovanni's love is constantly concerned with the production of "kleine[n] Epiphanien" (91). These epiphanies are occasioned both by their visual experience of the world and by the mutuality of their spiritual and emotional arousal: "*wir geraten miteinander, könnte man sagen, in einen Zustand der ununterbrochenen, begeisterten Unterhaltung. Es ist eine Art von Verzückung, einer Hyper-Erregung . . . vielleicht ist es wirklich etwas Mystisches, dann hätten die Theologen eben doch Recht. Schwärmerei, Sprach-Wollust, Welt-Verwandlung*" (120, italics original, HS).

Giovanni and Franca's ecstatic visual experiences are a reflection of the "Augenlust" of medieval aesthetics and their conception of the beauty of the world as transcendent "metaphysical certainty."[38] However, the above quote, particularly the term "Schwärmerei" (enthusiasm) in conjunction with the strong aesthetic component of Giovanni and Franca's love, points to the period of *Empfindsamkeit* with its reception and reflection of medieval mysticism, and ultimately to the meta-reflexive aspect of early German Romanticism, particularly to Friedrich Schlegel's novel *Lucinde* (1799).

Die große Liebe, Empfindsamkeit, and early Romanticism

With the reference to "Schwärmerei," *Die große Liebe* mentions one of the key terms of the period between *Empfindsamkeit* and *Sturm und Drang*, from the middle to the late eighteenth century.[39] Central aspects of medieval Catholic mysticism discussed above, including the rapturous "unio mystica," feed into the age of *Empfindsamkeit* via Protestant Pietism. A full exploration of the reception of medieval mystic traditions in the period of *Empfindsamkeit* and of the reception of Petrarchist motifs in its literature and the way they ultimately feed into early Romanticism would go beyond the remit of this chapter;[40] I am interested here predominantly in Ortheil's reception and use of central motifs from *Empfindsamkeit* and *Sturm und Drang* in relation to the literary reflection on love in *Die große*

Liebe, such as the issue of personal authenticity, the question of dialogicity, and the issue of fictionality.

As mentioned in the introduction, the period of *Empfindsamkeit* and *Sturm und Drang* is one of the threshold periods for the formation of modern bourgeois subjectivity, and love becomes one of its key themes. Early bourgeois society seeks to distinguish itself from a codified feudal ideal of behavior seen as false and inauthentic and cultivates a model of simplicity and personal authenticity in the cult of *Empfindsamkeit*.[41] The literature of the *Sturm und Drang* "embraces love as a central aspect of bourgeois identity driving the modernization process, while also pointing to the internal contradictions and the difficulties associated with this transition."[42] Gerhard Sauder comments that *Empfindsamkeit* "produziert ein neues . . . Selbstverständnis, das große, isolierte Ich, den Weltenschöpfer aus der eigenen Seele, die sich in Leidenschaft als (dichterische) Manie eingewurzelt hat."[43] These isolated subjects increasingly fail in their attempts to integrate the ideal of expression, authenticity, love, and harmonic communication in a society experienced as hostile to these ideals. For Gert Mattenklott, Goethe's *Werther* exemplifies the specific failure of this project: "Die Prämisse dieser radikalen Wende in der Kunstentwicklung des 18. Jahrhunderts lautet, daß der innere Reichtum des Subjekts in der äußeren Welt kein angemessenes Gegenüber mehr findet." This failure is expressed, among other aspects, in the monologic nature of Werther's writings, which Mattenklott reads as the cancelling out of the ideal of bourgeois "Geselligkeit."[44]

As indicated above, *Die große Liebe* can be read as a "correction" of the entire complex of the failed search for a harmonic love relationship in *Empfindsamkeit* and *Sturm und Drang*, insofar as it transfers this failed search into a success, a success that is explicitly configured as a dialogic relationship. This can be illustrated with the following comment on *Werther* by Wurst:

> Goethe's *Die Leiden des jungen Werthers* broke new ground by fusing Sentimentalist traits with a new, qualitatively different sense of an all-encompassing power of love as the force of creation and life. In the celebration of love as an almost religious experience, we see a search for alternatives to bourgeois rationality, to materialism, and also to an increasing bureaucratization of life . . . Modern romantic-erotic love becomes part of the search for a more authentic natural life, for an altered state of being, and for communication between highly individualized beings.[45]

It would be possible to apply all of the above statements to *Die große Liebe*, the celebration of an all-encompassing love with almost religious dimensions as well as the altered state of being of the lovers. The difference is that in Goethe's novel this search fails, whereas in Ortheil's novel it is successful, mainly because Ortheil's novel avoids any aspect of social reality that might interfere with the program of love's happiness. In contrast to Goethe's *Werther*, *Die große Liebe* is set in an almost idyllic Italian landscape that bears no relation to the social reality of the novel's German readers, an issue that I will address below.

Finally, *Die große Liebe* rejects one of the central aspects of *Empfindsamkeit*, that of subjective authenticity and sincerity. A number of scholars have commented on the critique of both artifice and fictionality of literature in the period of *Empfindsamkeit* and *Sturm und Drang*, especially in relation to fictional representations of love.[46] Wurst analyzes a number of central texts from the period where literature "turns out to be one of many ridiculous clichés that have no genuine role in the pursuit of authenticity, and even hinder it. Its false forms of communication take the place of potentially more authentic ones."[47]

Again, *Die große Liebe* turns the critique of fictionality and falseness in *Empfindsamkeit* on its head. Rather than a lament on the unreal fictionality of love in literary codes, it is a self-reflexive celebration of it. It is therefore important to note that both Goethe's *Die Leiden des jungen Werthers* and Ortheil's *Die große Liebe* are essentially novels about artists. Where Werther fails as an artist, Giovanni leads a successful creative existence. Moreover, in contrast to Goethe's novel, the female partner in *Die große Liebe* is also characterized as an aesthete with a tendency towards aesthetic production, despite her job as a scientist. As will be illustrated further below, Ortheil's novel operates with an ironic and self-confident conception of itself as literature that takes its cue from the "*potenzierte[n]* Reflexion"[48] of early Romanticism and particularly Schlegel's novel *Lucinde*, which is itself an anti-*Werther*-novel.

The love between Giovanni and Franca in *Die große Liebe* is an aesthetic engine for the creation of ecstatic moments of intensive experience. Apart from the documentary about the Institute of Marine Biology, the product of this love is love itself, which is described meta-reflexively by Giovanni as the "novel" written by both of them. When Franca's fiancé Alberti mocks Giovanni's description of their love as "*Die große Liebe*" with the remark that "diese Begriffe sind etwas für Romane und poetische Abhandlungen," Giovanni retorts:

> Wir befinden uns aber in einem Roman, sagte ich, Franca und ich—
> wir schreiben gleichsam an einem Roman, es ist ein beinahe klassischer Liebesroman, ein Liebesroman *in nuce* . . . ein Roman ohne wirkliche Hindernisse, ohne peinliche Irrtümer und Nebengedanken, es gibt auch keinerlei alberne Umwege und erst recht keine Skepsis, zwei Menschen erkennen, daß sie füreinander geschaffen sind, das ist es, und das ist so gewaltig, daß es alles andere zum Schweigen bringt, es ist *Die Liebe* pur, deshalb nenne ich diesen Roman ja auch *Die große Liebe* . . . (234–35)

Giovanni's description of their love as a "novel" reveals the poetological center of *Die große Liebe*. The novel's self- and meta-reflexivity creates a level of second-degree irony which transports the topic of the novel into the realm of literature and aesthetics, but *without* relativizing it, that is to say, without belittling it as "just" fiction. The harmonious and ideal consonance of the souls in a world-affirming existence and the ironic meta-reflexivity of the texts link *Die große Liebe* with Schlegel's *Lucinde*, the central Romantic novel on love.

Numerous parallels connect Ortheil's and Schlegel's novels. Schlegel's *Lucinde* is also an anti-*Werther*-novel that presents a successful union between two artistically minded lovers where Goethe's protagonist fails. Bobsin describes *Lucinde* as "gelingende Werther-Liebe."[49] Like Franca and Giovanni, Schlegel's protagonists Lucinde and Julius form a harmonious, equal, aesthetic unit in which they share "ihre Neigung zur Kunst."[50] Like Franca, Lucinde is an independent woman who lives according to her own rules: "Sie war eine von denen, die nicht in der gemeinen Welt leben, sondern in einer eigenen selbstgedachten und selbstgebildeten . . . Auch sie . . . lebte völlig frei und unabhängig."[51] Julia Bobsin notes that *Lucinde* "enthält . . . Aspekte einer Liebessemantik von Gleichheit und selbständiger Partnerschaft, die über das trivialisierte Modell der romantischen Liebe, wie sie bis Ende der 60er Jahre des 20. Jahrhunderts gültig war, hinausweisen." Lucinde is untypically conceived as a subject, not as a negative foil to the masculine subject: "sie ist ein 'Ich' oder auch ein 'Du,' keinesfalls aber ein 'Nicht-Ich.'"[52] Schlegel's conception of love in *Lucinde* as not only determined by equality but also as enveloping both partners equally, as a symbolic communion of hearts where spiritual and physical aspects unite, can be read as a model for the symbiotic understanding between Franca and Giovanni. Similarly to Giovanni, Schlegel's Julius notes "mit frohem Erstaunen, daß er ebenso unendlich geliebt werde wie er liebe" and sees "daß Lucinde von ähnlichem, ja gleichem Sinn und Geist mit ihm selbst war."[53] Finally, *Lucinde* also uses the term "große Liebe" in reference to Lucinde's importance for Julius.[54]

In *Lucinde*, too, love leads to the opening up of the world. Elke Reinhardt-Becker points out that in contrast to Werther's love, where passion alienates the subject from the world, in Romanticism passion is turned towards the world: "Das romantische Liebeskonzept . . . sieht seine Aufgabe nicht nur in der Herstellung von Identität, sondern will darüber hinaus auch noch den Einzelnen der Gesellschaft *zurückgeben*."[55] The conception of love in *Lucinde* thus shares the world-affirmative nature of love with the medieval "unio mystica" as discussed above. Christoph Huber notes a number of connections between Romanticism and medieval *Minne* such as the overwhelming force of sudden love, the idea of intensive, intimate closeness, the bridging of interpersonal distance, the ideal of the equality of the partners and devotion to a single person with a life-fulfilling bond, the conception of love as the highest value of life, and above all, the "ästhetische Selbstreferenz der Rede von der Liebe."[56] According to Huber, the "spezifisch 'romantische' Autoreferenz und die Erfüllung des Liebens in der Kunst und als Kunst" are central features of both medieval and Romantic literature.[57]

Like *Lucinde*, *Die große Liebe* contains a meta-reflexive allegory of itself, just as Schlegel's concept of irony is detectable in Ortheil's self-reflexive narrative strategies: "Die wahre Ironie . . . ist die Ironie der Liebe. Sie entspringt aus dem Gefühl der Endlichkeit und der eigenen Beschränkung und dem scheinbaren Widerspruch dieses Gefühls mit der in jeder wahren Liebe mit eingeschlossnen Idee eines Unendlichen."[58] This irony is not directed at the subject matter of love but at the text's identity as art.[59] In the novel, irony functions in a way "dass darin gar keine Rücksicht genommen wird, auf den Unterschied von Schein und Wirklichkeit, von Spiel und Ernst."[60] Bobsin has pointed out that the character of little Wilhelmine in *Lucinde* functions as meta-reflexive theory of the Romantic conception of poetry, as "intellektuelle Anschauung der intellektuellen Anschauung," and Schlegel's novel as a whole is an "allegoric representation of Schlegel's poetics."[61] *Die große Liebe* is likewise animated by a meta-reflexive textual allegory, the fish soup named *brodetto* that Giovanni and Franca eat at their first lunch. The *brodetto* contains "das halbe Meer *in nuce* . . . Der Sud ist hochkonzentriert, sie kochen ihn hier tagelang" (80). The *brodetto* represents in concentrated form the landscape of the Marches region as a union of land and sea; the soup is ideally created from species of fish "die sich im Sand vergrüben" (81). The term "*in nuce*" appears a second time in Giovanni's description of their love as a novel and thus marks the soup as the novel's own meta-reflexive concept of love: "ein Liebesroman *in nuce* . . . *die Liebe pur* . . ." (234–35). The repetition of the term "*in nuce*," italicized both times, thus aligns the *brodetto*, a concentrated union of sea and land, with the concept of the "große Liebe" as an intense union between man and woman, and with the self-reflexive idea of the love between Giovanni and Franca as a novel.

The literature of *Empfindsamkeit* and *Sturm und Drang* underlines the literary and thus unrealistic provenance of—frequently feminine—ideas of love with reference to the fictionality of literary representations in contrast to "realistic" expectations, often with reference to love as a "novel." Ortheil's novel turns this on its head and ironically presents the utopian couple as pure literary invention.

The auto-referentiality of *Die große Liebe* is not only an echo of Romantic tradition, but is already central to the medieval discourse on love. Huber notes that Romantic auto-referentiality and the idea of the fulfillment of love in and as art are already present in medieval notions of love.[62] Walter Haug argues that Gottfried von Straßburg's *Tristan und Isolde* represents the discovery of fictionality in European literature, simultaneously with the discovery of love as both personal and physical experience. Before *Tristan und Isolde*, says Haug, there is no discussion of love as "Erfahrung spezifischer Art."[63]

Gottfried's epic tale of doomed lovers is referenced in *Die große Liebe* in Giovanni's description of his and Franca's hotel room in Ascoli Piceno as "unsere einsame Höhle, die Höhle eines sehr alten Zaubers" (172), a reminder of the love grotto in *Tristan und Isolde*. Haug describes the lovers' grotto in *Tristan und Isolde*, where the lovers tell each other tragic ancient love stories as the auto-referential center of the novel that reflects upon the utopian unachievability of unity: "Auch in der idealen Minnegrotte braucht man Geschichten. Deshalb hat man im 12. Jh. die Liebe zugleich mit der Fiktionalität entdeckt. Und dies wiederum hängt zusammen mit der Differenzerfahrung . . . Personale Du-Erfahrung ist Differenzerfahrung, d.h. sie realisiert sich im Akt der Vermittlung, im Wort und in der Körpersprache als Verbindendem und Trennendem zugleich."[64] The discovery of fictionality and difference is thus, according to Haug, the discovery of the painfulness of love; with fictionality, love emerges as unhappy.

Die große Liebe transforms this entire historical context of unhappy love out of the untransgressible experience of difference into happiness, while maintaining the aspect of auto-referentiality. Like Schlegel's *Lucinde*, which plays off reality and fantasy against each other "zur wechselseitigen Relativierung,"[65] the center of *Die große Liebe* is its constant meta-reflexivity as literary construct. Consequently, there is no reference to any of the problems that characterize the tradition of the representation of love in both literature and reality, no doubt in the truthfulness and reality of the other's feelings, no semantic instability of the lover's discourse, and no tortuous attempts to authenticate emotions with a catalogue of expressions of questionable trustworthiness. Like Schlegel's *Lucinde*, Ortheil's *Die große Liebe* configures love as text and as "ästhetischer Zustand" that makes the world into an auratic spectacle.[66]

What is at stake in *Die große Liebe* is nothing less than the revision of the narrative tradition of literary love from the middle ages to modernity. In an interview, Ortheil has pointed out that he pursued an idea of love "die es in der Gegenwartsliteratur nicht mehr gibt, die es in der Moderne kaum mehr gegeben hat." He describes particularly the twentieth century as one "in dem der Selbsthass der Moderne sich geradezu manisch am Thema 'Liebe' austobt, um immer wieder vorzuführen, wie erledigt dieses Thema . . . ist."[67] Orteil's assessment of the hostility of modern literature is in accordance with Andrea Egger-Riedmüller's critique of the "Wortlosigkeit der erzählenden Literatur gegenüber dem Liebesglück."[68]

Against the Tradition of Unhappy Love:
Love vs. Eros—Psychoanalysis

One of the central aspects of the painful experience of insurmountable difference between the sexes is eroticism, which, specifically in modernity, through theories of psychoanalysis, comes to be associated with pain and death. Ortheil's avoidance of any aspects that might get in the way of the happy relationship means that the destructive aspect of Eros remains outside the confines of the novel, together with the entire field of psychology and of introspection. Following Freud, Georges Bataille links the power of Eros to the desire of humans for a suspension of their isolation and for continuity with death. He describes human desire as an "obsession with a primal continuity, linking us with everything that is."[69] For Bataille, eroticism is an expression of the desire "to substitute for the individual isolated discontinuity a feeling of profound continuity."[70] For Bataille, Eros is deeply connected to violence. He speaks of the "feeling of elemental violence which kindles every manifestation of eroticism. In essence, the domain of eroticism is the domain of violence of violation . . . Physical eroticism has in any case a heavy, sinister quality."[71]

Ortheil's conception of love lacks the aspect of violence, destructiveness, and excess that is characteristic of Bataille's conception of Eros. Sexual union between Giovanni and Franca takes place without the ideas of excess and the agony of the dissolution of selfhood that is essential in Bataille's concept of eroticism. The origin of the concept of Eros as agonizing dialectics between the burden of subjectivity and the desire for dissolution in Freud and Bataille, and for Horkheimer and Adorno in their *Dialectic of Enlightenment* is the thinking in categories of subject and object. This thinking is implicitly determined by the conception of a masculine subject, with a self that is held together by the pressure of civilization and who thus both desires and fears the suspension of these pressures. None of this plays any role in *Die große Liebe*. Although Ortheil's novel envisages the symbolic death of the isolated self in love as postulated by Bataille,[72] in contrast to Freudian "oceanic feelings" the transformation of the lovers is not characterized by ideas of dissolution and merging with the Other. Though metaphorically expressed in images of water and of diving, the dominating idea in the novel's representation of sexual union is that of duality, of the couple: "ich spürte, wie sie langsam auf mich sank, es war eine einzige, stille Bewegung, als fiele ein Tuch, sich langsam im Wind drehend, zur Erde . . . ich hatte das Gefühl, als stehe die Zeit still und als entfernten sich unsere beiden Körper in dieser Kapsel nun in die Tiefe . . . Ich sah uns als Paar und wie das Paar-Bild abtauchte, langsam drehten wir uns in der Tiefe des Meeres" (162–63).

Consequently, physical intimacy between Giovanni and Franca is described as distinct from sex and free from the agony of Eros and the "anguish of desire" as described by Bataille.[73] In Giovanni's view, sex is related to sports, something that is characterized by learnable techniques and staging of bodies, "*ein Ritual oder ein Spiel, eine Nummernfolge*" (185, italics original, HS). Sex is related to the efficiency principle and thus the enjoyment of the self.[74] Most commentators who refer to psychoanalysis point towards the separating aspects of sex. Alain Badiou has argued, with reference to Lacan, that sexual enjoyment is always one's own, "it does not unite, it separates."[75] Describing sex as "Konsum," Norbert Bolz maintains: "Im Geschlechtsgenuss verhalte ich mich gerade nicht zum anderen als solchem. Sein Selbst könnte da nur störend dazwischenkommen."[76] Giovanni, too, insists that "*die Einheit spielt beim Sex nur eine kurze und untergeordnete Rolle*," whereas his being with Franca evokes the image of a platonic completeness: "*ihr Körper und meiner gehörten zusammen . . . als hätten sie endlich, ja endlich, zueinandergefunden*" (185, italics original, HS).[77]

In its reference back to medieval literary and philosophical traditions, Giovanni and Franca's experience of love is not just set apart from modern literature but also in contrast to modern social theory, particularly Luhmann's theory of lovers' communication. Luhmann described the problem of lovers' communication as an unresolvable paradox, as each subject possesses a "world-constitutive individuality" and thus requires of the Other that it should be contained in their world.[78] In contrast to Luhmann's communication paradox, Giovanni and Franca develop a perfect and almost magically complementary form of communication. Ortheil describes the programmatically anti-modernist conception of his novel thus: "es geht um die Liebe zweier Menschen, ohne Vorbehalte, ohne lange Seitenblicke auf das, was dieser Liebe entgegenstehen, was sie verhindern, verschieben, umpolen könnte."[79]

Ortheil mentions explicitly the Petrarchism of the Italian Renaissance as a literary model for this type of love.[80] However, even Petrarch's poetry and the literature that emerged in its wake is dominated by an idea of love as suffering and as unfulfilled; the "dolce stil nuovo" is characterized by a bittersweet pain ("amore amaro").[81] Ortheil's novel, however, is free from the central metaphors of Petrarchism such as "die qualbekennende Werbung, die leidenschaftliche Klage ungestillter Sehnsucht, das grüblerische und gleichzeitig selbstbewusste Schwelgen in den Reizen des Leides . . . die Imagination des Scheinglücks im Traum, das Selbstverständnis des Liebenden als Märtyrer der Liebe, die Auffassung der Liebe als Krankheit, die Vorstellung von der Geliebten als Engel."[82] Whereas Goethe's *Werther* quotes and formalizes these Petrarchan motifs that by Goethe's time had deteriorated to a set of stock images, in order to expose them in a collision with realist psychology as empty rhetoric,[83] *Die große Liebe* celebrates the affirmative praise of love itself, the "'selbstlose' Freude der Liebenden an der Liebe": "die Liebe erscheint daher gleichsam wie ein Fest, ja, sie wird zelebriert wie ein Fest, das sich von Moment zu Moment steigert und immer intensiver wird."[84] What is at stake in *Die große Liebe* is thus the "Erweiterung der Liebesthematik um die narrative Darstellung erfüllter Liebe,"[85] something Ortheil has described as "Liebe an und für sich."[86]

In its rejection of psychoanalytic interpretations of love and desire, *Die große Liebe* echoes Günter Dux's thesis "dass der Liebende die Intimität der Kindheit auf dem Niveau autonomer Lebensführung zu reorganisieren sucht. Was der Liebende im anderen entdeckt, ist ein Moment an dessen Dasein, in dem er seine Erfahrung der Kindheit wiederfindet."[87] Love is thus an attempt to re-configure childhood experiences of intimacy on the level of adult life: "In der Liebe zum anderen kann ein Sehnen nach der Kindheit eingebunden sein. Dabei bleibt jedoch lebendig, dass sie gerade nicht wiederholbar ist . . . Die Reorganisation der Intimität steht unter Anforderungen einer autonomen Lebensführung."[88] In contrast to Freudian theory, which assumes that love relationships are an attempt to reconstitute the "primäre Verschmolzenheit der symbiotischen Phase,"[89] *Die große Liebe* stresses the "gemeinsame" aspect of the couple as individuals (120, 234–35).

The difference between Ortheil's conception of love and psychoanalytical conceptions is visible from the ideal of marriage expressed by Franca. Marriage is not envisaged as a union, a merging of two individuals into a symbiotic unity, but as a "duet" that leaves the individuality of both subjects intact: "*die Ehe* stellte ich mir nämlich sehr schön vor, immer eine Zeitlang für sich und dann eine Zeitlang zusammen, genau in einem solchen Rhythmus stellte ich mir die Ehe vor, wie ein fein abgestimmtes Duett, ruhig, harmonisch" (253).

A Poetics of Nonchalance

One intertext for the entire aesthetic programme of *Die große Liebe* is Baldassare Castiglione's (1478–1529) *Il Libro del Cortigiano* (The Book of the Courtier, 1528) with its courtly ideal of *sprezzatura*. Castiglione's book is of central importance for the transformation of medieval and Platonic conceptions of love into a secular and courtly ideal in Renaissance Italy, France, and England.[90] *Sprezzatura* is Castiglione's term for the ability "to steer away from affectation at all costs, as if it were a rough and dangerous reef, and (to use perhaps a novel word for it) to practice in all things a certain nonchalance which conceals all artistry and makes whatever one says or does uncontrived and effortless."[91] Through Castiglione, *sprezzatura*, or nonchalance, becomes an important behavioral ideal for the courts of the late Renaissance. Next to its importance as a behavioral codex of the courtier, it has an important aesthetic component. Castiglione's "universal rule"[92] of aesthetic nonchalance and of measure (*misura*) "transfers courtly conduct to the realm of poetic language and poetic language to the realm of courtly conduct. . . . "[93]

Die große Liebe articulates this ideal of aesthetic measure with respect to both form and content, on the one hand in Giovanni's perception of the Italian art of conversation and on the other in the tone of the novel itself. Giovanni stresses repeatedly the nonchalance with which Franca inhabits the world. She leaves no traces in their hotel room: "Gepäck hatte sie sowieso kaum dabei . . . natürlich nicht, sich nicht zu beschweren war die Grundregel jeder Äesthetik" (206). Franca speaks, "als habe sie auf alles . . . genau die richtige Antwort" (31). This aesthetic ease becomes an ideal for Giovanni, as twenty pages later, he refrains from complaining in a restaurant, as "sich zu beschweren ist gegen die Grundregel jeder Äesthetik" (229). To say and do the right thing in the right moment without effort is part of the aesthetic program of the novel; the text is littered with formulations like "genau die richtige Wendung" (15) or "der einzig richtige, große Moment" (94). Franca's statement at their first lunch, "Es ist schön hier mit Ihnen," comes "so selbstverständlich, genau im richtigen Augenblick" (82).

Furthermore, in Castiglione and in Petrarchism there is a "diskursive Verbindung von Liebe und Malerei, schöner Kunst und schöner Frau":[94] "Für die affektive wie intellektuelle Selbstfindung des Subjekts um 1500 war in Anlehnung an Petrarca das Wechselspiel von imaginärem, lyrischem und gemaltem Frauenbild noch konstitutiv. Die Malerei nimmt diesen Dreierbund zur Steigerung der Wirkungsmacht in sich auf, kann sie doch so den Rezipienten mit einem zugleich idealschönen wie besonderen Bild konfrontieren."[95] This connection between woman, love, and painting occurs at a central moment in *Die große Liebe*. In the parish church of Montefiore dell'Aso, Giovanni discovers a polyptych by the Venetian painter Carlo Crivelli (Venice 1430?-Ascoli Piceno 1495). The polyptych contains an image of St. Magdalen that shows a "geradezu unheimliche" (179) similarity with Franca.[96] However, in contrast to Petrarchism, where the ambivalence between the painted image and the distance of the real lover turns into a lament about the silence of the image, Crivelli's Magdalen does not remain a "Versprechen, das nie eingelöst wird."[97] For Giovanni, the painting does not mean distance but a quasi-mythical intimacy; "sie *war* es" (179, italics original, HS).

The ideal of *sprezzatura* is later enriched with Machiavellian motifs and ultimately develops into the French ideal of gallantry. Already in Castiglione's time, it was criticized for being little else but deception, as it describes social conduct as art and thus appears to give preference to appearance, rather than essence.[98] The problem of appearance vs. essence is central to all ancient rhetoric manuals[99] until it is finally substituted by Rousseau's ideal of genuine naturalness.[100] It is significant that this problem plays no role in *Die große Liebe*. The entire complex of

authenticity that is so central for the discourse on love and is still constitutive for Goethe's *Werther*, personal authenticity as well as that of the
lover, remains outside of the novel's frame of reference. Instead, the novel
focuses on the permanent evocation of the beauty of emphatically experienced moments—the term "schön" appears some fifty times in the text
in all its variants—and formally on its self-referential identity as literature.
Several times the novel mentions the "liebende, schwärmerische Suada"
(12) of the Italian conversational tone, "das schwärmerische, preisende
Sprechen, dass ich so an den Italienern mochte" (178). This enthusiastic
language dominates the novel as a whole, Giovanni notes at the end of
the text, "ich möchte, dass mein Schreiben einen hellen 'begeisterten'
Grundton erhält" (315).

This aesthetic self-referentiality is already a constitutive element of
Castiglione, who composed his *Libro del Cortegiano* as an aesthetic text
that oscillates between ideal and reality.[101] The constant focus in *Die große
Liebe* on the effortless appropriateness of moments, utterances, the order
of things in a room, and so forth, is a stylistic principle that self-referentially points to the artificiality and the aesthetic program of the novel itself.
It is an echo of Castiglione's artless art that hides the effort it takes for the
artlessness to appear artless. *Sprezzatura* is a "Lebenskunst," a term that
is central for Ortheil's writing:[102] "Castigliones Verbergungsforderung
basiert auf der Überzeugung von der Unmöglichkeit eines natürlichen
Erscheinens der Wahrheit, ist Zeigekunst angesichts der Tatsache, dass
ohne Kunst *nichts* zur Erscheinung kommt."[103]

I would argue that Ortheil's entire novel is underscored by an ideal
of effortlessness and artlessness that is part of the Italian Renaissance and
that expects the viewer of paintings, for example, to follow the artistic
hints of the painter.[104] Consequently, *Die große Liebe* self-referentially
exposes its own artificiality, but not the aesthetic effort and depth of its
program. One aspect of *sprezzatura* is concealment of one's erudition.[105]
Ortheil's novel is an effortless reflection on the entire discourse on love
in European literature, from Gottfried von Straßburg to modernity in
the guise of a happy holiday romance. As a programmatic revision of
the unhappy tradition of modern literary love stories *Die große Liebe* is
an implicit critique of both the negativity of modern literature and of
modern rationalizing discourses with respect to their representation of
love, desire, and intimacy. The meta-textual irony of the novel towards its
own status as fiction allows it to suspend any "realistic" engagement with
sociocultural realities.

Notes

[1] Denis de Rougemont, *Love in the Western World*, trans. Montgomery Belgion
(Princeton, NJ: Princeton University Press, 1983 [first 1940, revised 1956]), 15.

[2] See, e.g., Niklas Luhmann, *Love as Passion: The Codification of Intimacy*, trans. Jeremy Gaines and Doris L. Jones (Cambridge: Polity Press, 1986, first 1982), chapter 1; Ulrich Beck and Elisabeth Beck-Gernsheim, *The Normal Chaos of Love*, trans. Mark Ritter and Jane Wiebel (Cambridge: Polity Press, 1995 [first 1990]), introduction; Eva Illouz, *Why Love Hurts: A Sociological Explanation* (Cambridge: Polity Press, 2012), 12.

[3] See Karin A. Wurst, "'Wilde Wünsche': The Discourse of Love in the Sturm und Drang," in *Literature of the Sturm und Drang*, ed. David Hill, The Camden House History of German Literature, vol. 6 (Rochester, NY: Camden House, 2003), 217–40, here 220.

[4] Wurst, "'Wilde Wünsche,'" 220.

[5] Octavio Paz, *The Double Flame: Essays on Love and Eroticism*, trans. Helen Lane (London: Harvill, 1996), 90.

[6] On the specific modernity of Goethe's *Werther* see Julia Bobsin, *Von der Werther-Krise zur Lucinde-Liebe: Studien zur Liebessemantik in der deutschen Erzählliteratur 1770–1800* (Tübingen: Niemeyer, 1994), 16.

[7] Paz, *The Double Flame*, 95.

[8] Stefan Krankenhagen, "Gelingendes und beschädigtes Leben. Die Theorie der Unterhaltung im Licht der Ästhetik Adornos," in *Die Zweideutigkeit der Unterhaltung: Zugangsweisen zur populären Kultur*, ed. Udo Göttlich and Stephan Porombka (Cologne and Halem, 2009), 167–84, here 168.

[9] Krankenhagen, "Gelingendes und beschädigtes Leben," 169.

[10] See De Rougemont, *Love in the Western World*, 52.

[11] For a brief history of the romance genre see Emily S. Davis, *Rethinking the Romance Genre: Global Intimacies in Contemporary Literary and Visual Culture* (Basingstoke: Palgrave MacMillan, 2013), Introduction, 3–9.

[12] Illouz, *Why Love Hurts*, 197–215.

[13] Luhmann, *Love as Passion*, 155–71.

[14] Hanns-Josef Ortheil, *Die große Liebe* (2003), *Das Verlangen nach Liebe* (2007), *Liebesnähe* (2011), all Munich, Luchterhand Literaturverlag. Further references in the text in brackets. On the *Liebesroman* as subgenre of *Trivialliteratur* see Walter Nutz, "Trivialliteratur seit 1965," in *Deutsche Literatur in der Bundesrepublik seit 1965*, ed. P. M. Lützeler and Egon Schwarz (Königstein/Ts: Athenäum, 1980), 150–63.

[15] See for example Ulrich Greiner's review in *Die Zeit*, 25 September 2003, http://www.zeit.de/2003/40/L-Ortheil), and Reiner Moritz's review of *Das Verlangen nach Liebe* in *Neue Zürcher Zeitung*, January 23, 2008, http://www.nzz.ch/die-vollkommenheit-der-steinpilze-1.656054. Extracts of reviews of all three novels can be seen on perlentaucher.de.

[16] See Ortheil, "Die Liebe an und für sich. Hanns-Josef Ortheil im Gespräch mit Heinz-Jürgen Dambmann über 'Projekte des Liebesromans,'" in *Kunst der Erinnerung, Poetik der Liebe: Das erzählerische Werk Hanns-Josef Ortheils*, ed. Stephanie Catani, Friedhelm Marx, and Julia Schöll (Göttingen: Wallstein, 2009), 15–28, here 21.

[17] Gerhard Neumann, "Lektüren der Liebe," in *Über die Liebe: Ein Symposion*, ed. Heinrich Meier and Gerhard Neumann (Munich: Piper, 2001), 9–80, here 9.

[18] Hanns-Josef Ortheil, *Faustinas Küsse* (Munich: Luchterhand Literaturverlag, 1998). Quoted from the paperback edition (Munich: btb, 2005), 153–65.

[19] Julia Eckert, "Hanns-Josef Ortheils *Die große Liebe* als Anti-Werther-Roman? Zur Problematik des Konzepts der erfüllten Liebe in der Literatur," in *Kunst der Erinnerung, Poetik der Liebe*, 219–38, here 229.

[20] See Bobsin, *Von der Werther-Krise zur Lucinde-Liebe*, 76–78. See also Eckert, "Hanns-Josef Ortheils *Die große Liebe* als Anti-Werther-Roman?," 220–21.

[21] Johann Wolfgang Goethe, *Die Leiden des jungen Werthers*, in *Sämtliche Werke nach Epochen seines Schaffens*, Münchner Ausgabe, Vol. 1.2, ed. Karl Richter, with Herbert G. Göpfert, Norbert Miller, and Gerhard Sauder (Munich: Carl Hanser Verlag, 1987), 203.

[22] Bobsin, *Von der Werther-Krise zur Lucinde-Liebe*, 86.

[23] Eckert, "Hanns-Josef Ortheils *Die große Liebe* als Anti-Werther-Roman?," 221–22.

[24] Ortheil, "Die Liebe an und für sich," 21.

[25] Bardo Weiß, *Ekstase und Liebe: Die Unio mystica bei den deutschen Mystikerinnen des 12. und 13. Jahrhunderts* (Paderborn-Munich-Vienna-Zurich: Schöningh, 2000), 965.

[26] Ortheil, "Die Liebe an und für sich," 20–21.

[27] On the "subjektstabilisierende Funktion der modernen Liebe," see Bobsin, *Von der Werther-Krise zur Lucinde-Liebe*, 16.

[28] Ortheil, "Die Liebe an und für sich," 22.

[29] Eckert, "Hanns-Josef Ortheils *Die große Liebe* als Anti-Werther-Roman?," 222.

[30] See Weiß, *Ekstase und Liebe*, 628. Uta Störmer-Caysa, *Einführung in die mittelalterliche Mystik* (Stuttgart: Reclam, 2004), 143–44.

[31] Weiß, *Ekstase und Liebe*, 971. See also Störmer-Caysa, *Einführung in die mittelalterliche Mystik*, 10–17.

[32] Goethe, *Die Leiden des jungen Werthers*, 203.

[33] Weiß, *Ekstase und Liebe*, 90–91.

[34] Weiß, *Ekstase und Liebe*, 99.

[35] Weiß, *Ekstase und Liebe*, 596 and 599.

[36] Weiß, *Ekstase und Liebe*, 294, 299, and 965.

[37] Weiß, *Ekstase und Liebe*, 971.

[38] On the relationship between medieval mysticism, beauty, and vision, see Umberto Eco, *Kunst und Schönheit im Mittelalter*, trans. Günter Memmert (Munich: dtv, 1993), esp. the chapters "Das Schöne als Transzendentarium" (34–48) and "Die Ästhetiken des Lichts" (67–78), here 39.

[39] On "Schwärmerei" see the relevant section in Gerhard Sauder, *Empfindsamkeit: Vol. 1: Voraussetzungen und Elemente* (Stuttgart: Metzler, 1974), 137–43.

[40] On the reception of the Catholic mystic tradition in Protestant Pietism see Johannes Wallmann, *Pietismus und Orthodoxie: Gesammelte Aufsätze III* (Tübingen: Mohr Siebeck, 2010), esp. the chapter "Bernhard von Clairvaux und der deutsche Pietismus," 83–102. I am grateful to my colleague James Hodkinson for this reference. See also Douglas H. Shantz, *An Introduction to German Pietism: Protestant renewal at the Dawn of Modern Europe* (Baltimore, MD: Johns Hopkins University Press, 2013), esp. chapter 1, 15–41.

[41] See Gert Mattenklott, "Briefroman" in *Deutsche Literatur: Eine Sozialgeschichte, vol. 4: Zwischen Absolutismus und Aufklärung: Rationalismus, Empfindsamkeit, Sturm und Drang*, ed. Horst Albert Glaser (Reinbek bei Hamburg: Rowohlt, 1980), 185–203, here 185.

[42] Wurst, "'Wilde Wünsche,'" 217.

[43] Sauder, *Empfindsamkeit*, 137.

[44] Mattenklott, "Briefroman," 198.

[45] Wurst, "'Wilde Wünsche,'" 220.

[46] See, e.g., Georg Jäger, *Empfindsamkeit und Roman* (Stuttgart: Kohlhammer, 1969), esp. 57–63. See also Mattenklott, "Briefroman," 185–87, Wurst, "'Wilde Wünsche,'" 233–34.

[47] Wurst, "'Wilde Wünsche,'" 233.

[48] Sauder, *Empfindsamkeit*, 169.

[49] Bobsin, *Von der Werther-Krise zur Lucinde-Liebe*, 96.

[50] Friedrich Schlegel, *Lucinde*, in *Kritische Friedrich-Schlegel-Ausgabe*, ed. Ernst Behler, with Jean-Jacques Anstett and Hans Eichner, Vol. 5. (Munich: Ferdinand Schöningh, 1962), 56.

[51] Schlegel, *Lucinde*, 53.

[52] Bobsin, *Von der Werther-Krise zur Lucinde-Liebe*, 190 and 188.

[53] Schlegel, *Lucinde*, 56.

[54] Schlegel, *Lucinde*, 79.

[55] Elke Reinhardt-Becker, *Seelenbund oder Partnerschaft? Liebessemantiken in der Literatur der Romantik und der Neuen Sachlichkeit* (Frankfurt am Main: Campus, 2005), 119–20.

[56] See Christoph Huber, "'Romantische Liebe' und mittelalterliche Minne," in *Romantik und Exil: Festschrift für Konrad Feilchenfeldt*, ed. Claudia Christophersen and Ursula Hudson-Wiedenmann (Würzburg: Königshausen & Neumann, 2004), 224–34, here 230.

[57] Huber, "'Romantische Liebe' und mittelalterliche Minne," 230.

[58] Friedrich Schlegel, *Philosophische Vorlesungen insbesondere über die Philosophie der Sprache und des Wortes* [1830], in *Kritische Friedrich-Schlegel-Ausgabe*, Vol. 10, 375.

[59] See Bobsin, *Von der Werther-Krise zur Lucinde-Liebe*, 183.

[60] Friedrich Schlegel, "Gespräch über die Poesie," *Kritische Friedrich-Schlegel-Ausgabe*, Vol. 2, 284–351, here 334.

[61] Bobsin, *Von der Werther-Krise zur Lucinde-Liebe*, 220.

[62] Huber, "'Romantische Liebe' und mittelalterliche Minne," 230–31.

[63] Walter Haug, "Tristan und Lancelot. Das Experiment mit der personalen Liebe im 12./13. Jahrhundert," in *Über die Liebe*, 197–233, here 198.

[64] Walter Haug, "Die Entdeckung der personalen Liebe und der Beginn der fiktionalen Literatur," in *Aufbruch—Wandel—Erneuerung: Beiträge zur 'Renaissance' des 12. Jahrhunderts*, ed. Georg Wieland (Stuttgart–Bad Cannstadt: Frommann-Holzboog, 1995), 65–85, here 80 and 84.

[65] Bobsin, *Von der Werther-Krise zur Lucinde-Liebe*, 184.

[66] On love as an aesthetic state in Schlegel's *Lucinde* see Bernd Bräutigam, *Leben wie im Roman: Untersuchungen zum ästhetischen Imperativ im Frühwerk Friedrich Schlegels* (1794–1800) (Paderborn: Ferdinand Schoeningh, 1986), 13.

[67] Ortheil, "Die Liebe an und für sich," 21.

[68] Andrea Egger-Riedmüller, *Figurationen einer fortgeschrittenen Liebe: Eine topologische Suche nach dem Glück in Liebesgeschichten der deutschsprachigen Gegenwartsliteratur* (Innsbruck: Universität Innsbruck, 2004), 9.

[69] Georges Bataille, *Eroticism*, trans. Mary Dalwood (London: Boyars, 1987), 15.

[70] Bataille, *Eroticism*, 15.

[71] Bataille, *Eroticism*, 16 and 19.

[72] See Bataille, *Eroticism*, 21.

[73] See Bataille, *Eroticism*, 19–20.

[74] See Byung-Chul Han, *Agonie des Eros* (Berlin: Matthes & Seitz, 2012), 21.

[75] See Alain Badiou and Nicolas Truong, *Éloge de l'amour* (Paris: Flammarion, 2009), 23, my translation.

[76] Norbert Bolz, *Das konsumistische Manifest* (Munich: Fink, 2002), 127.

[77] Cf. Plato, *Symposium: Collected Works of Plato*, trans. Benjamin Jowett, 4th ed. (Oxford: Oxford University Press, 1953), 189c–192c, 520–223.

[78] Luhmann, *Love as Passion*, 21.

[79] Ortheil, "Die Liebe an und für sich," 20–21.

[80] Ortheil, "Die Liebe an und für sich," 22.

[81] See Gerhart Hoffmeister, *Petrarkistische Lyrik* (Stuttgart: Metzler, 1973), 27. See also Karlheinz Fingerhut, "Das versagte Glück 'uns zu lieben ohn' uns zu verstehen'. Goethe und Petrarca," in Fingerhut, *Kleine Blumen, kleine Blätter: Sieben Vorlesungen zu Goethe* (Freiburg im Breisgau: Fillibach 2007), 93–126, esp. 99.

[82] See Bobsin, *Von der Werther-Krise zur Lucinde-Liebe*, 92.

[83] On Petrarchism in Goethe's *Werther* see Bobsin, *Von der Werther-Krise zur Lucinde-Liebe*, 93–94 and J. U. Fechner, "Die alten Leiden des jungen Werthers," *arcadia* 17 (1982): 1–15.

[84] Ortheil, "Die Liebe an und für sich," 22–23.

[85] See Eckert, "Hanns-Josef Ortheils *Die große Liebe* als Anti-Werther-Roman?," 219.

[86] Ortheil, "Die Liebe an und für sich," 22.

[87] Dux, *Geschlecht und Gesellschaft*, 111.

[88] Dux, *Geschlecht und Gesellschaft*, 89.

[89] Dux, *Geschlecht und Gesellschaft*, 87. Like *Die große Liebe*, Dux refers back to the conception of the Other in Romanticism, especially the concept of the Other not as "not-I" but as "you," 92.

[90] See Sabrina Ebbersmeyer, *Sinnlichkeit und Vernunft: Studien zur Transformation der Liebestheorie Platons in der Renaissance* (Munich: Fink, 2002), 150–52.

[91] Castiglione, *The Book of the Courtier* (Harmonsworth: Penguin, 1967), 67.

[92] Castiglione, *Book of the Courtier*, 67.

[93] Joseph D. Falvo, *The Economy of Human Relations: Castiglione's "Il Libro Del Cortegiano"* (New York,: Peter Lang, 1992), 43.

[94] See Kia Vahland, "Wunschbilder und Augenschein. Zur Funktion innerer und äußerer Bilder bei Pietro Bembo, in Castigliones 'Hofmann,' sowie in der lyrischen Malerei de frühen Neuzeit," in *"Intellektuelle Anschauung": Figurationen von Evidenz zwischen Kunst und Wissen*, ed. Sibylle Peters and Martin Jörg Schäfer (Bielefeld: transcript, 2006), 61–76, here 72–73.

[95] Vahland, "Wunschbilder und Augenschein," 74.

[96] For a reproduction see: Wikipedia Contributors, "Trittico di Montefiore," *Wikipedia, The Free Encyclopedia*, accessed November 20, 2016, http://it.wikipedia.org/wiki/Trittico_di_Montefiore.

[97] Vahland, "Wunschbilder und Augenschein," 61: "Das Bildnis einer schönen Frau ist demnach ein Versprechen, dass nie eingelöst wird. Es verführt den Betrachter zur Liebe, verheißt ihm Seelenfrieden—und lässt ihn dann allein . . ."

[98] See Göttert, *Kommunikationsideale*, 129.

[99] See Göttert, *Kommunikationsideale*, 26.

[100] See Göttert, *Kommunikationsideale*, 129.

[101] See Falvo, *The Economy of Human Relations*, 6–7.

[102] Göttert, *Kommunikationsideale*, 37. On the concept of "Lebenskunst" in Ortheil see my "Hanns-Josef Ortheil: Das Erzählen der Welt," in *Poetologisch-Poetische Interventionen: Gegenwartsliteratur schreiben*, ed. Allo Allkemper, Norbert Otto Eke, and Hartmut Steinecke (Munich: Fink, 2012), 143–60.

[103] Göttert, *Kommunikationsideale*, 27.

[104] See Ernst H. Gombrich, *Art and Illusion: A Study in the Psychology of Pictorial Representation* (Princeton, NJ: Princeton University Press, 1969), 195.

[105] See J. R. Woodhouse, *Baldesar Castiglione: A Reassessment of "The Courtier"* (Edinburgh: Edinburgh University Press, 1978), 78.

Variations on Love
in the Contemporary

Healthy Socialists and Kinky Heroes: Carnivalesque Deconstruction of Heteronormativity in Thomas Brussig's *Helden wie wir*

Sven Glawion

"SIE STECKTE KERZEN an und setzte sich auf meinen Schoß. Wir küßten uns, und ich geriet in eine echte ethisch-moralische Notsituation, weil ich merkte, daß ich sie jetzt—nennen wir die Dinge beim Namen—*ficken* will. Kann ich es mit meinem Gewissen vereinbaren, einen *Engel* zu ficken? Noch dazu einen Engel, den ich liebe?"[1] Yvonne appears in the life of Klaus Uhltzscht, the GDR protagonist of Thomas Brussig's 1995 novel *Helden wie wir* (Heroes Like Us, 1997) almost as a celestial being. The young Klaus falls in love for the first time and his world is shaken up: Are love and sex compatible? Is he allowed to have sex with an angel?

Naive and inexperienced, Klaus works through the different narratives of love, partnership, and sexuality that are available to him. However, erotic encounters with women are extremely rare for him and always end in fiasco. He is an anti-hero with an unpronounceable name, a repressed nerd who refrains from masturbation for years only to later focus on it almost incessantly and with increasingly sophisticated methods. Over many pages of the novel he suffers from—what else could it be—"den kleinsten Schwanz, den man je gesehen hat" (*Hww*, 101), until multiple "Wenden" finally occur. Due to an accident and mysterious surgery, Klaus' genitals expand in such a way that they are eventually able to overcome the impotence of a self-repressed people and, in a virile act, cause a "Wende" of national proportions: while thousands of GDR citizens hesitantly stand at the border checkpoint exclaiming "Wir sind das Volk" (*Hww*, 315), Klaus unzips his fly and gets the border guards, who are paralyzed at the sight of his gigantic penis, to open up the Berlin Wall.

Thus, a historic event is swiftly turned into something lewd—a downright carnivalesque technique reminiscent of Bakhtin's culture of popular laughter.[2] Bakhtin looks at the medieval and early modern culture of laughter and describes ostentatiously staged bodies with oversized genitalia, who eat and excrete excessively and thus showcase "the grotesque image of the body."[3] In later literature—with its gaze increasingly focused inwards—this presentation of the physical is no longer present, although the grotesque image of the body survived in vulgar jokes and carnivals. Everything with a claim to greatness, majesty, and earnestness is met with fierce derision; everything turns into a "comic monster."[4]

Brussig's taunt is aimed less at the 1989 "Wende" itself and more at the heroic stories associated with it. As he explained to Herlinde Koelbl in an interview: "Bei den 'Helden' war es so, daß ich einen politischen Anspruch hatte. Im Osten hat mich der Umgang mit der Vergangenheit geärgert, daß alle nur von ihren Heldentaten erzählt haben, anstatt von ihrem Mitmachen. Ich dachte mir, daß einer über seinen Opportunismus, über seine Dummheit, über seine Verblendung reden muß."[5]

In order to deconstruct myths about the 1989 "Wende," Brussig satirically uses love, partnership, and discourses of sexuality, and sets stories of philistine mediocrity, stuffy uptightness, authority, and repression against stories of alleged heroic deeds. Klaus Uhltzscht's attention is completely focused on the quest of developing his sexuality in an impenetrable net of norms and prohibitions labeled "perversions," and only towards the end of the novel is he able to recognize the actual perversions of state socialism in which he as a Stasi employee is participating: surveillance, authority, inhumane actions against members of the opposition. Here, Brussig makes use of the figure of the Picaro[6] who, through his seeming incapability of understanding and low social status, is able to produce insight into society. Klaus tells his story in retrospect, which is reminiscent of Oskar Matzerath in Grass's *Die Blechtrommel* or Edgar Wibeau in Plenzdorf's *Die neuen Leiden des jungen W.*, but even more so of the protagonist of Philip Roth's *Portnoy's Complaint*: Just as the protagonist of Roth's novel tells a therapist about his sexual problems, Klaus tells the journalist Kitzelstein about his life and, in particular, about his sex life.[7] What is designed as a dialogue turns into a book-filling monologue recorded on seven tapes and fictionally played back for the reader. Since Klaus is, despite the occasional insight, convinced of his own grandeur even in retrospect, and presents himself as the "*Missing link* der jüngsten deutschen Geschichte" (*Hww*, 323), Brussig satirizes the very form of the confessional novel itself.

While it is not the first time in literature that the figure of a Picaro has been used to critically and satirically explore topics such as prudery and sexual taboos, Brussig addresses norms around love, partnership, and sexuality that were specific for state socialism in the GDR. As demonstrated below, he achieves this by contrasting cleanliness with dirt and sexual propriety with so-called perversion.

Healthy Socialists

Klaus's mother is a health inspector, a "Hygiene*göttin*" (*Hww*, 25), as Klaus calls her. Her hypochondriac advice (see, e.g., *Hww*, 33–36) and obsessive search for germs and dirt (see, e.g., *Hww*, 31) turn her into a caricature of an exaggerated state obsession with cleanliness, suggesting that the penis is "ein hygienisch heikles Ding" (*Hww*, 53) for which a separate bar of soap has to be used. Her encroaching mannerisms even include monitoring her son's excretions (see *Hww*, 43–45) or comments on his erections: "Hast du wieder daran rumgespielt" (*Hww*, 68). The "Hygienegöttin" (*Hww*, 25) focuses her attention on public spaces, the private flat, and also the personal hygiene of her family. She has Klaus's father on her side, who is "autoritär und rechtschaffen" (*Hww*, 9), and so prudish that Klaus calls his father's penis "sein geheimes Ding" (*Hww*, 66). In his portrayal of this family dynamic, "[der] bekennende Maaz-Leser Brussig"[8] is referring to Hans Joachim Maaz's book *Der Gefühlsstau*, in which Maaz examines the ramifications of repressive structures on the mental state of East German society and in this context also takes apart the state's norms regarding education, particularly in terms of teaching ideas of "Sauberkeit."[9] This education turns out to be tragically consequential for Klaus insofar as he is denied truthful information, both on the topic of sexuality as well as on his father's work as a Stasi employee. Klaus is always the last to know the truth and usually hears it from what he thinks of as debased and seedy "Ferienlagertypen" (*Hww*, 83, see also *Hww*, 49–51). Here, the satirical attack is aimed at a certain morality, which is articulated in the rhetoric of moral propriety that was typical in the GDR.

The German term "Sauberkeit" contains two meanings: on the one hand, "sauber" can refer to the condition of a person or thing as being "clean" and, on the other hand, can also mean "anständig, einwandfrei, korrekt, lauter,"[10] thus labeling a person or behavior as proper, morally sound, or healthy. Here the term "Sauberkeitsrhetorik" or "rhetoric of propriety" mainly refers to the second meaning. Therefore, "sauber" and "Sauberkeit" will henceforth be translated as either "healthy" and "health," or as "propriety." The wittiness of *Helden wie wir* is—amongst other things—derived from the way the novel plays on the different meanings of "Sauberkeit." It portrays an obsession with cleanliness and a form of sexual behavior that lies beyond the norms of morality and health; it both satirizes a normative—and, as will be argued, also heteronormative—value system which operates in private as well as within society.

"Sauberkeit" was indeed a guiding principle of the early GDR, and this is demonstrated most obviously in Walter Ulbricht's "Zehn Gebote für den neuen sozialistischen Menschen," proclaimed in 1958 at the Fifth

SED party conference.[11] The ninth commandment was: "Du sollst sauber und anständig leben und deine Familie achten."[12] Continuing in this vein, he also called them "Moralgesetze" and "Gebote der neuen, sozialistischen Sittlichkeit."[13] The "Wörterbuch der Sexuologie und ihrer Grenzgebiete" from 1964 also has its own entry for "Sauberkeit" and refers to both meanings, cleanliness as well as the—positively regarded— "saubere Einstellung zur Sexualität"[14] or "healthy attitude to sexuality." Under "Moral," Ulbricht's ninth commandment is quoted and its continuing validity stressed.[15] Even the law called for "saubere Beziehungen zwischen den Geschlechtern" as one of the "Charaktereigenschaften der sozialistischen Persönlichkeit" in the Uniform Socialist Education System Act (February 25, 1965).[16] Already in its 1952 constitution, the "Freie deutsche Jugend" had demanded that every member should create "saubere, gesunde Beziehungen zwischen Jungen und Mädchen zum inneren Gesetz seiner Handlung."[17]

However, the early GDR's attitudes towards morality and the values that were conveyed shifted over time. Initially, the goals of the state's policy regarding sexual and reproductive health were aimed primarily at reducing the number of sexually transmitted infections and pregnancy terminations as well as educating people about contraception.[18] For publications on sexual morality from this time until the 1970s, Joachim S. Hohmann observes that their authors frequently avoided developing an adequate position on the topic by making references to classic Marxist texts and the role of women, marriage, and the family described therein.[19] Things started to change in the 1960s, the "sexualpädagogischen Gründerjahre,"[20] when empirical research on citizens' sexual behavior started to be established.[21] Along with the growing interest in empirical research and the increasing professionalization of sexual counseling services, which had been taking place since the late 1960s, began a liberalization of sexual norms that led to an increasingly open relationship with sexual pleasure in the 1970s. The 1980s, then, saw a tendency to no longer pathologize homosexuality as "illness" or "perversion."[22]

Dagmar Herzog detects a "sexual evolution"[23] in this increasing openness and thus coins a term to counter West Germany's "sexual revolution." This sexual evolution can be seen as a mutually dependent process involving the Party softening its ideological stance on the one hand, and bourgeois emancipation on the other. However, due to the GDR's restricted civil liberties, this emancipation happened in a rather pragmatic manner where resistance was more often expressed through inconspicuous actions in everyday life than in the supposedly "revolutionary" manner adopted in West Germany, where the leftist student movement used deliberate provocation and the breaking of taboos to capture the media's attention when it came to transgressing accepted sexual norms. It is worth noting, however, that—despite the different systems and the striking lack of democratic structures in the GDR—a remarkable liberalization of sexual morals took place in *both* German states in just two decades. Josie McLellan therefore describes Herzog's juxtaposition of "sexual revolution" and "sexual evolution" as a "false dichotomy between East and West."[24] According to McLellan, this differentiation underestimates the diverse possibilities of revolutionary change: "The idea that a sexual revolution can take place, at least in part, 'from below,' rather than being shaped only by legislators, entrepreneurs, radicals, and sexual theorists, is highly relevant to the East German case."[25]

Despite all this liberalization, however, the guiding principle of "Sauberkeit" remained part of official GDR rhetoric. Until the late 1970s, the term "Sauberkeit" was used in sex education because all good Socialists should "sich offen zu ihren sauberen Einstellungen in den Geschlechtsbeziehungen bekennen."[26] This demand, which here is elevated to a quasi-religious status through the reference to confession ("bekennen"), also encompasses the use of language: even in the third edition published in 1989, a passage can be found in an encyclopedia on sexuality aimed at young adults that requests: "Vulgärbezeichnungen sollten von Jugendlichen und Erwachsenen, die auf einen guten und sauberen Umgangsstil Wert legen, nicht benutzt werden."[27] Klaus Uhltzscht, born on 20 August, 1968 (*Hww*, 5), experiences his childhood and youth in the 1970s and early 1980s, raised by parents loyal to the state who themselves had grown up in the spirit of the postwar period. Siegfried Schnabl's guidance book on sexuality, *Mann und Frau intim* (1973), becomes an important source of sex education for him. There, too, "Sauberkeit" features centrally in the description of proper socialist sexuality:

> Die marxistische Ethik bejaht die Liebe nicht nur als geistiges Band und tiefempfundenes Gefühl zwischen Mann und Frau, sondern auch als sinnlich-gegenständliches Erleben ihrer innigen Zuneigung in der körperlichen Vereinigung. Die sexuelle Partnerschaft wird moralisch nicht erst als eheliche Beziehung gerechtfertigt oder gar erst dann, wenn sie auf Fortpflanzung gerichtet ist, sondern auch als sich selbst genügende Beglückung der Liebenden in einer sittlich wertvollen und gesellschaftlich verantwortlichen gegenseitigen Beziehung. . . . Diese Bejahung der Sinnlichkeit war und ist allerdings für uns stets verbunden mit der Forderung nach moralischer Sauberkeit und Verantwortungsbewußtsein, nach Achtung und Vertrauen, nach Aufrichtigkeit und Ehrlichkeit.[28]

What is the moral core of this rhetoric of "Sauberkeit" or moral propriety that survives all forms of change, though? "Healthy" socialists, as Schnabl makes clear, do not need to renounce sexual pleasure and satisfaction. They are not asked—as in some religious contexts—to limit their sexuality to marital or even reproductive activities. The center of the socialist rhetoric of propriety, and, as such, the norm for a "healthy" sexuality, is "love." Josie McLellan, too, insists on the particular significance of love: "During the lifetime of the GDR, the connection between sex and love was central to all public discussions of sexuality. Sex advice books simply assumed that their readers were in a loving, heterosexual, monogamous relationship, and other publications continually stressed that sex without love was an empty activity, at best meaningless and at worst actively damaging."[29]

"Sauberkeit" is used as a term to describe the inseparability of love and sex, and also fulfilled a function for the building of state socialism. In 1965, Erich Honecker described the GDR as a "saubere Staat,"[30] with "unverrückbare Maßstäbe der Ethik und Moral, für Anstand und gute Sitte."[31] He distinctly distanced himself from the "kapitalistischen Unkultur und Unmoral, wie sie in der amerikanischen Sex-Propaganda . . . zum Ausdruck kommt."[32] In 1989, twenty years after the beginning of the "sexual revolution" in the FRG, an East German encyclopedia on sexuality aimed at young adults stated: "Überbewerten sollte man allerdings die Sexualität auch nicht, wie dies gegenwärtig z.B. in vielen kapitalistischen Ländern geschieht, um die Jugend von gesellschaftlichen Problemen (z.B. Arbeitslosigkeit) abzulenken. Dort wird 'Sex' zum Hauptzweck des Lebens erklärt und die 'sexuelle Freiheit' als die Freiheit schlechthin. Außerdem wird die Frau zum bloßen Sexualobjekt."[33] The rhetoric of "Sauberkeit" thus also served as a way for the GDR to distinguish itself from the West. The association of the West with questionable permissiveness, the objectification of women, dehumanization, and the use of sexuality for the purposes of political misdirection, also suggests that the West lacks love. The contrasting model was the supposedly loving relationship under socialism, which was based on fidelity, stability, and equality. This juxtaposition was indeed successful and frequently articulated in a romanticizing of love under socialism after the demise of the GDR in 1989, though it is not always possible to establish whether this idea of love was actually popular at the time or whether this is a retrospective idealization of the GDR. Pornography and prostitution, for example, were met with fierce opposition by East German sexologists.[34] Empirical studies have shown that young people who grew up in the GDR feel more strongly connected to the idea of monogamy,[35] and even Thomas Brussig spoke about Western permissiveness in 1997, when he said: "Es kotzt mich regelrecht an, dieses demonstrative Herausstellen von Sex."[36]

The fact that the political leaders of the GDR did not apply this much-lauded concept of "Sauberkeit" as strictly to their own actions—it makes sense, therefore, to refer to it as rhetoric of "Sauberkeit" or "propriety"—can be seen in the double standards of the SED and the Staatssicherheit (Stasi) when it came to loving relationships. It was, for instance, made very difficult for GDR citizens to have relationships with foreigners, and the Stasi destroyed intimate bonds by getting people to spy and inform on their partners.[37]

By reducing this rhetoric to absurdity in *Helden wie wir*, Brussig also deconstructs the concept of heteronormativity. However, heteronormativity is not to be equated with homophobia. It is about the norms, "die fordern, dass Sexualität Heterosexualität sein soll,"[38] and about a value system that delimits heterosexuality by subjecting men and women to heterosexual norms "wie zum Beispiel der Annahme der zugewiesenen Geschlechterrolle, dem demonstrativen erotischen Desinteresse an Menschen des eigenen Geschlechts, dem identifikatorischen Bezug auf gesellschaftliche Regulative wie der Ehe und der Familienplanung."[39] The linking of sex with love within the ideal monogamous partnership, as was demonstrated by GDR politicians and self-help literature of the time, produced many "impurities" such as, for example, promiscuity, polyamory, pornography, prostitution, and casual sex: topics which affected homo- and heterosexuals equally. It can be assumed that counselors and authors of sex manuals articulated some of the moral devaluations not according to their own perceptions but in regard to a powerful censorship. Siegfried Schnabl, for example, writes that "echte Liebe gibt es durchaus unter den Homosexuellen"[40] and that even homosexuality can be cultivated "durch feste, verantwortungsvolle, auf gegenseitige Treue, Liebe und Achtung gegründete Partnerschaft";[41] thus turning love, in perfect alignment with the rhetoric of "Sauberkeit," into the condition for recognition of homosexuality. Although Schnabl argued for the recognition of gays and lesbians, the heteronormative framing—possibly owing to censorship—remains intact: "Besondere Aufmerksamkeit müßte aber der Vorbeugung der Homosexualität geschenkt werden."[42]

Brussig's satirical attack on Schnabl's *Mann und Frau intim* in *Helden wie wir* is not concerned with fairness or historical contextualization, nor is it a comparison of the situation in the two German states. This is not about Brussig's perspective on Schnabl. There is no claim that the East German people had always taken this rhetoric of "Sauberkeit" espoused by the Party and self-help books seriously. Rather, it is a demonstration of how the "Kunstfigur"[43] Klaus Uhltzscht reads *Mann und Frau intim*. The typical satirical reversal—in which the Picaro takes certain statements literally without questioning them—ridicules not the supposed reality of East Germany but the rhetoric of its representatives in the worlds of politics and science.

Normativity, Progressiveness, and Feasibility

The norms surrounding partnership and sexuality are particularly distinct in East German self-help books. According to Regine Mahlmann, advisory books on marriage and sexuality "liefern das empirische Material, das die Liebenden darin unterweist, welche Zeichen sie benutzen dürfen" in a manner that is "exemplarisch und typisierend, beschreibend und norm-ierend."[44] However, in a society with no free book market, where pub-lications are legitimized from the top down, they have to be understood as directly bridging the gap between science, the general population, and state power, and therefore indicate the importance of the rhetoric of "Sauberkeit" as well as the liberalizations in society. Historically, as well as in terms of content, the guidance book *Mann und Frau intim* by Siegfried Schnabl, several editions of which were published since 1969, sits somewhere between the rigorous moralism of Rudolf Neubert—author of, amongst other things, *Das neue Ehebuch* from 1957[45]—and the more liberal approaches of *Liebe und Sexualität bis 30* from 1984 by Kurt Starke and Walter Friedrich.[46] Schnabl discusses medicine, sexol-ogy, biology, and psychology and uses case studies from marriage and sex counseling. This implies objectivity and pragmatism despite the fact that Schnabl consistently writes in a judgmental and moralistic manner. He does not intend to hand this "neue Wissen"[47] over to the readers for independent application but rather to explain how sexuality is *supposed* to be practiced in socialism.[48]

Besides this fundamentally normative attitude, another notable char-acteristic of Schnabl's book is its focus on the future. The new social-ist propriety was not just a program for the present but also for the years to come. The GDR established its identity officially as "Sieger der Geschichte"[49] and therefore victor over capitalism and fascism; com-munism was the future of state ideology. The route to communism was to form a society of socialist personalities, of people who had internal-ized and lived socialist values. This goal did not omit the realm of sexu-ality, and therefore norms for relationships were to be established that would satisfy the requirement of a Socialist society. In contrast to reli-gious norms, which constitutively entail failure (sin) and atonement, the application and fulfillment of these norms in everyday life was principally considered feasible.

In his guide, Schnabl uses a generalizing indicative that expresses an imperative heteronormativity: "Frau und Mann streben danach, sich zu vereinen, eine körperliche und geistige Gemeinschaft zu bilden."[50] This specifically includes an imperative for the man: Strive for the woman! It is the only way to become a man! Such an imperative character can be intrinsic to norms when they are not understood as averages (in the statistical sense) but as a moral model because then the norm has "über den deskriptiven Inhalt hinaus imperativischen Charakter, insofern alle der Norm unterworfenen Gegenstände ihrer Form nach mit der ihnen zugrunde liegenden Norm übereinstimmen sollen."[51] Schnabl elabo-rates stereotypically on the differences between man and woman; for example, he claims that a woman only starts desiring when she loves[52] and that a man only has one erogenous zone (his penis).[53] This difference is supposed to ensure attraction; however, the emphasis on binarity also articulates the concern that their differences may cause man and woman to pass each other by. Therefore, Schnabl offers a technical manual for intercourse:

> Die schwankende Libido der Frau wird durch das Verlangen und zärtliche Werben des Mannes angeregt, und es kommt bei ihr zu einer Sekretion. Diese erleichtert dem Mann, dessen Erektion jetzt leicht versagt, das Eindringen in die Scheide und erhöht das lokale Lustempfinden am Glied. Die Frau nimmt seine verstärkte Erregung und den Anstieg seiner Lust wahr. Das kann ihre Wollust fördern und die Auslösung des Orgasmus begünstigen.[54]

This implies that first the man has to arouse the woman with his desire, then there is the danger that his erection might fail just before "penetration," and once he is inside her she "can" experience lust but may not necessarily—a threefold possibility of failure. The reassurance lies in the basic feasibility of heterosexual intercourse, which Schnabl maps out in terms of a key and lock metaphor: the man has to "unlock" the woman ("aufzuschließen").[55]

Schnabl devotes more than one hundred pages to the possible problems of intercourse, while all other sexual options are relegated to the periphery in terms of focus and relevance. The male fear of problems during intercourse is contained in a union based on "Liebe und Verständnis."[56] Thus, the technical model is also emotionalized. This emotionalization aims at harmony and equality. In this, Schnabl indirectly distances himself from the sexological studies of capitalist countries (in particular from those of the Kinsey Institute and by William Masters and Virginia Johnson). While adopting their logic of technology, measurability, and feasibility, he incorporates it into state socialism by referencing "harmony," "collective," and "Sauberkeit."

Besides feasibility, however, sexuality is also aligned with a progressiveness in which man and woman are assigned different tasks. The woman has to become more carnal: "Der Mensch muß die geschlechtliche Erfüllung 'erlernen.' Für die Frau ist das schwieriger als für den Mann."[57] The man, on the other hand, is expected to become more civilized: He is supposed to "ihr seine Liebe bekunden, indem er mit ihr gemeinsam den Haushalt besorgt."[58] Man and woman become Socialist together. The ideal masculinity expressed herein matches East Germany's proclaimed demand for equality but is deeply invested in heteronormativity as it binds people to a heterosexual lifestyle and desire and compels them to form stable couples.

All that is "unclean" and "unhealthy" lies outside of the heteronormative imperative. Schnabl states that cases of premature ejaculation are common amongst "englischen Geistesarbeitern" and "Managertypen."[59] "Impotent" men are described as overbearing and egocentric, oversensitive and hypochondriac[60] or they are certified to suffer from "Denk- und Grübelsucht."[61] Men who cannot or will not perform coitus, as is necessary for "correct" heterosexuality, are thus characterized as some form of the intellectual, decadent-bourgeois, effeminate dandy. It is in distinction from these "countertypes"[62] that the model of the new Socialist masculinity becomes apparent: the healthy, proper, heterosexual and vital worker.

With the insistence on marriage, sexual fidelity, and the alignment of relationships with societal values—because "eine gehaltvolle, gemeinsame Stunde mit dem vielbeschäftigten Mann" can make a woman happier in the long term than "ewiges Schmusen mit einem Nichtstuer"[63]—Schnabl, furthermore, creates moral values which determine what heterosexuality should look like. In the light of the book's overall approach, his openness towards practices beyond vaginal intercourse does not appear credible. He dedicates over two hundred pages to problems related to sex but focuses on anorgasmia and frigidity for women, and impotence and premature ejaculation for men—all phenomena that make heterosexual vaginal intercourse difficult or impossible. Josie McLellan writes: "East German sexology was preoccupied with penetrative sex."[64] This might indicate a biopolitical intention, as the GDR was dependent on high birth rates to ensure the continuing existence of the state. On the other hand, this might be indicative of prudery, probably less on the part of sexologists and more on the part of the censors: although healthy socialists were allowed pleasure in love, there seems to have been a discomfort regarding individuals receiving "too much" enjoyment. Under the heading "Abwandlungen und Ersatzformen des Geschlechtslebens," Schnabl briefly describes practices such as petting, manual, and oral stimulation[65] but devalues them by subsuming them as activities to replace actual intercourse and assigning them an immoral ego-fixation. By this means, there is a constant reiteration of what makes heterosexuality the "right" sexuality (vaginal intercourse between man and woman). All that is left to homosexuals are "ungewöhnlich erscheinenden Koitusmethoden."[66]

In the novel *Helden wie wir* the reader gets acquainted with Schnabl's book from the completely uncritical perspective of a naive reader: Klaus. Schnabl's guide is a poor adviser for Klaus. He initially searches eagerly—though equally unsuccessfully—for information on the G-spot, until he finally concludes that it probably only exists in the West. Here, it becomes apparent that Klaus is incapable of questioning Schnabl's authority. Because of this uncritical fixation on authority, Schnabl's book finally turns against Klaus in an intimidating and repressive manner. When Klaus starts penetrating broilers, he tries to find a comment from Schnabl on the subject:

Was sagt Siegfried Schnabl dazu? Sind in seinem Buch "Mann und Frau intim" auch Fragen zum Thema "Mann und Broiler intim" Gegenstand von Erörterungen? Im III. Teil (Varianten und Abarten des Geschlechtslebens) mit seinem 9. Kapitel (Abweichungen des Geschlechtslebens) stand kurz etwas von *Zoophilie*, einer *Deviation*, auf die Schnabl nicht weiter eingehen wollte, um, wie er schrieb, seine Leser nicht zu langweilen. Auch die *Deformitätsfetischisten* und ihre *schwer nachvollziehbare Lust an verstümmelten Gliedmaßen* werden nur in einem Halbsatz erwähnt. Dafür widmet sich Schnabl ausführlich der *Pädophilie*, während wiederum *Nekrophilie* überhaupt nicht vorkommt (auch wenn im Abschnitt über den *Sadismus* der *perverse Lustmord*, der *Mord zur sexuellen Befriedigung* nicht verschwiegen wird). Dann gab es noch *Frotteure*, *Voyeure* und *Exhibitionisten* . . . *Unzucht mit Broilern* sprengte das 9. Kapitel! Ich trieb's *mit Tieren*! Mit *toten* Tieren! Toten *Jung*tieren! Die keinen Kopf hatten! Also mit verstümmelten! toten! Jung!tieren! *Vier* Perversionen auf einmal! (*Hww*, 240)

The inhibited delight in which taboos are pronounced in this passage creates a "polymorphous incitement to discourse."[67] At the same time, his compulsive confession and his self-pathologizing become overly hysterical as reinforced by the italics and exclamation marks in the typeface (which are also often used when Klaus recalls his mother's words). Penetration of broilers might be unusual and unsavory, yet Klaus has quite different problems to contend with: his real-life interactions with women turn into disasters, as will be shown below.

Marina, the "Sausage Woman," and Yvonne

Klaus's image of women turns any rhetoric of equality into absurdity: For him there are "whores" (Marina), "Madonnas" (Yvonne), and "leftovers" (the "Wurstfrau," *Hww*, 188). "Whores" seduce, "Madonnas" are practically untouchable, and "leftovers" become the target of crude violence. The three female characters respectively illustrate different traits of Klaus, the Picaro (inexperience, naive morality, and delinquency) while also satirizing a normative image of love and sexuality.

In the encounter between Klaus and Marina, it is Klaus's inexperience that is depicted:

Wo hatte sie das gelernt? Können das alle Frauen? Ich war so fasziniert—*fassiniert*—, daß ich mein Vorhaben vergaß, nach einem etwaigen G-Punkt zu suchen; wie oft hatte ich in Gedanken und unter Hinzuziehung anatomischer Skizzen aus dem Biologiebuch (8. Klasse) Stellungen projektiert, die meinem Dildo die nötige Bewegungsfreiheit—Stoßtiefe und Rührwinkel—bei der systematischen Suche nach einem G-Punkt gewährleistet hätten . . . Ich

lebte immer im Glauben, daß man vor, während und nach dem
Vögeln *Ich liebe dich* sagen muß. *Vor* und *während* war vorbei. Was tun?
    "Ich liebe dich," sagte ich probeweise.
    "Nun beruhige dich mal wieder," sagte sie.
    Was? Keine Liebe? War es der pure 6?
    "War doch sonst nix da," sagte sie und blies den Rauch aus.
(*Hww*, 122–29)

The joke here is that Klaus has planned a possible sexual act in detail but
never actually experienced it before. This is a parody of the normative
demand that a man must give a woman the greatest possible satisfaction
by use of his potency and technical virtuosity. But here, beyond anatomi-
cal sketch plans, it is the woman who is active, the man is surprised, and
in the end the woman's orgasm is never even mentioned. This is also a
derisive slur on Siegfried Schnabl's logic of feasibility with its quasi-tech-
nical manuals for intercourse. Finally, the rhetoric of love gets caricatured
by showing it—despite all fantasies of "Sauberkeit"—as not a necessarily inherent part of sexuality. At this point, Klaus is still caught up in his
inhibited propriety: By writing "6" instead of "sex," the author shows that
Klaus's mother (who always pronounces "sex" with a soft "s," *Hww*, 58),
now interposes as an internalized moral authority, which is confirmed in
the ensuing account of Marina's alleged lack of hygiene (see *Hww*, 129–
30). Klaus feels like he has been degraded to a "6maschine" (*Hww*, 129),
and leaves. The ambivalence of the term "Sauberkeit" is highlighted here
in a satirical manner as Marina lacks both cleanliness and moral propriety.
Concurrent with picaresque narrative patterns, this encounter results in
mishaps—Klaus infects himself with gonorrhea as a keepsake. In the context of his moral values, he can only interpret this infection as the inevitable and logical result of his intercourse (see *Hww*, 130).
    The encounter with the "Wurstfrau," as Klaus disparagingly calls her
because of her size, demonstrates the delinquency of Klaus Uhltzscht the
Picaro and thus—similarly to his position as a perpetrator in the Stasi—
the abysmal aspect of the upright and virtuous first-person narrator. At
the same time, this passage can be understood as a pun on the German
word "Fleischeslust," which is practically rampant in Klaus, who desires
sex with the "sausage woman" and penetrates broilers. Klaus's megalo-
mania and "*Gefühlsstau*" are expressed in his boundless misogyny: "eine
frustrierte, geschiedene, mausgraue Bürotussi . . . Sie ist *sitzengeblieben*,
niemand hat sie abgeschleppt, nur ich!" (*Hww*, 188, 190–91).[68]
    The tale of the attempted rape (*Hww*, 191–92) contains burlesque
and carnivalesque elements, such as when the woman laughs at the size of
Klaus's penis (*Hww*, 190–91). However, the narrator, and therefore the
author, does not utilize the mockery to justify the violence. The way in
which Klaus the narrator distances himself from Klaus the person signifies

that the deed is explicitly unacceptable, while the parody is aimed at Klaus's idea of sexuality when he masturbates for the first time following this scene as a sort of "sublimation activity" for the rape (see *Hww*, 193) and only then realizes that masturbation is not the "worst" way of handling sexual desire.

The narrative thread concerning Yvonne, introduced by Klaus as "die einzige Liebesgeschichte meines Lebens" (*Hww*, 214) is primarily about Klaus's morality. His portrayal of Yvonne is characterized by a (love-struck) idealization in which Yvonne the "Madonna" is set in contrast to Marina the "whore." While Klaus is not able to accept sex without love in his encounter with Marina, he now finds it hard to connect sex and love, as demonstrated in the quotation at the beginning of the chapter. The change in his language here, as well as in his encounter with the "Wurstfrau," is very noticeable. As a child, Klaus does not even know words like "Arschloch" (*Hww*, 33) or "Weitpissen" (*Hww*, 51) while he now showers the "Wurstfrau" with sexist epithets (even if just in his mind) and repeats the supposed "Ferkeleien" (*Hww*, 236) he intends for Yvonne almost compulsively: "Daß ich (ich!) ficken (ficken!) will (will!)" (*Hww*, 236). Where self-help literature for young people considers vulgar language to be impure, Klaus's use of language here demonstrates his progressive failure to become a healthy, proper socialist.

Klaus eventually manages to get over his qualms, but gets interrupted by Yvonne when she asks him to hurt her (see *Hww*, 237). Thereupon, he abandons the sexual encounter and leaves. For Klaus, love is associated with "cleanliness" and quasi-religious "Sauberkeit," and this morality makes him incapable of meeting Yvonne's supposedly "dirty" needs. Therefore, to come back to the initial question, he is indeed not permitted to have sex with an angel.

Klaus's encounters with the three women are used to show that the example set by his parents, the "healthy" Uhltzscht couple, and the reading of Schnabl's *Mann und Frau intim* have prepared Klaus neither for love nor sex. Klaus does not succeed in having a relationship and only manages one single act of intercourse, and even there, the idea of a male "Aufschließer," as Schnabl describes him, is shown to be preposterous. In terms of Socialist progressiveness, Klaus's relations also fail to achieve social significance, and he sublimely fails to meet the requirements of Socialist equality between the sexes: He is unable to come to an arrangement with Marina, almost rapes the "sausage woman," and stylizes and elevates Yvonne to the level of an angel. Finally, in an attempt to surpass everything that, according to state socialism's norms, is already impure in his love and sex life, Klaus creates a directory of his perversions, which he calls "Kartei neuen Typus" (*Hww*, 270). This is clearly a slur on Lenin's "Partei neuen Typus," indirectly turning socialism into a space of perversions. But the problem that Klaus actually faces is not his perversions but his inability to independently and confidently take a stand on the norms, idealizations, and pathologizations with which he is confronted. He does not succeed in emancipating himself from his mother's education and her voice, which he has internalized. He compensates this by attacking Christa Wolf, the GDR's most celebrated author (*Hww*, 282–88). On the one hand, Wolf appears as a laughable figure, dreaming of a Socialism "zwei Nummern zu piefig" (*Hww*, 287); on the other hand, the aggression is aimed at her eponymous novel *Der geteilte Himmel* and its depiction of love. When the book is referred to as an "Erektionstöter" (*Hww*, 307) and its title ridiculed and turned into "Der geheilte Pimmel" in the title of *Helden wie wir*'s last chapter, this is a renunciation of great, tragic, political, but non-erotic love stories, a cynical statement rebelling against the "politische Impotenz . . . der kritisch-betroffenen DDR- und Wendeliteratur."[69] Christa Wolf's 1989 speech at Alexanderplatz is reprinted in full in the novel (see *Hww*, 283–85)—this stylistic inconsistency within the text marks it as crucially important—and is commented by Klaus as follows: "Jede Revolution hat die Reden, die sie verdient" (*Hww*, 285). He even compares her 1990 preamble to the new GDR constitution to his mother's style: "Alles, aber auch wirklich *alles* Edle, Wahre, Hehre, Erbauliche usw. wurde dort hineingestopft, verkettet durch Partizipien, natürlich durch das aufdringlichere, das Partizip I. Ich kenne diesen Stil von meiner Mutter: Für den Badekappenzwang, aber sonst liberal" (*Hww*, 308). This symbolic matricide aims at the destruction of traditions and is also a rejection of highbrow GDR literature. Christa Wolf, a symbolic figure of civic and inner-socialist reform, becomes the embodiment of a once mighty but now powerless and defeated maternal principle which is juxtaposed with the "geheilte Pimmel," a male-connoted potency of revolution and radical change. This is emancipation from a state that provides and protects but that also controls and castrates: "Der geheilte Pimmel setzt den symbolischen Muttermord voraus (Ödipus re-gendered)."[70]

Klaus becomes fully aware of his own immaturity and his status as a mindless follower when he sees himself in citizens he meets at the Berlin Wall:

> So artig und gehemmt wie sie dastanden, wie sie von einem Bein aufs andere traten und darauf hofften, sie dürften mal—kein Zweifel, sie waren wirklich das Volk. So kannte ich sie, so brav und häschenhaft und auf Verlierer programmiert, und irgendwie hatte ich Mitleid mit ihnen, denn ich war einer von ihnen. (*Hww*, 315)

Maturity and Redemption

Brussig's novel does not merely target East German discourses of heroism, love, and sexuality, but also deconstructs other heteronormative patterns. One of those is the demand for maturity which was also raised (but not exclusively) in the GDR. Regarding homosexuality, the 1964 *Wörterbuch der Sexuologie und ihrer Grenzgebiete*, for example, states that "Jeder hat nur sein eigenes Geschlecht, so daß die Wirbildung im eigenen Geschlecht widernatürlich, infantil ist."[71] This thus implies that heterosexuality is something mature. Although such devaluation of homosexuality is time-specific and can no longer be found in *Mann und Frau intim*, Schnabl still deems it necessary to valorize homosexuality by saying that homosexuals can form clean relationships, too. For him, the goal of healthy, socialist romantic relationships pertains to everyone and constitutes (egalitarian) maturity for women and men, hetero- and homosexuals alike. Thus, maturing is a journey—a quest—and failure is, in principle, possible.[72]

The demand for maturity, however, is not unique to the GDR context: This normative objective can be legitimized theologically, psychoanalytically, and in terms of developmental psychology. By making the protagonist a Picaro, Brussig disavows both the psychological development from the oral through anal to the phallic stage, as well as the Socialist development model of the "new man." Klaus develops neither into a heterosexual man who has genital sex with women, nor into a good and "healthy," "proper" Socialist. The description of his regression into the anal stage is wickedly satirical when his mother, who monitored his excretions throughout his childhood (see *Hww*, 43–45) and is generally an "anal fixierte Mutter,"[73] still has to wipe the bottom of the 19-year-old Klaus when both of his arms are in a cast (see *Hww*, 24). With his verdict that "*Ficken* war was für gewöhnliche Menschen" (*Hww*, 245), and the decision to explore Schnabl's "*Abarten des Geschlechtslebens*" (*Hww*, 245), he becomes the exemplary figure of the "Polymorph-Perverse"[74] and thus the epitome of regression and infantilism. In its carnivalesque exaggeration this is, however, not a connection to but a satirical dissociation from psychoanalytical development models.

Even religion is not spared this deconstruction of greatness and is taken to the realms of the lewd. Klaus's birth is already a satirical allusion to the Christmas story (*Hww*, 20), he then proceeds to save Erich Honecker's life with an operation disguised as a "Blutspende" (*Hww*, 264), is incorrectly declared dead and, finally, his genitals, which swell to superhuman proportions, make him the "Erlöser mit dem großen Schwanz" (*Hww*, 316), who heralds a new age at the Berlin Wall. Brussig carves out these salvational Christian references to messianic birth, sacrificial death, symbols of blood, resurrection, and redemption in noticeable distance to his narrator. Klaus continuously uses the word "gleubisch" (*Hww*, 235, 294) instead of "gläubig," and describes the growth of his genital inappropriately as "biblisch" (*Hww*, 294); clear signs that Klaus—once again a typical Picaro—hardly has any knowledge of religion. The biblical references are not there to introduce the theme of Christianity, but neither do they, in their distortion of the story of Christian salvation, aim to be solely an anti-religious parody. Religion is referenced here in a similar way to Marxism: by using allusions to meta-narratives that stand for purpose and greatness, and also appeal to the good in people. There is nothing left of that in Brussig's novel: the people of the "peaceful" and therefore "good" revolution are silly extras; all that is left of their "savior" (a Picaro with airs and graces) and of his great act of redemption is his huge cock. It is difficult to find a more disrespectful and trivial example of religion being denigrated as a "comic monster." Nevertheless, this is not about religion itself, but about the negation of any promise of greatness and purpose. Religion finds itself in the company of communism, the belief in the "new human" of heroism, mature masculinity, and healthy love.

After everything that defines heteronormative masculinity—intercourse with women, maturity, sociopolitical integrity, coming of age—fails to materialize and greatness is reduced to a fantasy of potency, it becomes obvious: Klaus is not a "healthy," "proper" Socialist and not even a kinky hero. He is merely a picaresque figure through which Brussig reduces heteronormative norms to absurdity. Although Brussig particularly targets GDR culture with its rhetoric of "Sauberkeit" and its norms of love and partnership, his satirical deconstruction of maturity and greatness goes beyond the GDR. The real "comic monster" (Bakhtin) of the subversive carnival in *Helden wie wir* is heteronormative masculinity as such.

—*Translated from German by Scout Burghardt*

Notes

[1] Thomas Brussig, *Helden wie wir* (Frankfurt am Main: Fischer, 2002 [1995]), 235–36. Future references in brackets as (*Hww*).

[2] See Moritz Baßler, *Der deutsche Pop-Roman: Die neuen Archivisten* (Munich: Beck, 2000), 60 and Mirjam Gebauer, *Wendekrisen: Der Pikaro im deutschen Roman der 1990er Jahre* (Trier: Wissenschaftlicher Verlag, 2006), 30–34 and 90–93.

[3] Mikhail Mikhailovich Bakhtin, *Rabelais and His World*, trans. Helene Iswolsk (Bloomington: Indiana University Press, 1984), 303.

[4] Bakhtin, *Rabelais*, 26; see also Bakhtin, *Rabelais*, 29.

[5] Herlinde Koelbl, *Im Schreiben zu Haus: Wie Schriftsteller zu Werke gehen* (Munich: Knesebeck, 1998), 98.

[6] The "Picaro" (or "roguish hero" or "rascal") is the term for the antihero in a picaresque novel—a genre of fiction which combines realism with satirical and grotesque elements.

[7] See Mirjam Gebauer, "Milieuschilderungen zweier verrückter Monologisten. Philip Roths 'Portnoy's Complaint' als ein Vorbild für Thomas Brussigs 'Helden wie wir,'" *Orbis Litterarum* 3 (2002): 222–40.

[8] Heide Hollmer and Albert Meier, "'Wie ich das mit der Mauer hingekriegt habe.' Der 9. November 1989 in Thomas Brussigs 'Helden wie wir' und in Thomas Hettches 'Nox,'" in *Jahrbuch der Deutschen Akademie für Sprache und Dichtung 1999* (Darmstadt: Wallstein, 2000), 112–31, here 115.

[9] See Hans Joachim Maaz, *Der Gefühlsstau: Ein Psychogramm der DDR* (Berlin: Argon, 1990).

[10] See *Duden. Bd. 10: Das Bedeutungswörterbuch* (Mannheim: Dudenverlag, 2002), 754, left column.

[11] Otto Buchwitz, "Unsere zehn Gebote bringen den proletarischen und sozialistischen Internationalismus zum Ausdruck," in *Für den Sieg der sozialistischen Revolution auf dem Gebiet der Ideologie und Kultur*, ed. V. Parteitag der Sozialistischen Einheitspartei Deutschlands (Berlin [DDR]: Dietz, 1958), 74–77, here 74.

[12] Walter Ulbricht, "Die sozialistische Umwälzung der Ideologie und der Kultur," in *Für den Sieg der sozialistischen Revolution auf dem Gebiet der Ideologie und Kultur*, ed. V. Parteitag der Sozialistischen Einheitspartei Deutschlands (Berlin [DDR]: Dietz, 1958), 3–42, here 16.

[13] Ulbricht, "Die sozialistische Umwälzung," 16.

[14] Karl Dietz and Peter G. Hesse, *Wörterbuch der Sexuologie und ihrer Grenzgebiete* (Rudolstadt [DDR]: Greifenverlag, 1964), 245, left column.

[15] See Dietz and Hesse, *Wörterbuch*, 192, left column.

[16] Ministerrat der Deutschen Demokratischen Republik, Ministerium für Volksbildung, "Gesetz über das einheitliche sozialistische Bildungssystem der DDR" (Berlin [DDR]: Staatsverlag der Deutschen Demokratischen Republik, 1971), February 25, 1965, § 5, section 5, 16.

[17] Klaus Dieter Stamm, *Die Verfassen der Freien Deutschen Jugend*, accessed April 22, 2017, www.ddr-schulrecht.de/Schulrechtssammlung - DDR-Dateien/pdf/Statut-FDJ52.pdf.

[18] See Joachim S. Hohmann, "Einleitung: Geschichte, Ziele, Leistungen und Perspektiven der Sexuologie in der DDR," in *Sexuologie in der DDR*, ed. Joachim S. Hohmann (Berlin: Dietz, 1991), 9–50, here 9.

[19] Hohmann, "Einleitung," 29.

[20] Kurt Richard Bach, "Zur Entwicklung der Sexualpädagogik in der DDR," in *Sexuologie in der DDR*, ed. Joachim S. Hohmann (Berlin: Dietz, 1991), 228–38, here 231.

[21] See Hohmann, "Einleitung," 10–11.

[22] See Hohmann, "Einleitung," 15–22.

[23] Dagmar Herzog, *Sex after Fascism: Memory and Morality in Twentieth-Century Germany* (Princeton, NJ: Princeton University Press, 2005), 192–204.

[24] Josie McLellan, *Love in the Time of Communism: Intimacy and Sexuality in the GDR* (Cambridge: Cambridge University Press, 2011), 9.

[25] McLellan, *Love in the Time of Communism*, 11.

[26] Rolf Borrmann, "Pädagogische Grundlegung sozialistischer Sexualerziehung," in *Kinder- und Jugendsexualität,* ed. Heinz Grassel and Kurt R. Bach (Berlin [DDR]: VEB Deutscher Verlag der Wissenschaften, 1979), 176–94, here 179.

[27] Lykke Aresin and Anneliese Müller-Hegemann, *Jugendlexikon Jugend zu zweit* (Leipzig [DDR]: VEB Bibliographisches Institut Leipzig, 1989, first published 1978), 164, right column.

[28] Siegfried Schnabl, *Mann und Frau intim. Fragen des gesunden und gestörten Geschlechtslebens.* 6th unchanged edition (Berlin [DDR]: VEB Verlag Volk und Gesundheit, 1973), 58.

[29] McLellan, *Love in the Time of Communism*, 83.

[30] Erich Honecker, "Bericht des Politbüros an die 11. Tagung des Zentralkomitees der SED, 15.–18.12.1965," in *Kahlschlag. Das 11. Plenum des ZK der SED 1965. Studien und Dokumente,* ed. Günter Agde (Berlin: Aufbau, 2000, second extended edition; first published in 1991), 238–51, here 241.

[31] Honecker, "Bericht des Politbüros," 241.

[32] Honecker, "Bericht des Politbüros," 241.

[33] Aresin and Müller-Hegemann, *Jugendlexikon*, 140, left column.

[34] See Hohmann, "Einleitung," 35–37.

[35] See Kurt Starke, "Jugendsexualität," in *Sexuologie in der DDR*, ed. Joachim S. Hohmann (Berlin: Dietz, 1991), 209–27, here 218 and 220.

[36] Koelbl, *Im Schreiben zu Haus*, 100 (for information concerning the date of the interview: 254).

[37] McLellan, *Love in the Time of Communism*, 84 and 105–12.

[38] Sven Glawion, *Heterogenesis: Männlichkeit in deutschen Erzähltexten 1968–2000* (Darmstadt: Büchner, 2012), 77.

[39] Glawion, *Heterogenesis*, 79.

[40] Schnabl, *Mann und Frau intim*, 320.

[41] Schnabl, *Mann und Frau intim*, 327.

[42] Schnabl, *Mann und Frau intim*, 326.

[43] Koelbl, *Im Schreiben zu Haus*, 98.

[44] Regina Mahlmann, *Was verstehst du unter Liebe? Ideal und Konflikte von der Frühromantik bis heute* (Darmstadt: Primus, 2003), 31.

[45] Rudolf Neubert, *Das neue Ehebuch* (Berlin [DDR]: Volk und Gesundheit, 1957).

[46] Kurt Starke and Friedrich Walter (eds.), *Liebe und Sexualität bis 30* (Berlin [DDR]: VEB Deutscher Verlag der Wissenschaften, 1984).

[47] Schnabl, *Mann und Frau intim*, 9.

[48] See Sven Glawion, "Sauberkeit und Sozialismus. Heteronormativität, Männlichkeit und die DDR: Ein Blick in Siegfried Schnabls 'Mann und Frau intim,'" in *Unbeschreiblich männlich. Heteronormativitätskritische Perspektiven*, ed. Robin

Bauer, Josch Hoenes, and Volker Woltersdorff (Hamburg: Männerschwarm, 2007), 75–89.

[49] Peter Bohley, ed., *Erlebte DDR-Geschichte: Zeitzeugen berichten* (Berlin: Christoph Links Verlag, 2014), 19.

[50] Schnabl, *Mann und Frau intim*, 66.

[51] Annemarie Pieper, "Norm," in *Handbuch philosophischer Grundbegriffe, vol. 2*, ed. Hermann Krings, Hans Michael Baumgartner, and Christoph Wild (Munich: Kösel, 1973), 1009–21, here 1012–13.

[52] See Schnabl, *Mann und Frau intim*, 61.

[53] See Schnabl, *Mann und Frau intim*, 63.

[54] Schnabl, *Mann und Frau intim*, 122.

[55] Schnabl, *Mann und Frau intim*, 161.

[56] Schnabl, *Mann und Frau intim*, 66.

[57] Schnabl, *Mann und Frau intim*, 151.

[58] Schnabl, *Mann und Frau intim*, 168.

[59] Schnabl, *Mann und Frau intim*, 240.

[60] See Schnabl, *Mann und Frau intim*, 222.

[61] Schnabl, *Mann und Frau intim*, 220.

[62] See George L. Mosse, *The Image of Man: The Creation of Modern Masculinity* (Oxford: Oxford University Press, 1996), 56–57.

[63] Schnabl, *Mann und Frau intim*, 167.

[64] McLellan, *Love in the Time of Communism*, 90.

[65] See Schnabl, *Mann und Frau intim*, 276–80.

[66] Schnabl, *Mann und Frau intim*, 320.

[67] Michel Foucault, *The History of Sexuality. Vol. 1*, trans. Robert Hurley 1976 (New York: Pantheon Books, 1978), 34.

[68] The German original also contains this sentence, which is missing in the English translation: "Ich, historischer Missionar, der ich an meiner sexuellen Vervollkommnung arbeite, werde mich doch am Menschenmaterial eines Bumsschuppens ausprobieren dürfen" (*Hww*, 190–91).

[69] Baßler, *Pop-Roman*, 62–63.

[70] Baßler, *Pop-Roman*, 64.

[71] Dietz and Hesse, *Wörterbuch*, 260, left column.

[72] See Glawion, *Heterogenesis*, 13, 286–96.

[73] Baßler, *Pop-Roman*, 61.

[74] See Sigmund Freud, "Drei Abhandlungen zur Sexualtheorie," in *Studienausgabe. Bd. V*, ed. Alexander Mitscherlich, Angela Richards, and James Strachey (Frankfurt am Main: Fischer, 2000, first published 1905), 37–145, here 97.

Disembodied Love and Desire: Virtual Love in Daniel Glattauer's *Gut gegen Nordwind*

Angelika Vybiral, University of Vienna

PISTOLARY NOVELS BECAME increasingly popular in the eighteenth century as a consequence of two major developments: the emergence of the concept of romantic love[1] and the formation of modern reflexivity.[2] Epistolary novels like Richardson's *Pamela* (1740), Rousseau's *Julie ou la Nouvelle Heloïse* (Julie, Or The New Heloise, 1761), or Goethe's *Die Leiden des jungen Werthers* (The Sorrows of Young Werther, 1774) explore the potential of this genre to express modern subjectivity in the context of romantic love as a medium with its own codes of communication.[3] As a traditional genre of self-observation and observation of others, epistolary novels simulate face-to-face communication and are particularly suited to replicate modern forms of sociability and reflection. In the twenty-first century, even after the decline of letters as a preferred medium of communication, the genre is far from disappearing;[4] with the development of the e-mail novel, it has transformed and accommodated itself to contemporary conditions.[5]

This chapter explores the creation of intimacy and expression of love and desire in a twenty-first-century epistolary novel. Austrian writer Daniel Glattauer's *Gut gegen Nordwind* (translated as *Love Virtually*, 2006)[6] revives and updates the genre of the epistolary novel by using e-mails as the medium of communication. *Gut gegen Nordwind* was a major success in Austria, as well as internationally, and was translated into twenty-eight languages.[7] The novel is composed exclusively of e-mails exchanged between the protagonists Leo Leike and Emmi Rothner. An accidental conversation caused by a typographical error in an e-mail address soon turns into a contemporary romance, a virtual love story, as the English title anticipates. The novel tells the story of a fictionalized cyber-romance that mirrors literature's response to new information technologies. This chapter will study the narrative implications of the choice of a hybrid genre such as the e-mail novel. It will explore the possibilities and limits of the disembodied communication situation in the novel, and it will ask how the digital space shapes virtual desire and love.

Convergence of Media and Its Consequences

The novel itself classifies its genre as an "E-Mail-Roman" (*GgN*, 126), thus establishing a link to the tradition and genre of the epistolary novel. Readers are intended to establish a link between the genre of the epistolary novel and Glattauer's work, a process inherent in the reading process, as Dupont points out.[8] This link functions as an external structure and shapes the horizon of expectation of readers in matters concerning the novel's form, as well as its topic. *Gut gegen Nordwind* is in a hybrid genre, and some critics have even labeled it a modern epistolary novel.[9] Its "modernization" implies the convergence of two media: the letter and the e-mail. Ben-Ze'ev emphasizes that e-mails "are based upon an improved version of an old-fashioned way of communicating: writing. E-mail novels can thereby be considered a modern version of epistolary novels."[10] This modernization and mix of media allows for new narrative techniques. Every convergence of media creates a new genre and a new situation of communication.[11] The choice of using the computer as a means of communication in the novel is therefore inextricably linked to cultural changes. The birth of e-mail novels is a symptom of the current age, as their narrative structure mirrors a historic change in cultural practice.[12] Computer-based communication has consequences for everyday communication, including, but not limited to, narratives and literature, storytelling and stories about love. Dupont labels the inclusion of new media communication in literature a "Paradigmenwechsel."[13] However, e-mail novels should not be considered separately from their predecessors because they evolve from eighteenth century cultural practice. In her book *Letters, Postcards, Email: Technologies of Presence* (2010), Esther Milne relativizes views of new media as revolutionary and points out the evolutionary aspects of letters and e-mails.[14]

The mediality of a text shapes its communication strategies and narrative structure. Mediality is defined as a typical set of characteristics considered constitutive for a specific medium.[15] In fact, e-mails and letters share a multitude of characteristics. They both provide limited information about the other writer. According to Ben-Ze'ev, imagination plays a key role, and writing skills are crucial in regard to both text-based mediums for transmitting and deciphering information. In both media, the communication partners are physically and spatially separated, and their communication is discontinuous.[16] Polyphony and polyperspectivity are typical for both epistolary and e-mail novels. These genres present the voices of two (or more) characters who reflect upon and exchange their intimate feelings, frequently without an intervening narrator. A narrator may be present in the form of a (fictional) editor who frames the novel, as in Goethe's *Werther*. Where this "editor fiction" is absent, as in Glattauer's novel, the reader is presented with the exchange in apparently unmediated form. In *Gut gegen Nordwind*, the dialogue between the protagonists is interrupted only by e-mails from Bernhard, Emmi's husband, who contacts Leo after he becomes aware of his relationship with Emmi. This style of narration allows multiple narrative perspectives. It is not always immediately obvious who is writing because, in contrast to the traditional way of introducing letters in epistolary novels through giving the address of the recipient and a salutation, the corresponding electronic formatting of the e-mails, such as the recipient's email address, is not reproduced in the novel—to reduce complexity, as Kusche suggests.[17] Both genres often raise questions about identity and representation.[18] Unlike in traditional epistolary novels where the protagonists unveil their true selves, e-mail novels offer the possibility of creating multiple selves and fluid identities. Other features common to both genres are the creation of an enclosed virtual world detached from the surrounding world and an effort to bring those two together.[19] The epistolary novel serves as a "Bezugsfolie"[20] or reference context for the e-mail novel, which has, of course, its own features and characteristics due to the specific mediality of e-mails and the different cultural practices surrounding them.

The most striking difference between letters and e-mails is that computer-mediated communication offers a faster exchange of information. Emails "can take the form of both synchronous and asynchronous formats . . . In the new version of the epistolary novel, the temporal gap between writing, sending, receiving, and reading has been made almost instantaneous—the sender can receive a reply while still in the state of emotions in which they sent the original message."[21] Thus, e-mails offer the possibility to transcend both time and space.

Gut gegen Nordwind provides the emails with some of the formatting removed; as a compositional choice of the author, only the time intervals between consecutive e-mails are reproduced.[22] Consequently, the reader does not find precise information about who sent the e-mails or the dates on which they were sent. This creates a focus on the functionality of the format rather than on accuracy in every detail. At the beginning of the novel, the reader learns that the communication between Emmi and Leo starts in January. The novel's temporal setting stretches over one year and seven months, from January of one year to August of the following year. The reader knows this because the time interval between the e-mails is mentioned before every e-mail. This information is crucial in creating the narrative tension of a character impatiently waiting for a reply, contrary to the mediality of e-mails allowing almost simultaneous communication. As soon as the protagonists take advantage of the possibilities of the medium, its high speed also offers a higher degree of vividness. The language in the e-mails is lively and authentic in the sense of sounding like spoken language as the boundaries between orality and writing become blurred. The novel does not, however, exploit the full potential for reproducing orality, a characteristic of the medium,[23] as there are only a few examples of imitation of oral language. While Dupont emphasizes that the novel's language is linguistically and stylistically closer to a letter and literary, reflected language than to language typical of actual e-mails,[24] Wilke points out several elements of orality.[25] Indeed, there are several marks of orality in the e-mails, for example the forms of valediction (e.g., "Und tschüss!" *GgN*, 125) derive from oral practice, and grapho-stylistic expressions, for instance the excessive use of capital letters or exclamation marks (*GgN*, 13, 93, 161), express a virtual raising of the voice or stress the importance of the words (*GgN*, 20, 23, 24, 30, 97, 170), mimicking speech, volume, and prosody. This is characteristic for secondary orality. Additionally, at one point Leo uses a smiley-face emoticon (*GgN*, 12), moving to a more informal conversation.

What makes this novel interesting are the comprehensive metareflections about the medium in both Emmi's and Leo's writing. The novel clearly distinguishes between a textual virtual world and a textual actual world, and the protagonists are shown as balanced and torn between the two, each world affecting the other.[26] Thus the novel demonstrates how the internet has a profound impact on everyday life, social life, identity, and the body.

The continuities between old and new media show that "[n]ew communication technologies do not simply replace extant forms; instead, the more recent genre commonly borrows iconography, codes of composition, and modes of social practice from its predecessor. Rather than a process in which a new technology improves on and dispenses with earlier technologies, the relation between old and new technology is 'skeuomorphic.'"[27] This means that e-mails imitate and evoke an older form that is thought to be more authentic. Not only are the form of letters and e-mails akin, but characters in and readers of epistolary and email novels, respectively, have "remarkably similar experiences/fantasies of presence, intimacy and disembodiment."[28] The epistolary novel was considered an appropriate genre for love stories and related fantasies—and so is the e-mail novel, which, on the other hand, questions these assumptions of fantasies of presence, intimacy, and disembodiment, as this chapter will explore. The anonymity that is possible in virtual communication offers the opportunity to construct an image of oneself as a writer and imagine the other, the receiver, as a reader. Writing and reading are performative acts in both genres. The disembodiment of communication liberates the writers "from the socially constructed inequities of gender, race and class" and generates the ideal "communication or meeting of minds,"[29] an apparently immediate communication, independent of bodies and social settings, unlike face-to-face communication.[30] The spatial separation fires the desire of presence and longing for intimacy.

Constructing the Self and Imagining the Other

If e-mails "do not fully disclose the identities of the communication part-ners,"[31] then who are Leo and Emmi falling in love with? The protago-nists only become aware of each other's character as far as their dialogic e-mails allow. The only way of getting to know each other and presenting oneself is writing. Kusche emphasizes the dominating role of language in e-mails: "Die Sprache der E-Mails nimmt somit eine zentrale Stellung ein, denn sie wird zum einzigen Anhaltspunkt für die gegenseitige Konstruktion der Identitäten im sonst entkontextualisierten Cyberspace der E-Mail."[32] Identity is constructed through electronic communica-tion. Ascriptions and self-ascriptions are unstable because they rely exclu-sively on language in the virtual world, and might not have any point of reference in the actual world. In the case of Leo and Emmi and their adulterous affair, the distinction between virtual and actual world is made sharper as both characters create a virtual space through their e-mail com-munication that they experience as distinct and disconnected from their selves in their actual worlds. The novel thus stages a clash between textual virtual world and textual actual world.[33]

In the novel's textual virtual world, language is the only point of reference and thus is essential for online communication; refined psy-chological skills are required of an individual who wants to establish a connection through its use.[34] Both Emmi and Leo deal with the internet professionally, he as a psychologist doing research on e-mail as a way of transmitting emotions, and she as a homepage designer. There are numerous metareflections about their communication. Both are fully aware of the fact that everything they know—or think they know—about each other is solely based on their writing. Leo and Emmi both analyze each other's e-mails and attempt to gauge the personality behind them. From the very beginning of their conversations, Emmi is impressed by Leo's eloquence (*GgN*, 7). Leo likewise admires Emmi's linguistic elegance, which he analyzes syllable for syllable, drawing con-clusions about her personality based on her writing (*GgN*, 10–11). These are intimate and intense engagements with words that make the writers feel cherished and flattered for their skills.

In virtual encounters, there are no visible pre-existing identities that shape one's perception by the other. Therefore, every piece of informa-tion can be seen as performative self-construction. Identity is a choice. It is what you tell about yourself and what words you use to do so. Both of Glattauer's characters use a literary, artificial, playful language in con-structing their selves. Leo compares his writing to his personality: "Ich küsse so ähnlich wie ich schreibe" (*GgN*, 216). His is a narcissistic way of self-fashioning. Virtuality is the stage for the solitary performance; as Milne has written "the letter writer performs a version of self and the recipient reads that performance."[35] It requires a psychologically skilled reader to decipher the personality behind the letters. "Ich bin für Sie ein Fantasiebild, real daran sind nur ein paar Buchstaben, die von Ihnen sprachpsychologisch in einen klangvollen Zusammenhang gebracht werden können," observes Emmi (*GgN*, 43). Leo, as a professionally trained reader, comments: "Ich muss gar nicht wissen, wie Sie aussehen, wenn Sie mir solche Antworten geben, Emmi. Ich habe Sie ohnehin vor mir" (*GgN*, 18). He knows how to read her writing and imagines his own Emmi based on this information. However, when they arrange their first meeting at the Café Huber, Leo does not recognize Emmi. He "sees" her only through the eyes of his sister, who accompanies him there and describes the women present so Leo can maintain his language-based imaginations of Emmi. At their arranged first meeting Emmi compares the faces she sees at the café with Leo's way of writing but finds that none matches: "[an Leos] Art, mir schriftlich zu begegnen, kommt keines dieser faden Sonntagsnachmittagsgesichter im Café Huber auch nur im Entferntesten heran" (*GgN*, 49). Imagination exceeds reality. Corporeal co-presence, being together physically, threatens the "imaginary, incorporeal body."[36] After failing to recognize each other on their first date at the café, Leo proposes another date, as he is still convinced that they are going to recognize each other immediately based on their writing. Assuming that the style of writing matches the looks, Leo says: "Ich glaube, wir wissen es sofort, wenn wir uns sehen" (*GgN*, 91). Leo's idealized self-fashioning also appears to be successful when Emmi cannot reconcile her image of Leo from his e-mails with any of the faces she sees in the café. Both characters try to decipher the other's personality by reading each other's e-mails, while carefully choosing what they reveal to the other: "Wir versuchen zwischen den Zeilen zu lesen, zwischen den Wörtern, bald wohl schon zwischen den Buchstaben. Wir bemühen uns krampfhaft, den anderen richtig einzuschätzen. Und gleichzeitig sind wir akribisch darauf bedacht, nur ja nichts Wesentliches von uns selbst zu verraten" (*GgN*, 19). The described performative identity construction is doubled: "Subjects must negotiate not only the portrayal of self but also the audience response to this portrayal and, subsequently, their own response to the audience's reaction."[37] How they read the other's self and write their own is a crucial part of the attraction between Leo and Emmi. It is doubly narcissistic, both reading and imagining the other to their own pleasure on the one hand, and writing and imagining themselves as they want to be perceived, on the other. The communication partners set up a virtual stage where they, as writers, want to impress their reader who is deciphering the text as s/he in turn constructs her/his image of the other, adapting it to fantasies. Puzzling together the fragments to construct identities is an active process on both sides: "Je näher sich die Figuren kommen, desto vielfältiger und dichter werden die Identitäten, die sie dialogisch konstruieren."[38] E-mail novels open the stage to flexible, dynamic, fluid identities.

Disembodied Presence:
Establishing Intimacy through Words

In spite of the characteristics of the communication situation (spatial separation and exclusion of the body), e-mails have the performative power to construct the illusion of a co-presence through writing, creating "a spiritual, almost telepathic, sense of the other's presence" with words.[39] Particularly in love stories, the imagined presence is crucial to establishing intimacy, even when there is no body to serve as the basis for physical sexual attraction.

All literary works addressing love face the topos of the ineffability of love.[40] Epistolary and e-mail novels exacerbate this problem even more, as protagonists of such works rely exclusively on their own, perhaps limited, language to express love and desire. Glattauer's novel complicates this setting further by bringing together two characters who have never met before and never meet in the course of the novel.[41] The only way for them to develop and reveal their feelings, including those they have for each other, is through written language. Thus, they must narrativize their feelings if they are to be perceived by the other. Attraction, falling in love, and love itself become literary acts of visual-textual communication. The protagonists establish a literary intimacy, create literary emotions and literary erotic fantasies. The novel presents a meta-level reflection about the capacity of e-mail as a medium for the expression of love. Both protagonists are fully aware that their feelings are language-based and exclude any corporeality. Only what can be expressed in language is transmitted. This "verbal overshadowing," an "interference of verbal processes with visual ones,"[42] reflects their character and modes of behavior. Consequently, desire and writing become one: "Schreiben ist wie küssen, nur ohne Lippen. Schreiben ist küssen mit dem Kopf. . . . Emmi schreiben ist Emmi küssen" (*GgN*, 88–89), as Leo describes his erotic desires for Emmi, after falling in love with her words. Likewise, it is Leo's language that attracts Emmi. She expresses her longing for him and for reading his desired words and his words of desire (*GgN*, 139). Each word is weighed meticulously, and it is one word that keeps Emmi from meeting Leo at the end of the novel—when her husband calls her "Emmi" instead of the usual "Emma," exposing that he has read the hard copies of her conversation with Leo that she kept in a folder (*GgN*, 222–23). The exposure of the affair comes through an old-fashioned analog discovery, adding a moment of melodrama, similarly to traditional epistolary novels.

Language fuels imagination and replaces the absent body of the other; the subject's body is present.[43] Both are aware of their physical needs and feelings and in spite of the characters' virtual disembodiment, the realm of the senses find its way into the novel in various forms. The characters first discuss the absence of the sense of sight. Their conversation lacks visual stimulants because they never meet and do not describe their looks to each other. Leo's refusal to meet in person leaves Emmi, who longs for approval based on her looks, stunned (*GgN*, 17). Seeking Leo's praise of her beauty, she cannot believe that he does not want to see her (*GgN*, 32). Leo is critical of the emphasis that Emmi places on physical appearance (*GgN*, 44). He emphasizes at various points that he has absolutely no interest in knowing what Emmi looks like, for example when talking about their "Erkennungstreffen": "Interessant ist, ob und woran einer den anderen zu erkennen glaubt, nicht, wie wir beide tatsächlich aussehen, meine ich. Ich sage noch einmal: Ich will nicht wissen, wie Sie aussehen. Ich will Sie nur erkennen. Und das werde ich" (*GgN*, 35). Leo emphasizes reading and writing skills, while Emmi fantasizes about being perceived as an embodied person.

While sight is more important to Emmi, Leo mainly fantasizes about touch. During their first midnight conversation, Leo is drunk and asks: "Darf ich Sie umarmen, Emmi?—Darf ich Sie küssen?" (GgN, 87) He longs for her touch and her kisses without seeing her: "Wir müssen uns nicht sehen. Ich will Sie nur spüren" (*GgN*, 87). Though Leo only fantasizes about touching Emmi and does not even want to see her and find out what she looks like, sound on the contrary finds its way into their communication at three instances. Emmi's friend Mia hears Leo's voice on the phone and later describes it, after having met him in person, as an "angenehme Stimme" (*GgN*, 116). It is only towards the end of the novel that corporeality, or an indication of corporeality, enters the relationship of Emmi and Leo in the form of the sound of their voices, adding an aural level to their communication. Curious to hear his voice, Emmi asks Leo to exchange messages on their answering machines. This medium, unlike a phone call, allows a less intrusive, non-simultaneous, plannable, and recordable communication—it shares these major characteristics with e-mails. Both Emmi and Leo analyze each syllable of the voice messages and find doing so highly erotic (*GgN*, 170–77), something they also do with each other's emails. After hearing her voice, Leo expresses his wish to smell, kiss, and feel Emmi, and to spend a night with her: "Nur eine Nacht mit Emmi verbringen. Ich mache die Augen zu. Ich muss nicht wissen, wie sie aussieht. Ich muss sie nur riechen und küssen und spüren, ganz nah" (*GgN*, 178). Leo values words and imagined touch more than an actual being he could perceive with his eyes and touch with his hands. For Emmi, it is unsatisfying not to meet Leo in person, whereas Leo is content with his imagining of her. The reader might wonder whether Leo emphasizes his indifference to Emmi's looks on purpose to tease her or to maintain the idealized communication situation of a meeting of minds.

With the exception of the sound of their voices heard at one point of the novel, their sensory experiences of one another are exclusively inside the protagonists' heads, constructed by configurations of words to which they attribute a high importance—storing and remembering them by heart. The gender differences between Leo and Emmi regarding the hierarchization of the senses reverse traditional stereotypes as we can find them for example in *The Picture of Dorian Gray*: "We women, as someone says, love with our ears, just as you men love with your eyes, if you ever love at all."[44] Only towards the second half of the novel do looks and thus the body start to have less and less importance for Emmi and she is forced to discover the psychological techniques of writing and reading and their erotic possibilities. In a disembodied communication setting, imagined corporeal experiences are devices to create the feeling of proximity and presence.[45]

Milne has used the concept of "presence" in the context of written communication as "the degree to which geographically dispersed agents experience a sense of physical and/or psychological proximity through the use of particular communication technologies."[46] This virtually constructed "presence" in Emmi and Leo's textual actual world is crucial for enabling their intimacy, which is structured by the tension between emotional closeness and distance. When physical presence is not experienced, intimacy can only be established via a literary act. On a pragmatic level, we can observe a shift from formal to informal language mirroring different degrees of distance and closeness.[47] Merely strangers at the beginning, Leo and Emmi engage in a formal e-mail conversation using the polite and distant "Sie" and formal salutation formulas. However, Leo very soon turns his formal "MfG" (*GgN*, 7, 8) into the more friendly "Lg" (Liebe Grüsse), "Guten Abend" and "Gute Nacht" (*GgN*, 9, 10, 41) after Emmi's more personal message makes him chuckle. When Emmi experiences jealousy or anger, she switches to a more distant language, shown in the use of "Hochachtungsvoll" (*GgN*, 77, 146) and the sarcastic address "Meister Leo" (*GgN*, 80). Leo deliberately omits his last name, a tactic imitated by Emmi (*GgN*, 15). Their closeness is expressed by the frequent use of their first names when addressing each other; see for example Emmi's long e-mail to Leo where she uses his name multiple times in every paragraph (*GgN*, 98–100). As their bond grows closer, Emmi begins to end e-mails with "Bussis" (*GgN*, 35) as a first sign of affection. In spite of their intense conversations and expressions of desire, the personal "du" is only introduced moments before the last planned meeting, when Leo invites Emmi to his place for a romantic night that includes kissing. Emmi demands to switch to "du," as she states: "Und ich küsse niemand Fremden im Finstern, mit dem ich nicht per Du bin" (*GgN*, 219).

On a structural level, the ebb and flow of their intimacy is depicted in the novel by the frequency of e-mails. The novel uses the various capacities of email from bulk emails (or mass emails) to the possibility of holding a fast-paced, chat-like conversation. The frequency of their responses mirrors their excitement about each other. Compared to letters in epistolary novels, e-mails are particularly suitable for romances because immediate responses are more exciting, imitating a synchronous face-to-face communication. As Ben-Ze'ev notes: "The great temporal gap between one letter and another does not suit the impetuous nature of romantic affairs."[48] The bigger the desire, the higher the pace. From very early on, the protagonists feel uneasy when they have to wait longer than a day for a response (*GgN*, 16). The spatial distance is overcome by temporal closeness, which is highest when they engage in chat-like, fast paced e-mail exchanges during their romantic midnight-hour dates with wine in front of their computers, creating a "virtuelle Zweisamkeit" (*GgN*, 30). Seemingly unmediated communication creates a feeling of closeness and presence.[49] During the "romantische Mitternachtseinlage, vor dem jeweiligen Computer" (*GgN*, 37), highly involved in their virtual world, Leo and Emmi experience a feeling of presence, a feeling of "being there,"[50] that is, where the other one is. It is an incorporeal sphere of communicative closeness.

Another strategy to create a feeling of presence is the use of detailed descriptions of the surrounding world, exemplified by Emmi's description of her piano, which makes it "appear" in Leo's mind's eye (*GgN*, 126–27). It generates Roland Barthes's "effet de réel,"[51] the feeling of being part of the real world. Imaginary co-presence through words grows more and more important to both Leo and Emmi in the second half of the novel. Their togetherness is exclusively imaginary. Leo's desire for Emmi's physical closeness—"Ich hatte sofort den dringenden Wunsch, Sie noch näher an mich heranzulassen, Sie ganz nahe bei mir zu haben" (*GgN*, 77)—is never fulfilled. Their attempts to create a sensual, physical closeness fail every time: "Die Hauptfiguren tun alles, was in ihrer Macht steht, um sich einander so stark wie möglich anzunähern, ohne aus der Virtualität herauszutreten."[52] Their two worlds remain separated.

Torn between Two Worlds

Glattauer's narrative explores a love born of an accidental encounter as sudden and irrational, as a romantic "coup de foudre" that interrupts the daily routine and breaks into and re-creates the protagonists' worlds. The communicative situation creates a virtual sphere they at first try to keep separated from their real world. This virtual space can be defined as a heterotopia as defined by Foucault in his lecture "Of Other Spaces." A heterotopia is a space which does not, or does not completely, function according to the norms of society, or that functions according to its own laws. A heterotopia reflects social conditions by representing, negating, or reversing them.[53] Inside the boundaries of a heterotopia different rules apply. Virtuality is a heterotopia for the protagonists in the novel. In their virtual space, both Emmi and Leo are freed from any restraints and responsibilities of their real lives. For Emmi, virtuality is an escape from reality and everyday life, and for Leo it is a playground where he can explore and create identities. In each world, they both have different realities, different identities, and differently represented selves. The textual virtual world is tightly interwoven with the textual actual world. As they try to keep the two spheres separate, the protagonists are soon torn between them. At the beginning of the novel, the topics in Leo and Emmi's exchanges encompass mostly their feelings and thoughts about themselves and the other, and, only up to a certain degree, their pasts and only rarely their futures. Creating a "luftleeren Raum" (*GgN*, 19), they communicate in a virtual world where only the two of them are present, seemingly strictly separated from the surrounding world. At a certain point, both agree that their relationship can only be maintained inside their textual virtual world and try to keep everyone else outside of their virtual bubble (*GgN*, 39). Both protagonists clearly express interest in maintaining the conversation, even though meeting in person is not planned. This is a sign that they want to maintain their imagined personae unchanged. As Milne observes, "such readers often believe that the body imagined in epistolary intercourse is more real, in the sense of being more expressive of the writer's emotions and soul, than the actual body encountered in face-to-face communication."[54] The exclusion of the physical shows the idealized communication situation of the seemingly unmediated meeting of two minds. However, it is not disconnected from the actual world surrounding them.

The cyberspace Leo and Emmi generate is more a psychological reality than a social reality. The real world is the place of the physical, of erotics, and of "Zusammensein" (*GgN*, 213) while the virtual world is the "Kosmos der Wunschträume" (*GgN*, 183). The two worlds are incompatible, especially for Emma. Her virtual and actual identities exclude each other, especially since she has one man in each world: Leo as her virtual lover and Bernhard as her actual husband. Leo lets his private life enter the bubble and talks about his relationship to his ex-girlfriend (*GgN*, 21–22). Emmi, on the other hand, tries to compartmentalize the worlds and leave aside her family life, though Leo asks about her job, her children, and her husband (*GgN*, 33). Eventually, little by little, the two protagonists include the surrounding world in their conversation. The death of Leo's mother marks a starting point for that evolution (*GgN*, 72–74). The event causes Emmi to reveal some information about her children and her daily routines to him (*GgN*, 86–88).

The protagonists struggle to draw a sharp line between the actual and the virtual worlds, and the boundaries start to blur: "the virtual does indeed impact the real."[55] Leo quits his research project on e-mail as a way of transmitting emotions because he becomes personally too involved in it because of his relationship to Emmi. This is an instance of the virtual influencing the real. As for Emmi, her husband notices changes in her behavior. Leo is the one who wants to establish clear boundaries, but when he is drunk, he desires Emmi's body. Leo's libidinous desires focus on the feeling of body contact and overcoming the physical distance between himself and Emmi: "Ich habe im Traum weder Gesicht noch Busen noch sonst etwas Ihnen zugehöriges Körperliches gesehen. Ich habe alles nur gefühlt" (*GgN*, 158). To him, touching and physical closeness are paramount. Critiquing their conversation as not being an "Ausschnitt aus dem wirklich Leben" (*GgN*, 43), Leo's wish to get to know more about Emmi's life (*GgN*, 103) is contradicted by his belief that "[w]ir dürfen nicht beginnen, in die Privatsphäre des anderen einzudringen. Das kann zu nichts führen" (*GgN*, 77). Emmi is very clear when she describes Leo's place in her life as a "'Familienauszeit,'" as a "kleines Inselchen außerhalb meiner Alltagserlebniswelt" (*GgN*, 86). Communicating with Leo is a disconnection from the real world for Emmi, while Leo wishes to be allowed to enter her "Alltagserlebniswelt." Emmi responds in her next e-mail by attempting to describe her room (*GgN*, 104), but she fails. She also labels her inner world as undescribable and compares it to a stronghold that "[k]ann nicht erobert werden, duldet keine Eindringlinge, hält geschlossen dagegen" (*GgN*, 105). This stronghold offers no room for Leo and Emmi together. However, she needs her e-mail partner in order to be able to move outside of it: "Leo, ich brauche Sie! Ich muss mich auch außerhalb meiner Welt bewegen und spüren können. Leo, Sie sind meine Außenwelt!" (*GgN*, 105) Emmi distinguishes firmly between her inner world (her family life) and her outer world (her e-mails with Leo). The virtual world is a heterotopia the borders of which the two do not dare to cross, as it would endanger their love story (*GgN*, 20). But they fail at several instances in trying to protect their virtual universe because love, desire, and the longing to overcome their physical separation keeps blurring the line dividing the two spheres.

A harmless way for them to try to unify their worlds is talking about the weather, as they both live in the same city and experience the same weather conditions at the same time. Like meeting in person, talking about the actual weather in the real world is a "Dimensionssprung" (*GgN*, 217). The topic of weather ties the protagonists closely together, as the title of the novel suggests. After a dispute, Leo restarts the conversation by talking about the weather (*GgN*, 114–16). Another time, after a pause of three days without writing, both describe the weather, the heat, and a thunderstorm in front of the window (*GgN*, 120, 123). The passages recall one from Goethe's *Die Leiden des jungen Werthers,* in the letter dating from 16 June: "Wir traten ans Fenster. Es donnerte abseitwärts, und der herrliche Regen säuselte auf das Land, und der erquickendste Wohlgeruch stieg in aller Fülle einer warmen Luft zu uns auf."[56] The heavy rain leads to the most emotional moment in Goethe's epistolary novel, that of Werther kissing Lotte's hand and then breaking out in tears. Emmi does not share the enthusiasm for nature poetry, stating that "für Dialoge über das Wetter bin ich mir zu schade" (*GgN,* 123). However, she talks later about the north wind that is depriving her of sleep (*GgN,* 140). Followed by an intense exchange of e-mails, Leo and her meet virtually in her bed (*GgN,* 140–43) and his words soothe her:

> AW:
> Da kann der Nordwind jetzt blasen wie er will.
> *45 Sekunden später*
> RE:
> Leo, ich hab Sie sehr, sehr gern. Sie sind fantastisch gut gegen Nordwind. (*GgN,* 142)

Emmi feels better now and for the first time she expresses her affection for Leo. The weather is a re-enabler of communication when words dry up and a vehicle for expressing feelings, as "emotions are like storms."[57] The weather, experienced by both at the same time, unifies their worlds. The wind in the title is also found in the metaphor Leo uses to describe what he finds lacking in their relationship: "Endlich ein echter, physischer, befreiender, antivirtueller Luftzug!!!" (*GgN,* 161) The wind and the breeze are liberating and real, connecting them and ending their disunity. They both experience the sensation of the wind at the same time, the weather that brings them closer together. They can let in the outside world without the risk of destroying their virtual romance.

Material conditions threaten the characters' fantasies. The first materialization of the actual world is the introduction of Mia, Emmi's friend whom Leo dates as prospective girlfriend on Emmi's request. Mia becomes the "Verbindungsperson" (*GgN,* 148) between the two. Trying to connect Leo with Mia is Emmi's attempt to get access to physical aspects that are left aside in their relationship. Meeting Mia shows Leo what is missing from his relationship to Emmi: "Ich kann sie gleichzeitig sehen, hören, angreifen, riechen. Mia ist Materie. Emmi ist Fantasie. Beides mit all seinen Vor- und Nachteilen" (*GgN,* 126). Mia brings in the physical aspects that are excluded in cyberspace. Crossing the boundaries of the two worlds causes a dysfunction in the virtual relationship.[58]

Another instance of transgressed boundaries is the subject of Emmi's husband. Knowing that her two identities and worlds are incompatible, she vehemently refuses to talk about her husband Bernhard with Leo, repeatedly claiming she is happily married. Bernhard marks the boundary between her inner and outer worlds. Emmi's perfectly organized and harmonious life is perturbed by the appearance of Leo and the role he takes up in her life. However, despite Emmi's attempts to keep Leo outside of her inner world, she places him physically within it by printing out their e-mails and storing them in her room, compromising the immaterial form of the e-mails and their playful and intimate nature. She keeps the hard copies of the e-mail conversation "as if . . . they were adequate substitutes for Leo's body."[59] Her husband discovers Leo's intrusion after becoming suspicious. Like the breeze mentioned by Leo, the feelings have left the screen and entered the inner world of her family and marriage. It does not come as a surprise that the metaphor of the north wind is the subject of the last e-mail by Emmi: "Mein Gefühl hat den Bildschirm verlassen. Ich glaube, ich liebe dich. Und Bernhard hat es gespürt. Mir ist kalt. Der Nordwind bläst mir entgegen" (*GgN*, 223). The materialization of the textual virtual world makes it collapse. Bernhard breaks into their virtual togetherness by addressing an e-mail to Leo after having read their entire e-mail correspondence in hard copies. Bernhard asks Leo to meet Emmi in person in the hope that the real-life encounter will destroy all Leo's and Emmi's fantasies and desires (*GgN*, 181):

> Herr Leike, treffen Sie sich mit meiner Frau! Bitte tun Sie es endlich, damit der Spuk sein Ende hat! . . . Einem Geist kann man nichts vorwerfen. Sie sind nicht greifbar, Herr Leike, nicht antastbar, Sie sind nicht real, Sie sind ein einziges Fantasiegebilde meiner Frau, Illusion vom unendlichen Glück der Gefühle, weltferner Taumel, Liebesutopie aus Buchstaben gebaut. Dagegen bin ich machtlos, ich kann nur warten, bis das Schicksal gnädig ist und aus Ihnen endlich einen Menschen aus Fleisch und Blut macht, einen Mann mit Konturen, mit Stärken und Schwächen, mit Angriffsflächen. (*GgN*, 181)

A flesh-and-blood Leo can never correspond to the ideal like a virtual Leo can. The intrusion of Bernhard marks the beginning of the end of Emmi and Leo's relationship. Its collapse is ushered in by the materialization of the virtual romance as hard copies of their e-mails. While *Gut gegen Nordwind* ends with the separation of Emmi and Leo, the two worlds, the textual actual and the textual virtual, are finally—and predictably—united in the sequel *Alle sieben Wellen* (2009) when Leo and Emmi do meet in person.[60]

Superiority of Cyber Romance?

When two strangers meet in decontextualized virtuality, cyber writing offers them freedom on three levels. First, the disembodiment frees them from all preconceptions and directs the focus onto communication itself.

Illouz claims that the internet romance is superior to real-life romance because it erases the body and allows free expression of the self. Eva Illouz considers the internet positively as a technology of disembodiment.[61] Having a body is viewed as an obstacle in cyber writing, as the flesh is the dead flesh that contains the active spirit, which forms the authentic self.[62] Ben-Ze'ev writes that expressing the authentic self is easier online than in actual personal encounters: "A great emotional intimacy is achieved since the body . . . does not interfere; the possibility of leaving their bodies at home makes it easier for correspondents to reveal their thoughts and minds."[63] In their e-mails, Leo and Emmi talk openly about their feelings, sorrows, and desires. Illouz describes this as the "disinhibition effect" in non-face-to-face-communication.[64]

This is facilitated by the fact that, secondly, in cyberspace one is liberated from all social and moral frameworks. One can experiment with one's identity and how one wants to be perceived by the other. The identities Leo and Emmi present to each other are different from those they assume in the real world. The identities Leo and Emmi present to each other leave out most superficial information. The anonymity of cyberspace encourages experimentation with aspects of one's self and enables Leo and Emmi to construct a virtual self that is experienced as "more real": "Ich kann in meinen E-Mails an Sie so sehr die echte Emmi sein wie sonst nie. Im 'wirklichen Leben' muss man . . . ständig Kompromisse mit seiner eigenen Emotionalität eingehen, . . . schlüpft in die hundert kleinen Alltagsrollen, balanciert, tariert aus, wiegt ab, um das Gesamtgefüge nicht zu gefährden, weil man selbst ein Teil davon ist" (*GgN*, 98). The virtual self and the virtual other may be only loosely connected to the real self and the real other. We thus find in the novel a literary model of the paradigmatic contemporary self which is capable of conceiving and fashioning itself using language-based psychological technologies.[65] This self is different from the self in the textual actual world and claims to be more authentic. Fully aware of the nature of their relationship, Emmi and Leo raise the question of whether they really do know each other. The term "innige Unbekanntschaft" (*GgN*, 70) shows the tension between assumed authenticity and unstable identities.

Thirdly, in cyberspace one can fill the information gaps with fantasies and play with reality. Without ever meeting in person or describing their looks, both create a fantasy image about the "E-Mail-Partner(in)" (*GgN*, 138). Emmi wants to be a "Fantasiegöttin" (*GgN*, 38) a "Fantasiegestalt" (*GgN*, 116) because Leo's "Fantasievorstellung von mir kommt Ihrem Frauenideal sicher näher als irgendeine dahergelaufene Bekanntschaft aus einer vermutlich in rotem Plüsch gehaltenen Bar" (*GgN*, 38). Only in virtuality can Emmi meet the untouchable ideal (*GgN*, 31) that Leo has constructed of her: "Da sind Sie perfekt, die Schönste der Welt, da kommt keine an Sie heran" (*GgN*, 126). To preserve these fantasies,

Leo and Emmi avoid meeting. Leo is afraid that this artificial, virtual Emmi he created would collapse as soon as he touched her (*GgN*, 193). Quoting his sister, Leo knows that "[E]in Treffen wäre das Ende eurer Beziehung" (*GgN*, 108). Based on their imagination, both have high expectations about the other. Their love story starts from the end, lacking the "natürliche Anfang der Begegnung" (*GgN*, 103): "Wir starten von der Ziellinie weg, und es gibt nur eine Richtung: zurück. Wir steuern auf die große Ernüchterung zu. Wir können das nicht leben, was wir schreiben. . . . Emmi" (*GgN*, 161).

The detachment of Leo and Emmi's relationship from the actual world, and the characters' disembodied ideas of each other are both liberating and unsettling. The playfulness of identity construction and the fantastic idealization of the other are key elements of romantic love. In the same way, these elements render the relation in Emmi and Leo's cyber-romance highly unstable, and love becomes unattainable, as seeing the actual person would endanger it and take away the magic and excitement. This fragile construct is ultimately untenable for Leo, and when he ends the conversation before moving to Boston, he says that he wants to get to know a woman in a traditional way: "Zuerst sehe ich sie, dann höre ich ihre Stimme, dann rieche ich sie, dann küsse ich sie vielleicht. Und irgendwann später werde ich ihr wohl auch einmal eine E-Mail schreiben" (*GgN*, 192). Cyberromance offers endless perceived possibilities and transcendence. Its beauty and its downfall lie in virtuality, which, as Youngman argues, can be perceived as "a rupture in the 'social fabric,' or an intensification and expansion of the social realm."[66] Do exploratory identities result in better selves and better love?

Conclusion

How is an online romance different from an actual face-to-face romance? The elements of romantic love can be examined to explore whether and to what degree they characterize the love and desire experienced by Emmi and Leo in *Gut gegen Nordwind*. Romantic love is characterized by spontaneity, but in the novel, Leo and Emmi's interaction is not spontaneous but rather starts formally and then proceeds in a well-considered manner in which each word is carefully weighed. Additionally, Emmi's and Leo's relationship lacks the immediate physical attraction that is at the core of romantic love. The disembodied textual interaction lacks sexual/physical romantic attraction.[67] Consequently, attraction shifts to the imagined sensual experiences in the writing. Imagination is a key element in romantic love that elevates the beloved to a higher level and, in the case of Leo and Emmi, serves as a way of overcoming spatial distance. Lacking information, the protagonists imagine what the other could be like and idealize him/her, a common feature of blossoming romantic love of any kind. The separation of reality and fantasy is also typical. Lovers construct an ideal image that can be far from reality. In Glattauer's novel, since it is about a cyberromance, Leo and Emmi experience even more freedom, because they can conceive multiple identities that are different in the virtual and in the real world. This playfulness results in mystery and entails risks of disappointment and deceit as the virtual image of the other is detached from the actual world. Particularly Leo creates an enchanted vision of Emmi and imagines her as a fantasy goddess. The virtual world is the place for their love and this space with its fragile boundaries needs protection if the boundaries are to be maintained.

What makes this novel noteworthy are its meta-reflections about the fictional nature of literary love and its phantasmagorical aspects. Two fictional protagonists discuss cyber writing and cyber-romance as a flight from reality in a novel which itself offers an escape from reality for the reader. Comparing online communication to fictional literature, Ben-Ze'ev notes: "Cyberspace is similar to fictional space in the sense that in both cases the flight into virtual reality is not so much a denial of reality as a form of exploring and playing with it."[68] The novel explores the organization of the two different worlds in internet communication, as well as its contradictions. Cyber-romance puts the multi-faceted fragmented digital space into words. Digitalization and its impact on our social life entails changes in literature, its aesthetics and form and content. The novel creates a fictional concept of love and desire in the twenty-first century that assesses the impact of digitalization in our societies.

Today, eleven years after publication of Glattauer's novel, one can ask whether and how recent developments on the internet would affect the communication situation in the novel. In the last years, private internet communication has shifted from emailing to a variety of social media platforms with round-the-clock availability that include video options, that facilitate sending pictures and that simplify language further with the availability of emojis. Additionally, one is not dependent on one's computer anymore, as those applications are now available on our mobile devices, invading our actual world even more so than in the novel.

Notes

1 Werner Faulstich, *Die bürgerliche Mediengesellschaft (1700–1830)* (Göttingen: Vandenhoeck & Ruprecht, 2002), 112.

2 Anthony Giddens, *The Consequences of Modernity* (Stanford, CA: Stanford University Press, 1990), 36–45.

3 Niklas Luhmann, *Love as Passion: The Codification of Intimacy*, trans. Jeremy Gaines and Doris L. Jones (Cambridge: Polity Press, 1986 [first published 1982]), 20–21.

[4] See "List of Contemporary Epistolary Novels," *Wikipedia, The Free Enclyclopedia*, accessed July 2, 2017, https://en.wikipedia.org/wiki/List_of_contemporary_epistolary_novels.

[5] Apart from Glattauer's *Gut gegen Nordwind* and its sequel, *Alle sieben Wellen* (Vienna: Deuticke, 2009) see, e.g., Anja Nititzki's *Vermailt* (Halle: Mitteldeutscher Verlag, 2014) and *E-D@te* (Halle: Mitteldeutscher Verlag, 2015).

[6] Daniel Glattauer, *Gut gegen Nordwind* (Munich: Goldmann, 2008, first published Vienna: Deuticke, 2006), henceforth cited in the text as (*GgN*).

[7] "Übersetzungen von *Gut gegen Nordwind*," Daniel Glattauer.de, accessed December 17, 2016, http://www.daniel-glattauer.de/die-bucher/gut-gegen-nordwind/uebersetzungen/.

[8] Bruno Dupont, "Erzählen im Zeitalter des Internets," *Germanica* 55 (2014): 189–207, here 192.

[9] Sabrina Kusche, *Der E-Mail-Roman: Zur Medialisierung des Erzählens in der zeitgenössischen deutsch- und englischsprachigen Literatur* (Stockholm: Stockholm University Press, 2012), 32.

[10] Aaron Ben-Ze'ev, *Love Online: Emotions on the Internet* (Cambridge: Cambridge University Press, 2004), 26–27.

[11] Dupont, "Erzählen im Zeitalter des Internets," 153.

[12] Kusche, *Der E-Mail-Roman*, 31.

[13] Dupont, "Erzählen im Zeitalter des Internets," 190.

[14] Esther Milne, *Letters, Postcards, Email: Technologies of Presence* (New York: Routledge, 2010), 17–19.

[15] Knut Hickethier, *Einführung in die Medienwissenschaft* (Stuttgart: Metzler, 2003), 26.

[16] Ben Ze'ev, *Love Online*, 7.

[17] Kusche, *Der E-Mail-Roman*, 146.

[18] Kusche, *Der E-Mail-Roman*, 38.

[19] Kusche, *Der E-Mail-Roman*, 41–42.

[20] Kusche, *Der E-Mail-Roman*, 35–36.

[21] Ben Ze'ev, *Love Online*, 26–27.

[22] Dupont, "Erzählen im Zeitalter des Internets," 193.

[23] Kusche, *Der E-Mail-Roman*, 146.

[24] Dupont, "Erzählen im Zeitalter des Internets," 193–94.

[25] Beatrice Wilke, "Computerbasierte Kommunikationsformen in literarischen Texten (Sandra Hoffmann und Daniel Glattauer)," *Testi e linguaggi* 1 (2007): 151–68, here 162–63.

[26] Kusche, *Der E-Mail-Roman*, 79.

[27] Milne, *Letters, Postcards, Email*, 19.

[28] Milne, *Letters, Postcards, Email*, 190.

[29] Milne, *Letters, Postcards, Email*, 17.

30 Milne, *Letters, Postcards, Email*, 2.

31 Ben Ze'ev, *Love Online*, 26–27.

32 Kusche, *Der E-Mail-Roman*, 151.

33 See Kusche, *Der E-Mail-Roman*, 79.

34 Eva Illouz, *Cold Intimacies: The Making of Emotional Capitalism* (Cambridge: Polity, 2007), 107.

35 Milne, *Letters, Postcards, Email*, 9.

36 Milne, *Letters, Postcards, Email*, 2.

37 Milne, *Letters, Postcards, Email*, 197.

38 Dupont, "Erzählen im Zeitalter des Internets," 195.

39 Milne, *Letters, Postcards, Email*, 2.

40 On the topos of the ineffability of love see, e.g., Charles Lindholm, "Love and Structure," in *Love and Eroticism: An Introduction*, ed. Mike Featherstone (London: Sage, 1999), 243–63, esp. 246–48.

41 They only do so in the sequel *Alle sieben Wellen*.

42 Illouz, *Cold Intimacies*, 105.

43 Milne, *Letters, Postcards, Email*, 4.

44 Oscar Wilde, "The Picture of Dorian Gray," in *The Collected Works: The Plays, the Poems, the Stories and the Essays including De Profundis* (Ware, UK: Wordsworth Editions Ltd., 2007), 136.

45 Milne, *Letters, Postcards, Email*, 9.

46 Milne, *Letters, Postcards, Email*, 165.

47 Wilke, "Computerbasierte Kommunikationsformen," 162.

48 Ben Ze'ev, *Love Online*, 8.

49 Milne, *Letters, Postcards, Email*, 2.

50 Entry on "Presence," in *A Dictionary of Media and Communication*, ed. Daniel Chandler and Rod Munday (Oxford: Oxford University Press, ²2016), accessed December 17, 2016, http://www.oxfordreference.com/view/10.1093/acref/9780191800986.001.0001/acref-9780191800986.

51 Roland Barthes, "L'Effet de réel," *Communications* 11 (1968): 84–89.

52 Dupont, "Erzählen im Zeitalter des Internets," 196.

53 Michel Foucault, "Of Other Spaces," trans. Jay Miskoviec, *Diacritics* 16, no. 1 (1986 [1984]): 22–27.

54 Milne, *Letters, Postcards, Email*, 196.

55 Paul A. Youngman, *We Are the Machine: The Computer, the Internet, and Information in Contemporary German Literature* (Rochester, NY: Camden House, 2009), 146.

56 *Goethes Werke: Hamburger Ausgabe in 14 Bänden*, ed. Erich Trunz, vol. 6 (Munich: dtv, 1998), 27.

57 Ben Ze'ev, *Love Online*, 63.

58 Dupont, "Erzählen im Zeitalter des Internets," 197.

59 Youngman, *We Are the Machine*, 148.

60 Youngman, *We Are the Machine*, 152.

61 Illouz, *Cold Intimacies*, 75.

62 Deborah Lupton, "The Embodied Computer/User," in *Cyberspace/Cyberbodies/Cyberpunk: Cultures of Technological Embodiment*, ed. Mike Featherstone and Roger Burrows (London: Sage, 1996), 97–112, here 100.

63 Ben Ze'ev, *Love Online*, 29.

64 Illouz, *Cold Intimacies*, 95.

65 Illouz, *Cold Intimacies*, 129.

66 Youngman, *We Are the Machine*, 134.

67 Illouz, *Cold Intimacies*, 98.

68 Ben Ze'ev, *Love Online*, 3.

Thomas Mann in Furs: Remediations of Sadomasochism in Maxim Biller's *Im Kopf von Bruno Schulz* and *Harlem Holocaust*

Maria Roca Lizarazu, University of Warwick

AXIM BILLER IS in many respects a writer of extremes: as an author, journalist, and public persona, he is commonly associated with feelings such as hatred, hostility, and a notoriously provocative style. His 1980s *Tempo* column "100 Zeilen Hass" established his reputation as a polemicist and one of German literature's most renowned *enfants terribles*, while his more recent—and short-lived—contributions to the renowned *Literarisches Quartett* further cemented his image as "der Unzumutbare."[1] On the other end of the spectrum, the topics of love, desire, and sexuality emerge as central features of Biller's work, as is for example demonstrated by the 2007 collection of short stories *Liebe heute*.[2] However, love does not conquer hate in Biller's work: the majority of the (mostly German-Jewish) love relationships depicted in Biller's fiction fail miserably, and the surrounding erotic universe is populated by tabooed, unconventional, and provocative forms of desire, such as incest in *Die Tochter* (The Daughter, 2000), and sadomasochism in *Harlem Holocaust* (1998) and *Im Kopf von Bruno Schulz* (Inside the Head of Bruno Schulz, 2013). Biller's fascination with sadomasochism as a literary motif, figuration, and tradition is particularly noteworthy, as it forms a bridge between the early novella *Harlem Holocaust* and the more recent *Im Kopf von Bruno Schulz*.[3]

The reappearance of sadomasochism raises questions about the specific function of this discourse in the context of Biller's work. I want to argue here that *Im Kopf von Bruno Schulz* invokes the sadomasochistic constellation to reflect on and complicate the so-called German-Jewish symbiosis. In order to achieve this, sadomasochism is transposed from the realm of gender onto the terrain of ethnicity, which is staked out via the novella's fictional relationship between the Polish-Jewish writer Bruno Schulz and the German cultural icon Thomas Mann. Biller's text incorporates literary and iconographic traditions of sadomasochism, ranging from Bruno Schulz to Leopold von Sacher-Masoch, and then revaluates this heritage in the novella. This produces an interesting parallel to *Harlem*

Holocaust, which also uses a sadomasochistic relationship between a Jew and two Germans to comment on the state of German-Jewish relationships in postunification Germany.

As suggested in the title of my article, my analysis of these processes of borrowing and re-interpretation draws on Astrid Erll's reformulation of Jay David Bolter's and Richard Grusin's concept of "remediation":[4]

> With the term "remediation" I refer to the fact that memorable events are usually represented again and again, over decades and centuries, in different media . . . What is known about a war, a revolution, or any other event which has been turned into a site of memory, therefore, seems to refer not so much to what one might cautiously call the "actual events," but instead to a canon of existent medial constructions, to the narratives and images circulating in a media culture.[5]

Broadly speaking, remediation can thus be understood as the repeated representation and re-cycling of certain contents across various medial forms—as such it describes the principal dynamics of cultural memory.[6] What sets it apart from other concepts and practices of adaptation—such as for example intertextuality and/or intermediality—is the fact that remediation refers not to a specific text or image that gets recycled, but to an entire assemblage of various artistic forms, media, and discourses, as we can for example find in the sadomasochistic constellation that originated in Sacher-Masoch's writing but then traveled through and merged with discourses from the realms of psychiatry and psychoanalysis, literature, film, music, and popular culture. For the purpose of this article, I will focus particularly on Bruno Schulz's adaptations of Sacher-Masoch's writings. Schulz took up central motifs from Sacher-Masoch's universe in both his written and his graphic oeuvre; these then resurface in Biller's novella.[7] Biller's engagement with Sacher-Masoch's legacy is thus filtered through the lens of Schulz's adaptations and aesthetics, while possibly drawing on a broader discourse that links the Holocaust to tabooed forms of sexuality and desire, particularly in the form of sadomasochism.[8]

The process of remediation involves a diachronic as well as a transnational, transcultural, and transmedial dimension. Contents travel across different historical epochs and medial platforms, while also traversing national and/or cultural boundaries. Remediations of the sadomasochistic constellation in *Im Kopf von Bruno Schulz* thus knot together Sacher-Masoch's involvement in nineteenth-century Galician folklore with Schulzian traditions of "ghetto" and Eastern-Jewish writing at the beginning of the twentieth century. Biller's text re-interprets this legacy from the vantage point of Jewish existence in contemporary, post-Holocaust Germany. It should be noted that the process of remediation is never a "neutral" one—the travel through space, time, and various media engenders not only aesthetic and formal changes, but also affects the very quality of what is being transported. Remediation means re-interpretation *and* re-creation. Biller's re-purposing of literary and iconographic traditions of sadomasochism is thus more than a game of intertextual and intermedial references; it is a radical re-reading of a certain heritage that tries to intervene in the broader arena of German-Jewish relations and (cultural) memory after the Holocaust.

Traditions of Sadomasochism: Biller—Schulz—Sacher-Masoch

Biller's novella *Im Kopf von Bruno Schulz* is set in 1938 and focuses on a letter, written from the first-person perspective of the Polish-Jewish writer and art teacher Bruno Schulz, and addressed to the by then world-famous German author Thomas Mann. According to Schulz's German translator, Doreen Daume, the actual Bruno Schulz did really write a letter to Thomas Mann, which also contained a copy of Schulz's first German-language text, *Die Heimkehr*. Both the letter and the manuscript have been lost, however, which makes it impossible to verify her claim. In the novella, Schulz uses the letter to inform the German icon that a *doppelganger* of his is on the rampage in Schulz's (then) Polish hometown of Drohobycz. His detailed account of the fake Mann's grotesque and atrocious behaviors is frequently interrupted by a frame narrative in which a third-person narrator provides further insights into Bruno Schulz's mind. The contents of Schulz's letter become increasingly surreal as the novella progresses, and end with the revelation that the fake Thomas Mann is a secret agent who was sent to investigate and eventually eliminate Drohobycz's Jewish community. This revelation also illuminates the real motives behind Schulz's letter: in all likelihood, the fake Thomas Mann is Schulz's invention, created to attract his famous colleague's attention, in the hope that he may save Schulz from the advancing German troops. However, Schulz's endeavors are hopeless, and the novella ends with imagery that clearly anticipates the extermination policies of the Holocaust.

The life and works of Bruno Schulz are thus a central point of reference for Biller's novella. The text is dotted with numerous allusions to Schulz's writing and graphic work, most of which concentrate on Schulz's short-story anthology *Die Zimtläden* (translated into English as *The Street of Crocodiles*, 1933), whose main characters (the father, the mother, Adela) and motifs (the birds, the so-called cinnamon shops, the dog Nimrod) resurface throughout Biller's narrative, along with explicit references to Schulz's important poetological "Traktat über die Schneiderpuppen."[9]

Biller's intertextual engagement is seen mostly at the level of character constellations and motifs, rather than at the level of language and style, even though the text is inspired by Schulz's surreal aesthetics. The novella draws on two aspects of Schulz's writing in particular: Eastern-Jewish traditions of so-called "ghetto writing" on the one hand,[10] and the imagery of sadomasochism in Schulz's work on the other.[11] In its adaptation of Schulz's sadomasochistic universe, Biller's text also relies on Schulz's graphic oeuvre, specifically on a German edition of Schulz's drawings from 2000.[12]

Even though there is some continuity on the level of imagery, the two authors depict the sadomasochistic constellation very differently in their respective works. In Schulz's narrative, sadomasochism is tied to allusion; there are no explicit scenarios of physical punishment. In *Die Zimtläden*, the sadomasochistic figuration marks the relationship between the first-person narrator's father and the young housekeeper Adela, who rules the household (and the *pater familias*) with an iron fist and an acute awareness of her powers. Adela, who represents matter, the body, sensuality, and the lower regions of the house, uses her might to control the narrator's father, who occupies the house's upper realms, along with those of the mind. The gendered dichotomy of above/below is central to the story, as it encapsulates its main themes.[13] Above/below first and foremost describes the spatial location of the characters: Adela, although able to move freely around the house, usually works on the lower levels of the house, sweeping and scrubbing the floors, while the father prefers to spend his time in the attic, at times sitting on top of various pieces of furniture. Birds are his favorite animals, and he spends substantial amounts of time and money on importing and hatching exotic bird eggs. These locations and attributes carry symbolic significance, of course: Adela's association with the lower regions of the house can be read both in terms of class and in terms of her alignment with the lower regions of the body, that is, those parts that are the furthest removed from the brain and the powers of reason. She is all body (or rather: matter) whereas the father is all mind.

However, this very dichotomy is destabilized (and maybe even reversed) in the sadomasochistic scenario, in which Adela alternates between playfully teasing and openly challenging the father and his patriarchal power.[14] When the father explains the conflict between the (male) demiurge and the (female) material world in his speech on the "Schneiderpuppen," Adela disrupts his deliberations by tantalizing him with her foot: "Jetzt schob sie sich auf dem Stuhl eine Spanne weit nach vorn, hob den Saum des Kleides, steckte langsam den mit schwarzer Seide überzogenen Fuß vor und richtete ihn auf wie ein kleines Schlangenmaul" (*DZ*, 55). The father reacts "wie ein Automat" (*DZ*, 56), and falls to his knees. Ironically, this turns him into the type of mannequin that is the topic of his treatise—he is thus himself transformed from a (wannabe) active, male creator into a lifeless, passive automaton, while also being brought down from the realm of the mind (the above) onto his knees (the below). However, in Schulz's text any scenes of explicit sadomasochistic punishment are quite literally blanked out: "Adela erhob sich vom Stuhl und bat uns, die Augen zu schließen vor dem, was nun gleich geschehen würde. Sie ging auf meinen Vater zu und verlangte, die Hände in die Hüften gestemmt, was den Anschein betonter Entschlossenheit verstärkte, mit aller Deutlichkeit . . . -----------------" (*DZ*, 60, ellipses in the original, MRL).

Biller's text makes these allusions and omissions in Schulz's writing explicit: he transforms the multilayered sadomasochistic discourse in *Die Zimtläden* into a rather clichéd scenario of dominance, submission, and frequent physical punishment. The complex dependency and roleplay between the father and Adela is translated here into the openly sadomasochistic and violent relationship between the protagonist Bruno Schulz and Helena Jakubowicz, one of his fellow teachers. Schulz's masochistic urge is presented as a form of compulsive acting out that was caused by the frequent physical abuse he suffered from the housekeeper Adele[15] as a child. While being locked up in a wardrobe by Helena, Schulz begins to fantasize about other forms of punishment:

> Vielleicht, fügte sie hinzu, würde sie selbst kurz mit ihm in die Kammer kommen, sie könne, wenn er es wolle, in einem der chaotischen Läden hinter dem Marktplatz, . . . einige Dinge kaufen, die sie schon lange mit ihm ausprobieren wollte. Er konnte sich denken, was sie meinte! Nein, hatte er geantwortet, lieber nicht, obwohl er sich beim Gedanken an diese Dinge—venezianische Colombina-Masken aus schwarzem Leder, mit Sägemehl ausgestopfte, penisgroße Pierrots, aus Weidenruten geflochtene und mit dünnen Stahlketten durchwirkte Osterpeitschen, silberne Nippelklemmen und japanische Schungakerzen, deren tropfendes Wachs keine Brandblasen hinterließ—sofort sehr sicher und wohl fühlte . . . (*IKvBS*, 13–14)

What the novella presents as Schulz's deepest desires is more reminiscent of pop-cultural depictions of sadomasochism à la *Fifty Shades of Grey* than of the scenarios invented by Schulz as a response to Sacher-Masoch's *Venus im Pelz* (Venus in Furs, 1870). In their depiction of the sadomasochistic figuration, both Sacher-Masoch and Schulz rely on allusion, omission, and—as Gilles Deleuze has famously argued in connection with Sacher-Masoch—deferral and suspension.[16] Imagination and fantasy are generally more important than execution. Moreover, the dominant/submissive relationship is used to reflect on a whole range of topics, such as the relationship between the sexes, power, performativity, or, in

Schulz's case, the connection between mind and matter and the nature of creation and creativity. Despite these similarities, Schulz's collection of stories already transforms Sacher-Masoch's model in significant ways: in *Die Zimtläden*, Sacher-Masoch's cruel mistress loses her opulent gowns and furs and re-emerges as the housekeeper Adela. The sadomasochistic constellation is thus translocated from the aristocratic to the bourgeois milieu, while also being oedipalized via *Die Zimtläden*'s focus on the nuclear family.[17] In Schulz's graphic work in particular, the sadomasochistic figuration is supplemented by a foot fetish, which is not overly relevant for Sacher-Masoch's narrative. By going through yet another cycle of remediation, in Biller's writing, sadomasochism turns into a cliché, by being boiled down to a few potent scenes—involving mostly flagellation and genuflection—which are invoked mainly, albeit not solely, for the purposes of provocation.

The presence of traditions of sadomasochism allusions in Biller's novella is not limited to intertextuality; it also involves a strong visual component. I here want to explore in more detail the role of Schulz's drawings, arguing that they are the main source of sadomasochistic imagery in Biller's text, which makes repeated reference to a German edition titled *Bruno Schulz: Das graphische Werk* (Bruno Schulz: The Graphic Works, 2000).[18] However, the relationship between Schulz's drawings and Biller's novella is not a straightforward one, as the remediation of Schulz's oeuvre takes place on several levels: *Im Kopf von Bruno Schulz* includes six drawings by Schulz, which are inserted into the novella at regular intervals. While not intended as illustrations of any specific scenes in the text, they rather function as a general comment on the discourse of sadomasochism by adding an additional, visual layer. Five of the drawings show scenes of either social or sexual domination and submission, depicting the female in a position of power and superiority, expressed either in the form of spatial elevation (*IKvBS*, 25), or as an upwards movement of her head (*IKvBS*, 64). Furthermore, parts of Schulz's oeuvre are remediated in the text by way of ekphrasis: the character of Bruno Schulz for example describes his own (and the real Bruno Schulz's) drawings, using them as an inspiration for the letter he writes and the story he invents (*IKvBS*, 34). Finally, an examination of *Bruno Schulz: Das graphische Werk* reveals that, apart from the six drawings that are explicitly remediated in the novella, several more of Schulz's drawings have been implicitly remediated in the text, which draws on Schulz's works as an inspiration for central scenes, motifs, and constellations. This for example concerns Bruno's transformation into a dog (*BSgW*, 118), the human cart horses used by the fake Mann (*BSgW*, 61) as well as the scenes of collective adoration and submission that return in the bathroom sequence (*BSgW*, 57–59; 113).

Schulz's works of art were allegedly intended as illustrations of Leopold von Sacher-Masoch's *Venus im Pelz*.[19] They clearly draw on the precursor's imagery, by reiterating scenes of physical domination by a cold and aloof female, or by showing acts of flagellation. Biller's novella, however, downplays certain crucial aspects of Sacher-Masoch's influence on Schulz while highlighting others: *Im Kopf von Bruno Schulz* does not concentrate on the central figure of the unattainable, cruel woman and its complementary image of a man lying at the feet of his cold mistress, which are an integral part of literary and visual traditions of sadomasochism. Instead, Biller's textual rendition foregrounds scenes of violent punishment, especially the practice of whipping or flagellation. The topic of male adoration for a cold female thus plays a significant role on the visual level of Biller's novella—via the inserted drawings—while being downplayed on the level of narrative. Although the male/female sadomasochistic relationship is present in Biller's narrative (Schulz/Adele, Schulz/Helena), it is of secondary importance. Rather, the core sadomasochistic scenario is enacted through the relationship between Schulz/the town's Jews and Thomas Mann. While sadomasochism, in accordance with the literary tradition, is represented as an exclusively male/female scenario on the visual level, on the level of narrative it is coded as predominantly German-Jewish. Biller's text thus transposes the sadomasochistic complex from the realm of gender onto the domain of ethnicity and culture. However, this transposition only works with the help of a gendered strategy, which feminizes the fake Thomas Mann, and aligns him, in various ways, with the cruel and dominating females that play a role in Sacher-Masoch's, Schulz's, and Biller's texts. Sacher-Masoch's and Schulz's cruel mistresses are thus re-interpreted and re-emerge in the guise of Thomas Mann's character—Venus in furs becomes Thomas Mann in furs. This alignment becomes even clearer when the collection of Schulz's drawings that served as an inspiration for Biller's novella is considered. The drawings demonstrate that one of the central scenes of degradation in *Im Kopf von Bruno Schulz*—the scene in which the fake Thomas Mann uses the town's Jews as cart horses—redeploys an existing piece of art by Schulz, in which a female does the exact same thing to a group of naked men.[20] It is worth noting that the drawing is entitled "Auf Kythera," which in Greek mythology is the island belonging to Aphrodite, the Greek goddess of love and seduction. Another drawing by Schulz, which shows men crawling at the feet of a powerful woman, is entitled "Mademoiselle Circe und ihre Truppe," evoking yet another dangerously seductive female from the realm of Greek mythology.[21] By implicitly remediating these drawings, Biller's novella aligns the fake Thomas Mann (and German culture as a whole, which he epitomizes) with traditions of the seductive *femme fatale* whose presence proves to be fatal for the town's Jews.

The complex interaction between Biller's novella and Schulz's drawings points to remediation as a form of what Astrid Erll has described as "travelling memory."[22] Via remediation, the sadomasochistic constellation firstly "travels" from Sacher-Masoch's text into Schulz's written and graphic oeuvre, and then enters Biller's novella. Along the way, certain aspects of the sadomasochistic complex are highlighted while others are suppressed, and the issues attached to it change accordingly. Schulz's collection of stories sticks to the gendered constellation at the heart of Sacher-Masoch's writing, but re-interprets it in terms of class and a conflict between (male) mind and (female) matter. Schulz's *Zimtläden* also parodies Sacher-Masoch's model, at least to an extent. The transformation of the aristocratic and cruel mistress into the housekeeper, the translocation to the realm of the bourgeois nuclear family and the reversal of the dichotomy above/below can all be interpreted as forms of ironic debasement. Biller's text seemingly abandons the gender aspect by conceptualizing sadomasochism as an illustration of the (failed) German-Jewish symbiosis. At the same time, *Im Kopf von Bruno Schulz* incorporates certain misogynistic tendencies that are present in Schulz's oeuvre,[23] by revitalizing the topos of the *femme fatale*.

The Seductiveness of German Culture

Conceptualizing the German-Jewish relationship in terms of sadomasochism can arguably be read as a polemical demonstration of the dangerous seductiveness of German culture. According to this narrative, German culture, epitomized by the figure of Thomas Mann, lured Jews like Bruno Schulz into an act of submission that eventually cost them their lives. This dangerous constellation was sustained by the Jewish illusion that an untainted love for German culture and a German-Jewish symbiosis were possible.

In order to better understand this argument, it is important to consider the portrayal of Thomas Mann in Biller's novella, which encompasses three facets: firstly, there is the Thomas Mann that Schulz's fictional letter is addressed to. Known to Schulz only "von Fotografien und aus Zeitungen" (*IKvBS*, 7), this noble gentleman remains silent and absent throughout the text. This idealized Thomas Mann is gradually overwritten by the fake Thomas Mann, a "bösartiges Abbild" (*IKvBS*, 33), who roams the streets of Drohobycz and is physically and morally repulsive. Not only is he dirty, a slovenly dresser, and generally unkempt, he also abuses the town's Jews in increasingly sadistic ways and turns out to be an agent of Germany's secret police. Thirdly, there is the actual author Thomas Mann, who is supposed to help Schulz. It eventually becomes clear that both the ideal and its grotesque reversal spring solely from Schulz's imagination. There is no fake Thomas Mann in Drohobycz; Schulz has made him up to gain the actual Mann's attention and protection. The split Mann therefore exists exclusively in Schulz's mind, as an expression of the writer's ambivalent love-hate relationship with the idol. The sadomasochistic relationship between the fake Mann, Schulz, and the town's Jews is thus uncovered as a fantasy entertained by the book's protagonist. However, the neat separation between the fantasies of the novella's protagonist and its author's own opinions is complicated when Biller's autobiographically inspired "Selbstporträt" *Der gebrauchte Jude* (The Second-Hand Jew) is considered.[24] The text circles obsessively around Thomas Mann—there are at least ten episodes or dialogues that involve him—and Biller's personal love-hate relationship with the idol, so that Schulz's fantasies can be said to convey Biller's own negative sentiments towards the precursor:

> Thomas Mann ist der neue Goethe, und den Deutschen ist egal, dass fast alle seine Bücher einen dunklen Hinterausgang haben, durch den man direkt in die schmutzige Phantasiewelt der Rassentheoretiker des 19. Jahrhunderts gelangt. Die Juden bei Mann sind schnell, schmierig, gewissenlos und Demokraten. Sie haben platte Nasen und wulstige Lippen, und wenn sie wie Sieglinde und Siegmund in *Wälsungenblut* Geschwister sind, schlafen sie miteinander. (*DgJ*, 42)

Biller's novella thus uses an allegedly "real" historical event—Schulz writing a letter to Mann—to continue the writer's own dialogue with Thomas Mann. Similar to *Im Kopf von Bruno Schulz*, *Der gebrauchte Jude* also draws on the biography of a famous fellow Jewish writer to make a polemical point about the seductiveness of German culture and the futility of the German-Jewish symbiosis. Here it is the German-Jewish literary critic Marcel Reich-Ranicki who is under the spell of German culture and even goes so far as to reject Kafka, "de[n] Jude[n], der das schönste Deutsch des zwanzigsten Jahrhunderts schrieb," in favor of Thomas Mann, "der sich bis zu seinem Tod in der jüdischen Moderne so wohlfühlte wie ein niedersächsischer Pastor auf dem Geburtstagsfest des Zaddiks von Przemysl" (*DgJ*, 107). This betrayal of a Jewish heritage leads to harsh accusations from Biller's side: "Wie gerne wäre er [Marcel Reich-Ranicki, MRL] Deutscher gewesen—. . .—aber das ging wirklich nicht mehr. Und wenn doch? Also subtrahierte er sich seine Lebenswahrheit zurecht, wie so viele Davongekommene: Deutschland minus Hitler, Goebbels und Auschwitz gleich Heine, Rilke und Thomas Mann" (*DgJ*, 82–83). Biller's latest novella can in many ways be read as an attack on what he calls the "Reich-Ranicki-Syndrom" (*DgJ*, 117), that is, a belief in a German-Jewish symbiosis that is underpinned by the illusion that German (high) culture can somehow be separated from Nazi barbarism.

This suggests that, under the Damocles sword of the Holocaust, Schulz's personal perception of German-Jewish relations as a sadomasochistic dependency serves as a comment on the broader issue of the role of the Jew in German culture. Framed within the sadomasochistic constellation, Thomas Mann and German culture are imagined as feminine and highly seductive.[25] *Im Kopf von Bruno Schulz* features various scenes in which the people in the town are inexplicably drawn to the fake Mann, and this is so in spite of his repugnant physical appearance and atrocious behavior: "Die vielen wichtigen Leute aus unserer Stadt, die ihn seit seiner Ankunft wie der Bienenstaat die Königin umschwirren, ducken sich kurz und danach tauchen sie—die Mundwinkel zum unterwürfigen Lächeln hochgezogen, die Augen vor Schrecken gerötet und glasig—wieder auf und bitten ihn, ihnen weiter seine aufregenden Geschichten zu erzählen" (*IKvBS*, 17).

The comparison of the town's community to a "Bienenstaat" puts the fake Mann in the position of the proverbial queen bee. This link is further emphasized by Schulz's choice of words when describing the fake Thomas Mann. He mentions that the fake writer has come to the town to make everyone's head spin, and he admits: "Und so habe ich mich neulich auch, sehr verehrter Dr. Mann, wie jeder andere von Ihrem Doppelgänger einwickeln lassen" (*IKvBS*, 32). Verb constructions such as "den Kopf . . . verdrehen" (*IKvBS*, 32) and "einwickeln" (*IKvBS*, 32) form an imagery of seduction, ensnarement, and manipulation that is usually associated with the misogynistic topos of the *femme fatale*.[26] And even though the character of Schulz seems to take up a rather distanced, maybe even critical, stance towards this senseless admiration, he himself is also not immune to the charms of Mann, and, just like Reich-Ranicki in *Der gebrauchte Jude*, finds himself trapped in his love for the German language and German culture as a whole: "Die biegsamen Regeln der Mischna, die fast beschwingte Schwermut des Predigers, die sanfte Klarheit des Schulchan Aruch? Nein, das war nie etwas für mich. Ich sehne mich eher mit Malte Laurids Brigge und Gustav von Aschenbach nach einem Ende, das uns alle ohnehin erwartet, dessen Schönheit und Zeitpunkt wir aber selbst bestimmen sollten . . . " (*IKvBS*, 62).

Yet, as is well known, flirting with the *femme fatale* usually does not end well for the male characters. This is not any different for the Jews who have fallen prey to the temptations of Thomas Mann and German culture. The fake Mann lures them into a profoundly sadomasochistic constellation of dominance and submission that eventually leads to their death. This is epitomized in the bathroom scene, which, situated at the center of the narrative arc, forms the climax of Biller's text (and Schulz's fantasy). The scene relies on the provocative image of the *doppelganger* giving the town's Jews a whipping inside a bathroom that evokes the iconography of the gas chamber: "Sie hatten ihre Kleider an die Haken gehängt, sie saßen stumm oder übertrieben leise miteinander sprechend auf den Bänken und warteten. Als der Meister mit dem Direktor und mir reinkam, erhoben sie sich fast gleichzeitig, sie verdeckten mit den Händen ihre nackten Brüste und Genitalien, und auch die letzte, allerleiseste Unterhaltung brach ab" (*IKvBS*, 34–37).

References to the gas chambers are of course anachronistic from the viewpoint of the novella, which it set in 1938. However, they also suggest that Schulz's fantasies are actually a form of premonition. The superimposition of the iconographies of sadomasochism, the Holocaust, and anti-Semitic violence in the bathroom scene thus indicates that the blind and masochistic love for German culture on the part of the Jews—that is, the belief that something like a positive German-Jewish symbiosis is possible—makes them follow the fake Mann like lambs to the slaughter, which anticipates future historical events. The violence is sparked when the Jews start to harass the fake Mann in response to his announcement that he is leaving Europe for America to escape the advent of German fascism. The physical contact made by the Jews is thus a cry for help, but their actions could also be interpreted as the culmination of their desire for symbiosis and amalgamation, which, however, provokes fear in the German author, leading to his violent response.

What begins as a sadomasochistic orgy eventually turns into a pogrom, an act of anti-Semitic destruction. Schulz's narrative positions the fake Mann within a genealogy of anti-Semitic excess, which logically leads to the Holocaust as the endpoint, making him part of the perpetrator collective:

> Doch allmählich wurden die Hiebe des Deutschen schwächer, seine Stimme auch, in der silbernen Rauchwolke formten sich für einen Moment die wabernden Konturen des traurigen Kindergesichts von Leutnant Alfred Dreyfus, aus dem französischen Offizier wurde die weinende und blutende Jagienka Łomska, dann schaute ich mich selbst aus dem Rauchschleier an, und schließlich drehte sich die Wolke, sie zog sich zusammen und stieg zur Decke auf, wo sie mit einem lauten Zischen in den Düsen der Duschen verschwand—und gab so den Blick frei auf einen großen Haufen nackter Körper, die leblos um den vor Erschöpfung knienden, falschen Thomas Mann herumlagen. (*IKvBS*, 40–41)

Yet again, the recourse to Holocaust imagery—of the gas chamber in particular—is undeniable in this passage. The fake Thomas Mann, suddenly referred to solely as "the German," is represented as a Nazi perpetrator executing anti-Semitic violence, while the townspeople are integrated into a transhistorical community of eternal victims with the prophetic Schulz as their latest addition. Among the palls of smoke, it thus becomes clear that German-Jewish relations can only ever result in anti-Semitic excess, and that sooner or later, any German will turn into a perpetrator. According to this scenario, German-Jewish relations function as a one-sided dependency, based on an act of delusional submission on the side of the Jews, which inevitably entails their destruction. The introduction of Mann as "Meister" at the beginning of the scene thus carries multiple meanings: not only is he a master commanding words and slaves, he is also the "Meister aus Deutschland" that haunts Celan's poem "Todesfuge" (Death Fugue, 1948), and thus an emblem of Nazi extermination policies.[27] The Schulz in Biller's story aims to exploit the difference between his grotesque invention and the actual Thomas Mann, who he hopes will save him. However, the fact that Mann remains silent and Schulz's fantasies eventually become real—Drohobycz is overrun and destroyed by Nazi troops at the end of the novella—implies that the difference between the fake and the real Mann is not that substantial, and that Schulz himself fell prey to a delusional belief in German culture as the opposite of and antidote to Nazi barbarism. The novella hence employs Schulz's pre-Holocaust interpretation of German-Jewish relationships as a masochistic dependency on the side of the Jews to express a post-Holocaust consciousness. In contrast to Schulz's illusions, the novella is firmly based on the conviction that, after the attempted extermination of an entire people, Jews and Germans are "für immer geschiedene Leute" (*DgJ*, 107).

(De-)Constructing the Jewish Monster in *Harlem Holocaust*

The connection between sadomasochism and the German-Jewish symbiosis surfaces at an earlier stage of Biller's writing career, in the 1998 short story *Harlem Holocaust*.[28] It depicts the problematic triangular relationship between Efraim Rosenhain, a German son of perpetrators, his German (ex-) girlfriend Ina Polarker, and the American-Jewish linguistics professor turned writer Gerhard "Gary" Warszawski. During the course of his narration, the first-person narrator Rosenhain delivers a deeply unsympathetic portrayal of Warszawski who, as a "Zerrbild deutscher Schuldprojektionen,"[29] has come to haunt Germany and destroy everything Rosenhain holds dear. Warszawski's oeuvre endlessly recycles a story of Holocaust survival that he has stolen from his cousin Leo Schneider, while his public career and personal relationships ruthlessly exploit the masochistic German "Gier nach Schuld und Entsühnung" (*HH*, 9). Warzawski instrumentalizes what Rosenhain describes as his "Auschwitzbonus" (*HH*, 52) in the most brutally calculating and sadistic manner, subjugating the German public in general and Rosenhain in particular. While Biller's short story is on the one hand a bitter parody of the deeply ritualized, commodified German *Vergangenheitsindustrie* and its "fascination for things Jewish,"[30] it on the other hand comments on the post-Holocaust state of German-Jewish relationships via recourse to the sadomasochistic complex.

The relationship between the two Germans and their Jewish counterpart is depicted as a sadomasochistic *ménage à trois* in which they succumb all too willingly to the lure of the Jewish monster Warszawski.

While Rosenhain, who embarks on a desperate search for the long lost "Seelenverwandtschaft" (*HH*, 49) between Germans and Jews, is in equal parts attracted and repelled by Warszawski's demeanor and physique, Ina has become totally enslaved by Warszawski's irresistible air of "'Angst' und 'Reue' und 'Todeserotik'" (*HH*, 24). Warszawski wields power over the two Germans by physically and mentally abusing and demeaning them (especially Ina, who is repeatedly coerced into humiliating sex acts). Because he draws sadistic joy from these various acts of degradation, the reader cannot help but sympathize with the victimized Germans. Throughout most of the story the reader therefore willingly embraces Rosenhain's anti-Semitic portrait of Warszawski as the sex-hungry, money-grabbing Jew. However, the reader's sentiment is radically called into question by the story's ending: *Harlem Holocaust* finishes with a note written by a man called Hermann Warschauer, which uncovers the entire narrative as the posthumously released manuscript of a certain Friedrich (not Efraim) Rosenhain, who Warschauer claims was mentally ill. It remains unclear whether Friedrich imagined the entire story (along with his hyper-Jewish name) or whether Warszawski/Warschauer, in a final masterstroke, added this note to permanently discredit the (by then dead) Rosenhain. In any case, this ending makes the reader question the accuracy of the picture painted by the first-person narrator Rosenhain—was his portrayal of Warszawski rooted in his paranoid, anti-Semitic fantasies? And why did the reader embrace it so willingly?

Biller's literary sleight-of-hand thus forces the reader into a critical self-examination as to why s/he took the parodic image of Warszawski as the Jewish monster at face value, especially since Rosenhain is presented as an unreliable narrator. He himself admits that he suffers from repeated bouts of dizziness and a propensity for hallucinations and wild fantasies: "Dabei machte das mir ja auch Spaß, es war eine verzweifelte Spielerei, die mich mitunter dazu antrieb, mir mein Leben anders und besser vorzustellen, was immer funktionierte und manchmal sogar so weit ging, dass ich mir, zum Zeitvertreib nur, etwa auf der Straße die Gesichter der Passanten in surrealistischer Manier zurechtbog" (*HH*, 10).

Although *Harlem Holocaust* reverses the constellation depicted in *Im Kopf von Bruno Schulz*—here it is the Jew who is in power and sadistically abuses this privilege—the text still comments on the German-Jewish symbiosis, which is presented as a "negative Symbiose," to quote Dan Diner.[31] The disturbing relationship between Rosenhain and Warszawski—and the reader's reaction to it—serves as an impressive illustration of what Dan Diner has described as an unsolvable, unintended, and most undesired bond between perpetrators and victims:

> Seit Auschwitz—welch traurige List—kann tatsächlich von einer "deutsch-jüdischen Symbiose" gesprochen werden—freilich einer

negativen: für beide, für Deutsche wie für Juden, ist das Ergebnis der Massenvernichtung zum Ausgangspunkt ihres Selbstverständnisses geworden; eine Art gegensätzlicher Gemeinsamkeit—ob sie es wollen oder nicht. Denn Deutsche wie Juden sind durch dieses Ereignis neu aufeinander bezogen worden. Solch negative Symbiose, von den Nazis konstituiert, wird auf Generationen hinaus das Verhältnis beider zu sich selbst, vor allem aber zueinander, prägen.[32]

The short story demonstrates exactly this "gegensätzliche Gemeinsamkeit," albeit in a grotesquely exaggerated manner. It shows that neither Rosenhain nor Ina can free themselves of their obsession with Warszawski and their feeling of perpetrator guilt, while Warszawski—at least according to Rosenhain's portrayal—cannot stop tormenting them (and the German public) on the basis of these feelings. In both cases, the central characters are unable to construct an identity that does not take the Holocaust as its "Ausgangspunkt," which gridlocks them (and the Other) in the roles of either perpetrator or victim. This unavoidably leads to a state where Germans and Jews are perpetually "aufeinander bezogen," without, however, being able to meaningfully relate to one another. Any possibility for empathy on the interpersonal level is eroded—a situation that is further aggravated by the total commodification of Holocaust memory in the story, which also forestalls any meaningful responses to German-Jewish history on the collective level.[33] The text demonstrates that for Germans and Jews alike the perception of the other is not possible beyond the level of clichés, stereotypes, and projections. The perverted and darkly grotesque depiction of German-Jewish (love) relationships in *Harlem Holocaust*—and in any other Billerian story that concerns this topic—is thus merely the "Wiedergabe einer Situation, in der Deutsche und Juden alle Unmittelbarkeit im Umgang miteinander eingebüßt haben und nur noch in Rollen und Masken miteinander reden und so verkappt sogar miteinander ins Bett gehen."[34] When considering *Im Kopf von Bruno Schulz*, the idea of a *loss* of "Unmittelbarkeit" is called into doubt, however, as the novella strongly emphasizes that "Unmittelbarkeit im Umgang" never existed between Germans and Jews in the first place. Biller's text demonstrates that the German-Jewish symbiosis has always been a wishful fantasy, entertained by naïve Jews and violated by cruel Germans, as the example of Mann shows. A similar point is made in *Harlem Holocaust*, as the text suggests that any notion of a German-Jewish "Seelenverwandtschaft"

> ... war, im kleinen, genauso eine Illusion und ein eskapistischer, verzweifelter Rettungsanker gewesen wie, im großen, die von so vielen propagierte deutsch-jüdische Symbiose, der historische Schulterschluß zweier Völker, der mal Genies, mal Leichen produzierte. Ja, und wir Idioten glaubten immer noch daran, an die

einträchtige Kraft von George, Musil und Kisch, an die Einsichten
von Freud und Schopenhauer, an die gemeinsamen Visionen von
Rilke, Fritz Lang und Billy Wilder, an diese ganze romantische,
germanisch-hebräische Mitteleuropa-Idee also, an die Metapher von
Kultur und Kaffeehaus. (*HH*, 50)

Although both texts employ the sadomasochistic configuration to negotiate the German-Jewish relationship, there are crucial differences: in
Harlem Holocaust, the imagery of sadomasochism is decipherable as the
paranoid template applied by Rosenhain, who, following German anti-
Semitic traditions, sees the omnipotent Jew as a threat to himself and
his culture. In *Im Kopf von Bruno Schulz*, this constellation is reversed,
while also being uncovered as the protagonist's (Bruno Schulz's) fantasy. However, in contrast to Rosenhain's projections in *Harlem
Holocaust*, Schulz's invention in *Im Kopf von Bruno Schulz* is not called
into question by the narrative construction of the text—his fantasy in
the end becomes a reality, turning him into a prophet and one of the
many Jews who fell prey to the lures of German culture. While sadomasochistic discourse in *Harlem Holocaust* is thus inextricably linked to the
"negative Symbiose," and the persistence of certain discursive patterns,
Im Kopf von Bruno Schulz can be read as a polemic against the ideal of
the German-Jewish symbiosis, attacking the "Reich-Ranicki-Syndrom."
As such, Biller's novella, set in a pre-Holocaust world, expresses a post-
Holocaust consciousness, which is in itself shaped by the dynamics of
the negative symbiosis.

Alternative Genealogies

I want to conclude by showing that the recourse to Schulz and Sacher-
Masoch in Biller's writing serves a purpose that goes beyond mere polem-
ics. Both Sacher-Masoch's and Schulz's works are inextricably caught up
with the lost world of Galicia and traditions of Eastern European and
Eastern-Jewish culture and writing. This suggests that Biller's text draws
on Schulz's oeuvre to inscribe itself into a specifically Eastern European
Jewish genealogy, which is pitted against a German tradition represented
by Thomas Mann. This also explains the epigraph that precedes the
novella, quoting the Nobel Prize-winning Galician writer Shmuel Josef
Agnon: "Gelobt sei, der seltsame Wesen schafft" (*IKvBS*, 5). Agnon was
famous for his depictions of Jewish life in Galicia, making him a prime
exponent of the literary tradition of "ghetto writing." The Agnon quote
therefore links Biller's own text to the wider canon of ghetto literature,
while also firmly aligning Schulz with the traditions of Galician or Eastern
Jewish writing. The emphasis on the themes of sadomasochism in Schulz's
writing and drawings further strengthens these affiliations, as it references

Leopold von Sacher-Masoch's work. Even though Sacher-Masoch was not Jewish himself, he is renowned for his—personal and literary—interest in Galician folklore and local Jewish communities.

The Agnon quote, "Gelobt sei, der seltsame Wesen schafft" (*IKvBS*, 6) may furthermore be seen to refer to Kafka's *Die Verwandlung* (The Metamorphosis, 1915) and surrealist traditions more generally: Biller's novella features a protagonist who is trapped in a basement and undergoing a gradual transformation from human to animal, while obsessing about the relationship with a father figure. This obvious reference to Kafka's *Die Verwandlung* is reinforced by the fact that Schulz and Biller repeatedly destabilize the human-animal divide; their writing examines the bond between humans and animals alongside the transformation of humans into animals. In Biller's novella, human-animal relationships, especially man/dog and man/bird relations, function as intertextual reworkings of Schulz's writing, which also allude to Kafka. This creates a second, specifically Jewish genealogy and creative alliance between Kafka, Schulz, and Biller.

Im Kopf von Bruno Schulz thus engenders "negative" and "positive" practices of remediation. References to various authors, their works, and the literary and visual traditions in which they were embedded become the battle ground on which a general conflict of belonging and dissociation is staged and acted out, which uses allusion to connect to some traditions, while aggressively warding off others. A positive relationship is established with the works of Bruno Schulz, which inserts Biller into a specifically Eastern European Jewish tradition. This heritage encompasses "ghetto writing" and sadomasochistic discourse (Sacher-Masoch, Agnon, Schulz), alongside a Kafkaesque surrealism, all of which intersect in Schulz's oeuvre. Biller's novella furthermore uses a fictionalized Schulz and the sadomasochistic constellation to act out a broader conflict with Thomas Mann, which links back to Biller's autobiographical self-portrait *Der gebrauchte Jude* (The Second-Hand Jew, 2009). The relationship with Schulz and his oeuvre is thus characterized by an ambivalent mix of adoration and appropriation, commemoration and erasure, homage and criticism. By contrast, the relationship with Thomas Man is less ambiguous: it is driven by hatred. Since Biller's texts do not engage with Thomas Mann's oeuvre as such, the German writer fulfils a synechdochical function, representing German cultural tradition as a whole. By contrast, the relationship with Reich-Ranicki is defined by identification—Biller sees himself in Reich-Ranicki and claims that the opposite is also true. Nonetheless, Biller's writing discredits Reich-Ranicki by merging him with Bruno Schulz's character, accusing both of a blind infatuation with German culture. The danger of this infatuation is highlighted in the sadomasochistic submission of the Jews by Thomas Mann, which, in the case of Schulz, can only end in annihilation.

Biller's relationship with various writers, texts, and traditions illustrates my initial point about the transformative powers of remediation and its contribution to the larger dynamics of cultural memory. By converting the game of dominance and submission between a man and a cruel, cold female into the violent and abusive relationship between Thomas Mann, the epitome of German culture, and Bruno Schulz, who symbolizes the destroyed world of Eastern Jewry, Biller's novella seeks to intervene in existing memorial discourses: the sadomasochistic constellation is invoked to demonstrate the futility of the German-Jewish symbiosis. Biller's text can thus be said to perform the violent separation that he deems necessary and inevitable in a post-Holocaust world: "Juden und Deutsche [sind] seit Birkenau für immer geschiedene Leute" (*DgJ*, 107). Simultaneously, Biller's literary career and self-understanding as a pariah presuppose some form of connection to his German audience, thus exemplifying the unavoidability of a symbiosis that is, however, fundamentally negative. In response to this conundrum, references to Schulz and Sacher-Masoch seek to establish an alternative, untainted genealogy and a specifically (and exclusively) Jewish memorial space that draws on the rich traditions of Eastern European "ghetto writing" and a specifically Eastern-Jewish surrealism.

Notes

[1] Stefan Willeke, "Der Unzumutbare," *Zeitmagazin* 10/2017, 17 March 2017.

[2] Maxim Biller, *Liebe Heute* (Cologne: Kiepenheuer & Witsch, 2007).

[3] Maxim Biller, *Im Kopf von Bruno Schulz* (Cologne: Kiepenheuer & Witsch, 2013); henceforth cited in the text as *IKvBS*. In English: Maxim Biller, *Inside the Head of Bruno Schulz* (London: Pushkin Press, 2015).

[4] See Jay David Bolter and Richard Grusin, *Remediation: Understanding New Media* (Cambridge, MA: MIT Press, 2000); Astrid Erll and Ann Rigney, eds., *Mediation, Remediation, and the Dynamics of Cultural Memory* (Berlin/New York: de Gruyter, 2009); Astrid Erll, "Literature, Film, and the Mediality of Cultural Memory," in *A Companion to Cultural Memory Studies*, ed. Astrid Erll and Ansgar Nünning (Berlin and New York: de Gruyter, 2010), 389–98.

[5] Erll, "Literature, Film, and the Mediality of Cultural Memory," 392.

[6] On the interrelation between "remediation" and cultural memory see Astrid Erll and Ann Rigney, "Introduction: Cultural Memory and Its Dynamics," in *Mediation, Remediation, and the Dynamics of Cultural Memory*, 1–11.

[7] Both Schulz's *Die Zimtläden* and his graphic oeuvre contain obvious references to Leopold von Sacher-Masoch's seminal text *Venus im Pelz*, see Leopold von Sacher-Masoch, *Venus im Pelz* (Frankfurt am Main: Fischer Verlag, 2013).

[8] On the interrelation between fascism and tabooed forms of sexuality and desire see for example Marcus Stiglegger, *Sadiconazista: Faschismus und Sexualität im Film* (St. Augustin: Gardez! Verlag, 1999).

9 The "Traktat über die Schneiderpuppen" can be regarded as the centerpiece of *Die Zimtläden*, as it outlines Schulz's aesthetic program and provides crucial insights into Schulz's poetics. See Schulz, *Die Zimtläden*, 51–66. Henceforth cited in the text as *DZ* and page number.

10 On the topic of "ghetto writing" see *Ghetto Writing: Traditional and Eastern Jewry in German-Jewish Literature from Heine to Hilsenrath*, ed. Anne Fuchs and Florian Krobb (Rochester, NY: Camden House, 1999) and Gabriele von Glasenapp, "Deutsch-jüdische Ghettoliteratur," in *Handbuch der deutsch-jüdischen Literatur*, ed. Hans-Otto Horch (Berlin and Boston: de Gruyter/ Oldenbourg, 2015), 407–21.

11 On the theme of sadomasochism in Schulz's work see S. D. Chrostowska, "'Masochistic Art of Fantasy': The Literary Works of Bruno Schulz in the Context of Modern Masochism," *Russian Literature* 55 (2004): 469–501.

12 I am referring to an edition of Schulz's work published by the German dtv-Verlag that resulted from a 1992 exhibition in the *Münchner Stadtmuseum*. I thank Ulrike Henneke from Kiepenheuer & Witsch for her generous help with tracking down this source.

13 On this and other dichotomies in Schulz's text see Iwona Janicka, "Mapping the Father. The Application of Greimassian Semiotics to Bruno Schulz's *Sklepy Cynamonowe*," *Welt der Slaven: Internationale Halbjahresschrift für Slavistik* LV (2010): 45–66.

14 The subversive potential of Adela's actions is also stressed by Chrostowska, along with the irony resulting from the role reversal she provokes—the formless, passive female ultimately dominates the active, male (wannabe) demiurge, see Chrostowska, "'Masochistic Art of Fantasy,'" 475–77.

15 It should be noted that Biller changes the housekeeper's name slightly, compared to Schulz's original text; she is transformed from Adela into Adele.

16 Gilles Deleuze, *Masochism: Coldness and Cruelty & Venus in Furs*, trans. Jean McNeil (New York: Zone Books, 1991).

17 However, Schulz's writing is still marked by the anti-oedipal impulse which, according to Deleuze, is at the heart of the masochistic figuration—the father slowly but surely vanishes from the fictional universe of *Die Zimtläden*; see Deleuze, *Masochism*, 47–68.

18 *Bruno Schulz. Das graphische Werk 1892–1942* (Munich: dtv, 2000); henceforth cited in the text as *BSgW*.

19 See Chrostowska, "'Masochistic Art of Fantasy,'" 497n13.

20 See *Bruno Schulz: Das graphische Werk*, 61.

21 See *Bruno Schulz: Das graphische Werk*, 63.

22 Astrid Erll, "Travelling Memory," *Parallax* 17, no. 4 (2011): 4–18.

23 Chrostowska also points to "misogynistic impulses" in Schulz's writing. Moreover, visual references to the topos of the *femme fatale* can be frequently found in Schulz's graphic works. See Chrostowska, "'Masochistic Art of Fantasy,'" 489.

24 Maxim Biller, *Der gebrauchte Jude: Selbstporträt* (Frankfurt am Main: Fischer Verlag, 2001); henceforth cited in the text as *DgJ*.

[25] Feminizing Thomas Mann could point to either an ironic reversal of the anti-Semitic stereotype of the effeminate Jew, or to Gustav von Aschenbach's character in *Der Tod in Venedig* and thus an allusion to the real Mann's alleged homosexuality. The fact that the fake Mann is described as wearing make-up in the novella (*IKvBS*, 50) points to the latter explanation.

[26] The fake Mann is not only connected to the *femme fatale*. Because his fakeness and status as a mere "Abbild" (*IKvBS*, 33) are continually stressed, he is also cast as a "false idol" and thus connected to the practice of idolatry, one of the worst transgressions in Judaism.

[27] I am referring to the iconic stanza from Celan's *Todesfuge*: "Schwarze Milch der Frühe wir trinken dich nachts / wir trinken dich mittags der Tod ist ein Meister aus / Deutschland / wir trinken dich abends und morgens wir trinken und trinken / der Tod ist ein Meister aus Deutschland sein Auge ist blau / er trifft dich mit bleierner Kugel er trifft dich genau / ein Mann wohnt im Haus dein goldenes Haar Margarete / er hetzt seine Rüden auf uns er schenkt uns ein Grab in der / Luft / er spielt mit den Schlangen und träumet der Tod ist ein / Meister aus Deutschland." The complete poem can be found in Paul Celan, *Ausgewählte Gedichte. Zwei Reden* (Frankfurt am Main: Suhrkamp, 2nd ed., 1969), 18–19.

[28] Maxim Biller, *Harlem Holocaust* (Cologne: Kiepenheuer & Witsch, 1998); henceforth cited in the text as *HH*.

[29] Barbara Beßlich, "Unzuverlässiges Erzählen im Dienst der Erinnerung. Perspektiven auf den Nationalsozialismus bei Maxim Biller, Marcel Beyer und Martin Walser," in *Wende des Erinnerns? Geschichtskonstruktionen in der deutschen Literatur nach 1989*, ed. Barbara Beßlich, Katharina Grätz, and Olaf Hildebrand (Berlin: Erich Schmidt Verlag, 2006), 35–52, here 43.

[30] Jack Zipes, "The Contemporary German Fascination for Things Jewish: Toward a Minor Jewish Culture," in *Reemerging Jewish Culture in Germany: Life and Literature Since 1989*, ed. Sander L. Gilman and Karen Remmler (New York: New York University Press, 1994), 15–45.

[31] Dan Diner, "Negative Symbiose. Deutsche und Juden nach Auschwitz," in *Ist der Nationalsozialismus Geschichte? Zu Historisierung und Historikerstreit*, ed. Dan Diner (Frankfurt am Main: Fischer Verlag, 1987), 185–97. On the issue of the negative symbiosis in *Harlem Holocaust* see also Rita Bashaw, "Comic Vision and 'negative Symbiosis' in Maxim Biller's *Harlem Holocaust* and Rafael Seligmann's *Der Musterjude*," in *Unlikely History: The Changing German-Jewish Symbiosis, 1945–2000*, ed. Leslie Morris and Jack Zipes (New York, NY: Palgrave, 2002), 264–76.

[32] Diner, "Negative Symbiose," 185.

[33] On the commodification and hypermediatization of Holocaust memory in *Harlem Holocaust* see Jefferson Chase, "Shoah Business. Maxim Biller and the Problem of Contemporary German-Jewish Literature," *German Quarterly* 74, no. 2 (2001): 111–31.

[34] Gustav Seibt, "Der letzte Augenblick der Unschuld. Ein Nachwort von Gustav Seibt," in Biller, *Harlem Holocaust*, 65.

Love and Cultures
of Exclusion

Precarious Subjects, Vulnerable Love: Thomas Melle's *3000 Euro*, Feridun Zaimoglu's *Isabel*, and Julia Wolf's *Alles ist jetzt*

Silke Horstkotte

OW CAN WE TALK ABOUT LOVE, how can we tell love stories in a contemporary situation characterized by precarity, vulnerability, and a persistent sense of crisis? A situation in which senses of the self and of its relation to its environment have become radically uncertain, fractured, and tenuous? In the past decade, "precarity" and "vulnerability" have become key concepts through which the humanities and social sciences address changing conditions of life and work in the present age, including the increase in non-permanent forms of work, casual labor, unpredictable life stories, erratic career patterns, and a lack of material and psychological welfare.[1] While "precarity" is most often associated with economic risk and social disenfranchisement, "vulnerability" commonly describes risks resulting from environmental and climate change, although the two terms are also sometimes used interchangeably.

From a philosophical perspective, "precarity" and "vulnerability" can also express a more general sense that the position of humans in this world is tenuous, that we are not masters of the world but are vulnerable to disease and death. It is in this sense that the two terms are introduced in Judith Butler's collection of essays *Precarious Life* (2004), one of the earliest works of cultural theory to engage with precarity and vulnerability on a conceptual level.[2] Originally written in the wake of the 9/11 attacks and intended as a critique of the ways in which some lives have become more precarious than others in the ensuing wars in Afghanistan and Iraq, Butler's essays have wide-ranging consequences for a philosophy of the subject. They propose a concept of the self that is not autonomous and self-determined but fundamentally dependent on others, not a disembodied inner sense of self but one embodied and embedded in an intersubjective web of relations.

In this chapter, I draw on Butler's subject philosophy to analyze three recent German novels which explore the narrative and aesthetic consequences of precarity and vulnerability in the context of love stories. Thomas Melle's *3000 Euro* (2014), Feridun Zaimoglu's *Isabel* (2014), and Julia Wolf's *Alles ist jetzt* (Everything is Now, 2013) present us with protagonists on the social margins whose lives are coming apart, who are radically dependent on others. By telling their stories as love stories— disappointing and failing love stories, to be sure, but love stories none- theless—these novels highlight the subject-philosophical side of precarity, although they also tell of economic precarity. While it is possible to read the texts as sociocritical interventions in contemporary public debates about economic poverty, their literary impact goes beyond such immedi- ate concerns, as the novels by Melle, Zaimoglu, and Wolf also participate in the development of a new poetics of the precarious subject and its vul- nerable relationship to others.

This development stands in a longer literary tradition of portraying weak or failing subjects and making them the focal points of an aesthetic investigation of subjectivity. Core texts in the literary history of the modern subject such as Karl Philipp Moritz's *Anton Reiser* (1785/86) or Johann Wolfgang von Goethe's *Die Leiden des jungen Werthers* (The Sorrows of Young Werther, 1774) trace unsuccessful individuation processes and nar- rate the failure of their protagonists to achieve an autonomous subjectiv- ity. *Werther* in particular is an important intertext for Melle, Wolf, and Zaimoglu because it explores, in a way that has become highly canonic in the German literary tradition, the ambivalent role of love in healing or else in deepening a precarious subjectivity. For Werther, love provides the means to experience himself as an individuum. But such an absolute view of love raises expectations that can never be fulfilled, as the novel's climax makes abundantly clear. Many twentieth-century writers, especially in the Expressionist movement of the 1910s and the *Neue Sachlichkeit* movement of the 1920s, have therefore been extremely critical of the exalted ideal of love in the *Sturm und Drang* and its Romantic legacy.

My chapter considers the precarious subjects and vulnerable love sto- ries in Melle, Wolf, and Zaimoglu in light of this literary history, with a particular emphasis on Thomas Melle's *3000 Euro*, since it is the one among my sample texts that most emphatically cites the ideal of love's healing power. But Melle is not naïve about the power of vulnerability and mutual recognition to institute a new community. In *3000 Euro*, he uses the meeting of two different types of precarious subjects to not only narrate a new type of love story on the edges of society, but also to ques- tion the aesthetic means by which novels represent people who are barely self-aware. The novel's distanced attitude towards its protagonists refer- ences narrative techniques from Expressionist writing and from 1920s *Neue Sachlichkeit*.

Wolf and Zaimoglu, too, draw on Weimar-era tropes, but combine them with the brutally disillusioned description of sexuality that Elfriede

Jelinek developed in her novels. While Melle pays elegiac reference to the trope of Romantic love (and shows how it does not work), the other writers reject the idea of love's healing power outright. The severity of their rejection, the close connection they draw between a vulnerable subjectivity and economic precarity, and the cold style in which these are registered, reveal *Alles ist jetzt* and *Isabel* to be indebted to the more radical novels of the late Weimar Republic such as Erich Kästner's *Fabian* (1931). When read against this background, the novels by Melle, Wolf, and Zaimoglu can function as a critique both of the concept of the autonomous individuum and of the literary discourse of love associated with it. The next sections of this chapter begin by outlining the historical and philosophical background to my argument before focusing on the two key concepts of precarity and vulnerability through which I read the three novels.

Love and Literature

Since the mid-eighteenth century, the discourse of love in German literature has been intimately linked to a new understanding of individuality. The "Sattelzeit" of German history from 1770 to 1830 marks not only a radical semantic shift in which many key concepts of modernity such as "history" or indeed "modernity" acquired the meaning they still possess today,[3] but also witnesses a deep-seated shift in the history of mentalities. A new, heightened awareness of contingency—the idea that the world can be changed—led to a new self-description of the human person as an individuum who emerges from such awareness.[4] But the idea of change has a dark, depressive back side: it can be experienced as a loss of a structuring and stabilizing exterior environment. Released from a fixed and stable order, the new individuum only ever has the whole of the world, another absolute, as its counterpart.[5]

In this development of a new idea of the self, literature played a key role, as the new experience of the self as an individuum was first explored in love novels of the period and through the literary practice of letter writing. In the late eighteenth century, the novel was the key medium which shaped understandings of the self and of its relationships with its environment, providing codes of speech and behavior that were often explicitly intended to regulate love relationships in real life. In the earliest study of the idea of love in eighteenth-century German literature, first published in 1922, Paul Kluckhohn outlines the development of two distinct but related discourses of love—sentimental love and metaphysical or religious love—and describes their impact on contemporary readers, which can be traced through love letters written in the period.[6]

The sentimental model of love presented in, for instance, Christian Fürchtegott Gellert's *Das Leben der schwedischen Gräfin von G**** (The Life of the Swedish Countess of G***, 1747/48) or in Sophie von

La Roche's *Geschichte des Fräuleins von Sternheim* (The Story of Miss Sternheim, 1771) conceives of love as an emotion closely related to friendship. Love makes and maintains connections, and the patterns of speech and behavior through which it does so can be learned from literary presentations of it. Indeed, the German authors who drew on this model have themselves acquired it from the English sentimental tradition, especially from Samuel Richardson.[7] Metaphysical love, on the other hand, is less regulated and almost impossible to police. This religiously exalted view of love was developed and popularized in the poetry of Klopstock, but found its most influential presentation in Goethe's *Werther*. Kluckhohn describes how Goethe's readers reveled in the feeling of being completely filled by love, to knowing nothing but love, to becoming better and more truthful through love, and relegating the hopes that remain unfulfilled by love in this world to eternity—just like Werther.[8]

A closer reading of *Die Leiden des jungen Werthers* reveals that both the sentimental and the metaphysical/religious model of love are present in the novel. Lotte and Albert closely follow the sentimental code of love as it was established in the novels of Richardson and Gellert.[9] Unlike Lotte and Albert, however, Werther refuses to participate in this code of behavior. Werther believes that an absolute love exists and is possible. Yet he is happiest not when he is with Lotte, but when he sits in Wahlheim, the village where he lives (literally, "chosen home"), growing peas, reading Homer, and thinking about Lotte.[10] This is presented as an idyll, but the problem with idylls is that they are located in the past and have no place in the present—even the ancients knew this. Werther's suicide is not the tragic result of insurmountable social circumstances but an inevitable and logical outcome of the metaphysical model of love; this is a love that can be consummated only in the other world. For this reason, it does not matter to Werther that Lotte is promised to another man, and he does not even attempt to win her over when this is still possible at the beginning of the novel, when Lotte is only "as good as" betrothed to Albert.[11]

It is precisely because it presents a love that is dissolved from all social context that the Werther model continues to speak to readers to this day, whereas the sentimental novels of Gellert and La Roche have been largely forgotten. But that does not mean that Goethe's novel itself is devoid of context. On the contrary, as Karl Eibl has convincingly shown, the literature of the *Sturm und Drang* reacted to a historically and culturally specific shift of mentalities, and it found a way of symbolically expressing the unsolved problems associated with this shift—experiences of contingency and an isolated individuum—by connecting them to three absolutes: society, love, and death, all of which are constituted in *Sturm und Drang* writing as liminal areas in which the absolute will of the individuum fails because of the world's contingency.[12] Love is for Werther an expression of his individuality, a medium for realizing the wholeness and integrity of his interior.[13] On the one hand, the novel emphatically celebrates the new experience of individuality; on the other hand, however, it presents a perceptive analysis of the problems and dangers that go along with being a self-determined individuum.[14] In the character of Werther, Goethe drafts a model of individuality, makes that model fail, and dismisses it.[15] The novel also shows that this failure is closely linked to the exalted concept of love which it receives from Klopstock and to its inheritance of functions which were previously associated with religion: guaranteeing the highest form of human life and experience.[16]

Beyond the Self

Our present age can be seen as a second "saddle period" of social and semantic change, in which new concepts of the self seek to describe a new sense of being in the world. Aspects of this wide-ranging change include a shifting sense of time and place produced by the interlinked phenomena of globalization, acceleration, and the rise of the "network society";[17] the crumbling of old political institutions under the weight of populist movements across Europe; fundamental changes in the organization of paid employment; and a persistent sense of cultural lateness that has been identified as a new historical mood after the end of postmodernism.[18] Many of these changes have been linked to the dismantling of the "human" as a category, the disappearance of the human subject, and to the apprehension that we have entered a "posthuman" phase of history.

According to the posthuman theory of Rosi Braidotti, "posthumanism" expresses a "life beyond the self" that results from the insight that "contemporary science and biotechnologies affect the very fiber and structure of the living and have altered dramatically our understanding of what counts as the basic frame of reference for the human today."[19] Posthuman theory has as its premise the "global sense of inter-connection" provided by the network society—a sense of connection not only between humans but also "between the human and the non-human environment, including the urban, social and political, which creates a web of intricate inter-dependencies."[20] From a philosophical perspective, the human subject is reconceived as an embodied, embedded, and relational process that can overcome old boundaries between people, things, and animals.[21]

Other theorists take a darker view of the dismantling of the human subject. In the essay collection *Precarious Life*, Judith Butler unfolds a philosophy of human life under conditions of precarity and vulnerability. Her view of the human subject as not strong, not autonomous is based on the insight, gained throughout the twentieth century but sharpened by the 9/11 attacks, that "we can be injured, that others can be injured, that we are subject to death at the whim of another."[22] Butler concludes that we are fundamentally reliant on others on whom our lives depend, including "people I do not know and may never know."[23] Vulnerability, thus understood, constitutes a universal condition of being human. According to the legal scholar Martha Fineman, "[the] vulnerable subject is the embodiment of the realization that vulnerability is a universal and constant aspect of the human condition. Dependency and vulnerability are not deviant, but natural and inevitable."[24] Together with other "weak" conceptions of subjectivity which have been devised to critique the "strong," autonomous subject of Western idealist philosophy, the concept of vulnerability highlights phenomenological aspects of subjective experience, especially embodiment and embeddedness. For Judith Butler, "[loss] and vulnerability seem to follow from our being socially constituted bodies, attached to others, at risk of losing those attachments, exposed to others, at risk of violence by virtue of that exposure."[25] At the same time, however, vulnerability is also the basis of our political and ethical responsibilities, so much so that "each of us is constituted politically in part by virtue of the social vulnerability of our bodies."[26]

Butler sees political as well as corporeal forms of weakness as crucial aspects of contemporary subjectivity that philosophical theories of the subject have to account for more closely. In the essay "Violence, Mourning, Politics," Butler considers a "dimension of political life that has to do with our exposure to violence and our complicity in it."[27] Looking at the uneven distribution of grief for victims of the 9/11 attacks and the wars fought in their wake, Butler concludes that non-Western victims are not considered "grievable" by the media and public, that they "cannot be mourned because they are always already lost."[28] For Butler, non-grievable lives challenge our very understanding of what it means to be human, as "humans not regarded as humans" lay bare a "restricted conception of the human that is based upon their exclusion."[29] The corporeal and social vulnerability that becomes discernible in these lives necessitates a different view of the human subject. Butler argues that the language of distinct, autonomous, individual subjects is important legally and politically because it allows us to claim equal rights for all. But it is not an adequate description of who we really are: corporeal beings, bounded by "passions of grief and rage, all of which tear us from ourselves, bind us to others, transport us, undo us, implicate us in lives that are not our own."[30] Faced with the open-ended incarceration of so-called "enemy combatants" at Guantánamo Bay, which violates international law, Butler distances herself from philosophical deconstruction of the subject. In a global political situation in which life has become "precarious," an important task for the humanities consists in regaining an integral idea of subjectivity—but one that at the same time acknowledges that the self is not as autonomous as we like to think.

Against a Cartesian mind-body dualism, the concept of vulnerability emphasizes that we relate to the world through our bodies, through senses and emotions, and thus highlights conditions of selfhood such as passivity and the dependence on others that have been marginalized or silenced in earlier conceptions of subjectivity. In literary engagements with subjectivity, however, vulnerability has long been an integral aspect—especially, as the example of the eighteenth-century novel shows, in the context of love stories. But when vulnerability, a general condition of being human, becomes compounded by precarity, a more specific economic and/or political condition, the individuum in love becomes much more radically unstable than its eighteenth-century predecessors were.

Precarity in Melle's *3000 Euro*

Someone or something is "precarious," according to the *Oxford English Dictionary*, when they are vulnerable to the will or decision of others; dependent on chance or circumstance; or fraught with physical danger or insecurity.[31] A precarious person is at risk, insecure, unstable. When Judith Butler published *Precarious Life* in 2004, calling a human life (rather than a thing, structure, or argument) "precarious" was quite unusual. Since the 2008 global financial crisis, however, "precarious" and "precarity" have become important bywords for social and economic insecurity. The terms are frequently used in the emerging field of poverty studies, which associates precarity with such contemporary concerns as migration and globalization and their effects on the labor market;[32] protest movements and the sustainability crisis;[33] insecure employment in the creative professions, especially the arts and media;[34] and youth unemployment.[35]

Literary studies, too, contribute to this discourse of precarity as an economic condition in times of crisis. In the edited collection *Narrating Poverty and Precarity in Britain*, Barbara Korte and Frédéric Regard define precarity as referring to "insecure existential conditions that result from economic and social circumstances."[36] Precarity is here seen as the human face of poverty, the existential feel of being poor or in danger of becoming poor. The representation of poverty in literature often deals with this phenomenal quality, rather than with economic conditions per se; it "coincides with periods of a heightened social awareness of poverty," for instance the peak of poverty literature in 1930s Britain,[37] without being identical with such awareness. Literary representations contribute to a wider discourse on poverty by giving faces and voices to poverty, asking readers to see situations from the perspective of those who are afflicted.[38] It is this face-giving aspect that Korte and Regard have in mind when using the term "precarity." Judith Butler's concept of "precarious life," however, reminds us that precarity runs deeper than that. Precarious conditions that are caused by external (economic or political) factors have important implications for our understanding of subjectivity, of agency, and of life itself. The new interest in human weakness and vulnerability reacts to the loss of optimistic belief in progress after the disillusionment with the political utopias of the twentieth century and to the experience of war, violence, and disenfranchisement after 9/11. At the same time, discourses of weakness and vulnerability are effects of a philosophical critique of the autonomous subject which ensues from these historical developments.

Thomas Melle's *3000 Euro* studies these two dimensions of precarity through a tightly interwoven double plot.[39] The novel's title draws immediate attention to the precarious existence of its two protagonists: 3,000 Euro is an almost unachievable sum for Anton, a failed law student who piled up a debt of over ten thousand Euros during a psychotic breakdown and now lives in a homeless hostel, and for Denise, a single mother who tries in vain to collect the pay she is owed for a porn shoot. Ironically, however, three thousand Euros happens to be not only the portion of his debt that Anton has to go to court for, but also the sum Denise is owed by the producers of the porn films she acted in. Throughout the novel, their two stories move in parallel as the narrative perspective switches back and forth between the protagonists. Anton and Denise meet in the supermarket where Denise works as a cashier and where Anton cashes in the beer bottles he finds in the trash. Both are drawn to each other because each recognizes that the other stands out from their own social situation. Denise had done well at school and even planned at one time to study for a teaching degree, but ultimately did not have the courage to leave her working-class background behind. Anton, too, comes from a working-class family, the gifted child of a single mother with mental problems. He went to university on a scholarship, but became increasingly mentally unstable, dropping steadily down the social scale from long-term student to taxi driver to sleeping rough and eating in soup kitchens.

Further parallels between the two storylines concern the characters' skirmishes with the recalcitrant bureaucracy of social services. Anton drowns in applications for housing, for a bank account, and for social benefits, while Denise is fighting to get her young daughter, who suffers from a learning disability, into a special education program. Finally, Anton resorts to begging old friends and former lovers for cash, and Denise goes back to the porn producers to personally demand her outstanding payment—only to be coerced into performing in yet another porn shoot. All of these details are reminiscent of the social drama in social realist films by British director Ken Loach (*Riff-Raff,* 1991; *Ladybird Ladybird,* 1994) or by the Belgian director duo the brothers Dardenne (especially *Deux jours, une nuit,* 2014). However, the overt focus of *3000 Euro* is not on the characters' economic struggles but on their subjectivity and mental health, although the novel also foregrounds other dimensions of precarity: class and culture, subjectivity, and intersubjectivity. Anton's and Denise's loss of identity deeply impacts on their unfolding love story. Anton is initially uncomfortable with dating a supermarket cashier, both because this seems somehow below the social position into which he was once expected to move, and because he now does not know how to position himself at all any more:

> Noch nie hat er eine Kassiererin gedatet. Dabei hing er in seiner Kindheit nur mit Arbeiterkindern ab, denn er war ja selbst eines. Aber das blendende Abitur und das angefangene Jurastudium haben ihn der eigenen Klasse entrissen und—ja, was? Auf eine andere soziale Ebene gehoben? Einem unaufhaltsamen Aufstieg zugeführt? Nein, im Ungefähren belassen, nirgendwo wirklich abgesetzt. (*3000 E*, 68)

However, Anton's precarity goes beyond his social situation. The narrative discourse of the novel situates him on the outmost margins of humanity, deliberately presenting him as a test case for what it means to be alive and human. On the scale of grievable lives, Anton lies far outside anything imagined by Judith Butler. The novel makes this point when the very first sentence asserts Anton's humanity only to call that very humanity, and our recognition of it, into question: "Da ist ein Mensch drin, auch wenn es nicht so scheint. Unter den Flicken und Fetzen bewegt sich nichts. Die Passanten gehen an dem Haufen vorbei, als wäre er nicht da. Jeder sieht ihn, aber die Blicke wandern sofort weiter. Zwei Flaschen stehen neben dem Haufen, trübe und abgegriffen. Die Sonne knallt herunter. Es riecht streng, nach Urin, nach Säure und frühem Alter" (*3000 E*, 7). In this as well as in other passages, the novel's impersonal narrator speaks over Anton's head, addressing an audience that might include the pedestrians passing Anton by, and calling on our empathy: should we stop and take notice of Anton, really see him? Would that make him more human, a more grievable life? The narrator's attitude, however, is not empathic. The narratorial consciousness is situated at a level far above Anton's twitching body. The same elevated narratorial position continues in the following paragraphs, in which Anton serves as the focal character: "Anton träumt einen dünnen Traum, in ihm sind alle Arschlöcher weg. . . . Wenn Anton träumt in diesen Wochen, dann von den alten Zeiten, die es so nie gab" (*3000 E*, 7). The novel's narration is omniscient in a peculiarly selective manner: the narrative can zoom into Anton's consciousness and let us see the world through him, but can also keep its distance, evaluating his dreams and thoughts with an almost clinical precision and coldness—and it can frequently do both things at once, resulting in a mutually contradictory combination of internal and external focalization in which Anton's focal filtering of the novel's world is subject to a higher-level filtering by the narrator which goes against the grain of Anton's prior filtering. Thus, we are made aware of Anton's thoughts, feelings, and perceptions, but we are simultaneously warned not to trust Anton's fallible sense of self.

Alternating sections of *3000 Euro* focus on Denise, towards whom the narrative's attitude is far less distanced. Readers get a more direct, and less conflicting, insight into Denise's thoughts and perceptions. The narrative makes frequent use of free indirect discourse, which double-voices the narrator's voice and the character's vision, and is generally less outspokenly judgmental towards Denise. It is important to take precise note of this varying treatment of the two protagonists because large parts of the novel are explicitly concerned with the characters' perception of the world and with their impression of being perceived by others. It is Anton's and Denise's peculiar individual experiences of being in the field of vision that constitute the strongest expression of a precarious subjectivity in *3000 Euro,* and the slanting of that experience through the voice and style of the narrator acts as a commentary on these experiences that is directed at the novel's readers. Frequent attention is drawn, for instance, towards Denise's feeling of being watched by shoppers in the supermarket where she works as a cashier. Her feelings of being sexualized by the gaze of others stem from the shame she feels at having acted in the two porn films. Denise is convinced that every customer has seen the clips online and will recognize her—as some of the shoppers, indeed, do. But Denise is not defenseless. She returns the customers' gaze, evaluating shoppers based on the groceries in their carts (even though her employers discourage this). Just as the customers' gaze robs her of her subject status by turning her into a sexual object, so Denise's gaze in turn objectifies the customers, making them data in a statistic: "Es stellen sich keine Bilder der Wohnungen und Kühlschränke dazu mehr ein, es ist eher wie eine Notenvergabe, ein schnelles Einschätzen des Lebensstandards, was eigentlich verboten ist. Man soll blind sein" (*3000 E*, 13).

Such defense mechanisms are not open to Anton, who only slowly (and never fully) begins to realize his own situation. "Wenn Anton zurückdenkt, fragt er sich, wann die Weichen gestellt wurden, wo er die Abzweigung genommen hat, die ihn nach und nach von den alten Freunden und Kommilitonen entfernte" (*3000 E*, 85). The novel implies that this wrong turn was not one that Anton deliberately took but that it is his mental illness that radically separates him from all other characters. In his autobiographical essay *Die Welt im Rücken,* Thomas Melle reveals that Anton's story is a loosely fictionalized version of Melle's own.[40] Close similarities concern not only the framing data—family history, academic career, debts, and trial—but also the neurological condition of character and author, and the style in which their psychotic breakdowns are presented in the two books. Thomas Melle describes how his first manic episode began with a "Gefühlsüberschuss": "Ein Schock durchfährt die Nerven, Kaskaden von ungerichteten Emotionen schießen hinab und schwappen wieder hoch. Die Empfindung völliger Haltlosigkeit stellt sich ein" (*WiR*, 42). In a later passage, he connects this unanchored state with the image of his brain running away on its own: "Das Hirn stürzt herrenlos davon" (*WiR*, 43). In the fictional context of *3000 Euro*, Melle uses a different metaphor for the same feeling of the brain getting out of control: "[Anton] kann es nicht mehr genau sagen, aber eines Morgens dann, nach mehreren wilden Nächten des Ausgehens und Trinkens, schien sein Hirn umgekippt zu sein wie ein vergifteter See. Das wusste er zu dem Zeitpunkt jedoch nicht. Er wachte auf und hatte Gedanken an Gott" (*3000 E*, 122). *Die Welt im Rücken* similarly describes grandiose delusions of a religious nature.

For Thomas Melle, having a neurological disorder causes a radical rift between the sick person and the rest of humanity, creating two categories of subjects: vulnerable and non-vulnerable ones. In *Die Welt im Rücken*, he explains:

> Hier die Normalen, selbst von Neurosen, Phobien und echten Verrücktheiten durchzogen, aber alle liebenswert, alle mit einem Augenzwinkern integrierbar, während dort die Verrückten mit ihren Unverständlichkeiten hadern, schlichtweg nicht mehr einzuordnen sind, nicht zu ironisieren oder durch Humor kommensurabel zu machen. Das ist das Fatum der Irren: ihre Unvergleichlichkeit, der Verlust jeglichen Bezugs zum Leben der restlichen Gesellschaft. Der Kranke ist der Freak und als solcher zu meiden, denn er ist ein Symbol des Nichtsinns, und solche Symbole sind gefährlich, nicht zuletzt für das fragile Sinnkonstrukt namens Alltag. Der Kranke ist, genau wie der Terrorist, aus der Ordnung der Gesellschaft gefallen, gefallen in einen feindlichen Abgrund des Unverständnisses. (*WiR*, 15)

Despite the similarities between the two books, this rift is much more radical in *3000 Euro* than it is in *Die Welt im Rücken*. There are two reasons for this. The first lies on the level of plot and concerns the different outcome of the two stories. When Thomas Melle ends up in a homeless hostel, he is saved by love. His girlfriend Ella brings him food, battles bureaucracy on his behalf, and helps him regain an independent life. Anton, on the other hand, only has a brief affair with Denise. Ultimately, Denise decides to spend the three thousand Euros on herself and her daughter. The second reason lies on the level of discourse and concerns the narrative voice through which these stories are presented. In *Die Welt im Rücken*, Thomas Melle boldly claims his story as his own, characterizing his rendering of it as "eine Form von Wahrhaftigkeit, von Konkretion, jedenfalls . . . den Versuch einer solchen" (*WiR*, 56). Although his autobiography tells of a repeated and growing loss of control over his own self, the act of telling that story in his own voice re-establishes that control. In *3000 Euro*, as I have already pointed out, the narrative address is directed towards the audience, but away from Anton. The novel's narrative discourse, then, is set up to distance itself and its readership from the protagonist. This is made explicit in a passage shortly after the novel's opening sentences quoted above:

> Humpeln die Penner an uns vorbei, berührt uns das unangenehm. Nicht nur ist es eine ästhetische Belästigung, sondern auch ein moralischer Vorwurf. Wieso bitte ist dieser Mensch so tief gesunken, welche Gesellschaft lässt einen derartigen Verfall zu? Das ist schon kein Mensch mehr, das ist ein Ding. Dann geht man weiter, angewidert fast, und verscheucht den Eindruck, lässt das Ding hinter sich zurück. Ein Schicksal, ja, unter vielen, und sicher nicht meins. (*3000 E*, 15)

The use of the plural pronoun "uns" and the impersonal "man" creates a community between the narrator, the novel's readers, and the passersby in the scene that is evoked, even if the narrative is also critical of the views ascribed to that community. This creates a double bind: at the same time as the narrative invites us to step out of a perception that regards Anton as "kein Mensch mehr, . . . ein Ding," it reinforces Anton's dehumanization through its distanced attitude.

Vulnerability in Zaimoglu's *Isabel* and Wolf's *Alles ist jetzt*

As a concept, vulnerability draws attention to the corporeal side of subjectivity, which is highlighted in phenomenology.[41] Vulnerability is a condition of our embodiment; when we speak about vulnerability, we are inevitably speaking about subjects who are not autonomous because they are bound up in intersubjective relationships and in subject-object relationships through which they come into being. Vulnerability accentuates the negative side of intersubjectivity: a vulnerable body is susceptible to wounding and exploitation, the passive recipient of external harm and injury. But for Judith Butler, vulnerability also has a positive side, as it enables a rethinking of new forms of bonding, pointing out that openness is an inevitable condition of our relational being. If conceived as such a double-faced concept, how does vulnerability relate to love, which itself marks off an autonomous subjectivity because in love, one surrenders to another person? How is vulnerability imagined in the novels, and what consequences does the imagination of vulnerability have for literary discourses of love? Can vulnerability transcend the negativity that is often associated with it?

Like *3000 Euro*, the novels by Feridun Zaimoglu and Julia Wolf rely on stylistic means to create a distance towards their characters. That distance has consequences for the implicit view of human life and the possibility of human love presented in both texts. *Alles ist jetzt* and *Isabel* portray people on the margins of society as existences that are coming apart.[42] Zaimoglu's heroine Isabel stumbles aimlessly through the dark underbelly of Berlin, through the misery of soup kitchens and pedestrian subways. Isabel meets the soldier Marcus, who has been suffering from PTSD since his deployment in Kosovo, and she falls in love with him. Together, the two set out to discover the circumstances that led to their mutual friend Juliette's suicide. Isabel and Marcus spend a night together, but the image of love presented in the novel is so bleak that nothing can ever come of this, and the night remains inconsequential. The reasons for this are much less obvious than in *3000 Euro*. Isabel has become estranged from her Turkish family, and her economic situation is precarious, but no external factor can explain the protagonist's existential forsakenness. From a self-chosen Bohemian precarity, Isabel seems to have descended into real poverty, yet the novel does not make any effort to explain the circumstances that led to this descent. Unlike the sociocritical literature of the 1970s and 1980s, for instance Günter Wallraff's documentary *Ganz unten* (Lowest of the Low, 1983), Zaimoglu does not aim to compel his readers to investigate social ills. Instead, Zaimoglu focuses on aesthetic innovation by translating Isabel's poverty of being into a depleted language that he drives to the boundaries of literary style.

Especially when presenting Isabel's consciousness by way of free indirect discourse, the narrative relies on very short sentences, often without a verb, some consisting of only one word: "Sie legte auf und schämte sich. Dummer Einfall. Auf der Küchenanrichte stand ein großer Saftbeutel mit Zapfhahn. Morgentrunk" (*I*, 10). Sometimes these snippets of thoughts contain highly creative metaphors: "Draußen: tropfender Mond" (*I*, 11). This creativity, however, finds no outside expression in Isabel's precarious life. Besides Isabel, Marcus serves as a second focal character whose mental life is rendered in a distinctive "mind style":[43] "Lästiges Insekt fliegt ihm um den Kopf. Keine Wespe, kein Grund, es wegzuwedeln. Sollte er an der Tür klopfen? Stramme, magere Frau—würde auf ihn losgehen. Würde schreien" (*I*, 48). Like scribbled shorthand notes, these short statements serve as abbreviations for the more complex thought processes and ideas of the two characters. Both their style and their imagery can be traced directly to the legacy of German Expressionism—the moon metaphor, for instance, recurs in the expressionist poems collected in Kurt Pinthus's *Menschheitsdämmerung*, for instance in Jakob von Hoddis's "Die Stadt," Georg Heym's "Die Dämonen der Städte," and Alfred Lichtenstein's "Nebel."[44]

Zaimoglu's characters are a kind of shorthand too. The narrative habitually refers to Marcus merely as "Soldat," without even a definitive article, framing his actions in prototypical soldier-ese: "Soldat stieg aus— Eingriff sofort" (*I*, 136). Isabel, meanwhile, is revealed to be the victim of her restrictive Turkish upbringing, from which she never entirely escapes. She refuses her parents' choice of partners for an arranged marriage, but she has internalized her parents' prudish view of sexuality so much that she can think of lovemaking only in the most brutal terms: "Dort hinter den Büschen rissen sie sich auf, seine Hände unter ihrem Pullover, sie saß mit nacktem Unterleib auf seinem Schoß" (*I*, 15). Her relationship with Marcus is entirely lacking in a conventional language of love: "Sie fühlte sich traurig gut, sie wollte ihn schlagen, er saß zu nah bei ihr. Kalter Kerl" (*I*, 158). When Isabel and Marcus finally make love, the novel again resorts to a violent language of ripping open that is reminiscent of the novels of Elfriede Jelinek, especially *Lust*: "Nackte Frau, nackter Mann, sie lag auf dem Sofa, er lag auf dem Boden. Es war wieder geschehen, sie hatte sich auf ihn gestürzt und mit ihm gerauft. Hatte fest in sein Ohrläppchen gebissen, als sie aufplatzte. Er fiel aufgerissen herunter" (*I*, 215–16).

As Jens Jessen remarks in his perceptive review for *Die Zeit*, *Isabel* is an anti-psychological novel: there are no discernible reasons for Isabel's hatred of all men. The novel goes to great pains to subvert possible attempts to find causes in Isabel's biography for her fear of sex and for her neurotic preoccupation with sexual purity. Isabel has come to Germany from Turkey, but her story does not follow the typical migrant experience. Her Turkish parents are modern, well-off, and oriented towards the West; in Germany, Isabel seeks a life in the gutter although there is no apparent need for her to do so. She has an apartment but prefers to spend her days with the homeless, sleeping under bridges, crawling through rubbish-infested bushes, and eating her meals in soup kitchens run by watery-eyed pastors. Jessen points to the important role that the novel's artificially scarce language plays in this subversion of psychological explanation, linking both the literary style and the rejection of psychology to the legacy of German Expressionism: "Mit *Isabel* sind wir nur topografisch in der Berliner Gegenwart, atmosphärisch sind wir um hundert Jahre zurück in der dampfenden, selbst in der Sentenz noch ekstatisch erhitzten Ausdruckswelt des jungen Brecht, bei Ernst Toller, Georg Kaiser und in der brachialen Verkürzung bei Carl Sternheim."[45]

The novel's disillusioned view of human existence and of human love can also be traced back to Expressionist literature and its interest in sick, disfigured, and dying bodies, as for instance in Gottfried Benn's early cycle of poems "Der Arzt," which begins with the emphatic statement "Mir klebt die süße Leiblichkeit / wie ein Belag am Gaumensaum,"[46] and which envisages love-making as something that takes place not between individuals but between bodies, and diseased and smelly bodies at that, a mechanical action devoid of emotions: "Mit Pickeln in der Haut und faulen Zähnen / paart sich das in ein Bett und drängt zusammen / und säet Samen in des Fleisches Furchen."[47]

Julia Wolf similarly uses a reduced language to make accessible a reduced experientiality. For narrative theorists such as Monika Fludernik, David Herman, or Marco Caracciolo, it is not plot, but experientiality, or the "impact of events on an experiencing mind" which constitutes narrativity: stories are imaginative experiences that engage the experience of readers.[48] Like in *Isabel*, however, readers of *Alles ist jetzt* do not get much access to the way in which the novel's characters experience events and situations—not because their consciousness is closed off by the narrative, and their thoughts are hidden, as, for example, in the camera-eye narration of Ernest Hemingway, but because the characters of *Alles ist jetzt* do not appear to have much of an inner life to begin with. As a consequence, here, too, love is reduced to sex and sex to something between violence and a commodity. Yet at the same time, the vestiges of the Romantic ideal of love remain on the horizon, serving as a measuring stick that indicates the failure of the novel's characters.

Wolf's heroine Ingrid lives an economically precarious life, always on the verge of bankruptcy, surrounded by broken characters, broken families, in a broken world. Ingrid's father left her mother without warning or explanation; now her mother has become a depressive alcoholic. Ingrid works in a cheap nightclub where Eastern European women perform live sex acts. These are described in a cold technical idiom even when Ingrid herself is anally raped on open stage at the request of a customer. The club's customers are members of a porn-satiated generation for whom sex constitutes a commodity unconnected to any emotions. "Die Show beginnt. Mona stakst auf die Bühne, Stilettos, sie nimmt auf spitzen Pobacken Platz, klappt ohne Umschweife vor den Jungs ihren Leib auseinander. Kein Raunen, ein Schnaps, ein alltäglicher Anblick" (*Aij*, 14). In an allusion to Irmgard Keun's novel *Das kunstseidene Mädchen* (The Artificial Silk Girl, 1932), Ingrid thinks of herself as a "kunstseidenes Mädchen . . . das gerade zur Arbeit geht" (*Aij*, 11). The sex scenes in *Alles ist jetzt*, too, build on styles developed in the context of Weimar-era *Neue Sachlichkeit*. But the prototype for Ingrid is less Irmgard Keun's heroine Doris, a naive girl with ideas above her station who hopes to be saved by the love of a wealthy man, than it is Erich Kästner's eponymous hero Fabian, an unemployed journalist for whom love equals sex, and sex is for sale in any brothel. Like Kästner's *Fabian*, *Alles ist jetzt* is couched in a style that is specifically designed to circumvent any "Pathos von der Stange"[49] and thus to prevent its readers from developing any emotions apart from disgust. Love, in *Fabian*, is "ein Zeitvertreib / Man nimmt dazu den Unterleib."[50]

But while in *Fabian* it is bigoted socialites who meet in the brothel, in *Alles ist jetzt* the haggard dead souls from Eastern Europe perform a globalized version of the disillusionment, the provincial version of which can be found in the stylistically similar sex scenes of Elfriede Jelinek and Marlene Streeruwitz. In particular, the staccato style through which Julia Wolf gives expression to her heroine's lack of development, playing it off against the norm of development which inheres in the form of the novel, seems indebted to the peculiar *écriture féminine* of Streeruwitz. The eternal now of Wolf's motto "Alles ist jetzt und alles wie immer" (*Aij*, 26 and passim) becomes particularly tortured in the sacrificial imagery of the rape scene, in which "Ingrid wird aufgebaut. Alle sind da, glotzen im spöttischen Halbkreis. Ingrid wird hingestellt, auf allen vieren, mit hängenden Brüsten, vor den senfgelben Kerl. Der reibt sich die Wampe und grinst" (*Aij*, 148). While she is being raped, Ingrid imagines her former lovers Jenny and Moritz attending the occasion, even fancying herself drawing strength from their presence—but these imaginings remain futile in the face of Ingrid's brutal violation, as she feels her skin tearing and bleeding: "Später ist alles jetzt und vorbei, die Bühne leer" (*Aij*, 151).

Love, Again

In his seminal study *Die Entstehung der Poesie*, Karl Eibl connects the development of a new language of love around 1800 with a new function of literature: that of processing unsolved social problems without coming to definitive solutions, because such solutions are impossible.[51] One of these unsolved problems, to which the new discourse of love seeks to provide answers, concerns the modern individual's lack of a fixed position in society. The period from about 1770 to 1830 marks the transition from a stratified (hierarchical) to a functionally differentiated society, characterized by a much more varied number of personal and social systems; single individuals no longer act in only one subsystem of society, but in many.[52] In this process, the individual self becomes the focus of experience, while its environment grows increasingly faceless, causing the individual to seek recognition and affirmation in a private sphere "that is still understandable, intimate and close," a sphere of family and friendship.[53] Romantic love, as we still know it today, becomes the medium in which a sheltered individuality may be facilitated and nurtured, and through which it is communicated.[54] Love, in this context, is understood as a cultural discourse produced in the sentimental novel from Richardson to Goethe. However, the concept of love that is developed in these texts is so fraught with expectations that it can only fall short. In his analyses of *Sturm und Drang* texts, Karl Eibl shows how fictional literature processes the problem of the placeless and fractured individual by offering a space of wholeness: love. But at the same time, literary texts since

Goethe's *Werther* show that such an absolute love, dissolved from other social bonds, is impossible, or is possible only in death.

Yet despite these conceptual problems, the sociologist Eva Illouz argues that love continues to be of overwhelming importance for the constitution of a social sense of worth.[55] Even today, "in the conditions of late modernity, it is the erotic question that best articulates the problem of reassurance, and . . . this has replaced the epistemic question in a shift that is fraught with the aporias of the self in modernity."[56] The three novels by Melle, Zaimoglu, and Wolf consider the problem of love—its promise of individuation and its well-known failure to guarantee individuation—in the particularly difficult context of precarious subjects. Anton, Isabel, and Ingrid are deeply affected by the economic forces of globalization, precarious employment, and the loss of significance of the working class. The general sense of crisis that surrounds them only deepens their failure to individuate, and it provides them with a radically disillusioned love language: "Ratten fraßen Ratten, Liebe ging zu Ende, Liebende lagen wie glühende Leichname nebeneinander," Isabel thinks as she moves out of the apartment she shared with her ex-boyfriend at the beginning of the novel (*I*, 7). Illouz argues that self-doubt in love is unequally distributed, with women being more vulnerable to doubts and failure. *Isabel* and *Alles ist jetzt* take such a gendered view of vulnerable love. In *3000 Euro*, however, the novel that most closely builds on Romantic love discourse, it is Anton who is the weaker partner. When he receives help, it is predominantly from women—his social worker Sonja, his friend Herrmann's wife Cathrin with whom he once had an "Ausrutscher" (*3000 E*, 29), his mother—and it is implied that these strong women emasculate him. Even before his descent into homelessness, Anton has been particularly vulnerable in love, holding a highly Romantic view of love that always gets disappointed: "So wurde seine erste Liebesbeziehung denn auch von der überhitzten Hochromantik erstickt, die Anton ausstrahlte und zugleich zu verstecken versuchte, die aber dennoch die Atmosphäre süßlich vergiftete und kein normales Gespräch zuließ" (*3000 E*, 93).

Isabel and *Alles ist jetzt* paint a consistently bleak picture of love: love is a myth from the past that has no place in a precarious present; only trashed fragments remain of it. *3000 Euro*, however, reinforces the old storylines: when Anton and Denise meet on a park bench, both feel that they can be honest with each other without having to conform to social stereotypes. But the novel also offers a counterperspective to Anton's Romantic view of love through the unromantic Denise, who decides: "Denise wird sich Anton einfach nehmen. Das hat sie entschieden. Wenn es ihr guttut, warum nicht. Es ist egal, ob sie zusammenpassen oder nicht. . . . Sie mag seine Nähe und fühlt sich von ihm angezogen. Mehr braucht es nicht" (*3000 E*, 156). The novel's climactic scene mediates the two protagonists' attitudes by having them make love while watching one of Denise's porn flicks together. Anton alleviates Denise's unease about the films by saying "Sieht doch ganz geil aus" (*3000 E*, 192); then, while both are getting dressed again, Denise checks her bank account and discovers that the outstanding porn money has finally arrived. But instead of helping Anton, she decides to take her daughter to New York on the vacation she has always wanted. Even when it is upheld, the old storyline of the love narrative does not lead anywhere anymore—not to healing and wholeness, but also not to death. We do not learn whether Anton is really dead, as Denise suspects. The best we can hope for from a love story about precarious subjects is a temporary and inconsequential connection.

Notes

Research for this chapter was generously funded by the European Union's Horizon 2020 program.

[1] See, e.g., Andrew Ross, *Nice Work If You Can Get It: Life and Labor in Precarious Times* (New York: New York University Press, 2009); Isabell Lorey, *State of Insecurity: Government of the Precarious* (London: Verso, 2015); Michael Curtin and Kevin Sanson, *Precarious Creativity: Global Media, Local Labor* (Oakland: University of California Press, 2016); Kiyoko Hagihara and Chisato Asahi, *Coping with Regional Vulnerability: Preventing and Mitigating Damages from Environmental Disasters* (Wiesbaden: Springer, 2016); Judith Butler, Zeynep Gambetti, and Letitia Sabsay, *Vulnerability in Resistance* (Durham, NC: Duke University Press, 2016); Tadeusz Rachwal, *Precarity and Loss: On Certain and Uncertain Properties of Life and Work* (Wiesbaden: Springer, 2017).

[2] Judith Butler, *Precarious Life: The Powers of Mourning and Violence* (London: Verso, 2004).

[3] Reinhart Koselleck, "Einleitung," in *Geschichtliche Grundbegriffe*, vol. 1, ed. Otto Brunner, Werner Conze, and Reinhart Koselleck (Stuttgart: Klett Cotta, 1979), xv. Kossellek's concept of the "saddle period" is metaphorically derived from the mountain saddle or col and describes the epoch threshold between early modernity (the period prior to the French Revolution) and modernity proper (nineteenth and twentieth centuries).

[4] Karl Eibl, *Die Entstehung der Poesie* (Frankfurt and Leipzig: Insel, 1995), 114.

[5] Eibl, *Die Entstehung der Poesie*, 128.

[6] Paul Kluckhohn, *Die Auffassung der Liebe in der Literatur des 18. Jahrhunderts und in der deutschen Romantik* [1922], 3rd ed. (Tübingen: Niemeyer, 1966).

[7] Friedrich, Hans-Erwin, "'Ewig lieben', zugleich aber 'menschlich lieben'? Zur Reflexion der empfindsamen Liebeskonzeption von Gellert und Klopstock bis Goethe und Jacobi," *Aufklärung* 13 (2001): 148–89.

[8] Kluckhohn, *Die Auffassung der Liebe*, 186.

[9] Friedrich, "'Ewig lieben,'" 174.

[10] Goethe, *Werther*, letter of 21 June, 28–30.

[11] Goethe, *Werther*, 25, "so gut als verlobt."

[12] Eibl, *Die Entstehung der Poesie*, 117.

[13] Friedrich, "'Ewig lieben,'" 170.

[14] Dirk Kemper, *"ineffabile": Goethe und die Individualitätsproblematik der Moderne* (Munich: Fink, 2004), 74.

[15] Dirk von Petersdorff: "'Ich soll nicht zu mir selbst kommen'. Werther, Goethe und die Formung moderner Subjektivität," *Goethe-Jahrbuch* 123 (2006): 67–85.

[16] Petersdorff, "'Ich soll nicht zu mir selbst kommen,'" 73.

[17] Hartmut Rosa, *Beschleunigung: Die Veränderung der Zeitstrukturen in der Moderne* (Frankfurt am Main: Suhrkamp, 2005); Manuel Castells, *The Rise of the Network Society* (Oxford: Blackwell, 2000).

[18] Jeffrey T. Nealon, *Post-Postmodernism, or, The Cultural Logic of Just-in-Time Capitalism* (Stanford, CA: Stanford University Press, 2012).

[19] Rosi Braidotti, *The Posthuman* (Cambridge: Polity, 2013), 40.

[20] Braidotti, *The Posthuman*, 40.

[21] Braidotti: *The Posthuman*, 41 and 49.

[22] Butler, *Precarious Life*, xii.

[23] Butler, *Precarious Life*, xii.

[24] Martha Albertson Fineman, "Equality, Autonomy, and the Vulnerable Subject in Law and Politics," in *Vulnerability: Reflections on a New Ethical Foundation for Law and Politics*, ed. Martha Albertson Fineman and Anna Grear (Farnham, Surrey and Burlington, VT: Ashgate, 2013), 13–28, here 17.

[25] Butler, *Precarious Life*, 20.

[26] Butler, *Precarious Life*, 20.

[27] Butler, *Precarious Life*, 19.

[28] Butler, *Precarious Life*, 32–34.

[29] Butler, *Precarious Life*, 33.

[30] Butler, *Precarious Life*, 25.

[31] *Oxford English Dictionary*, art. "precarious," acessed June 18, 2017, http://oed.com.

[32] Carl-Ulrik Schierup, Ronaldo Munck, Branka Likic-Brborić, and Anders Neergaard, *Migration, Precarity, and Global Governance: Challenges and Opportunities for Labour* (Oxford: Oxford University Press, 2015).

[33] Sanford F. Schram, *The Return of Ordinary Capitalism: Neoliberalism, Precarity, Occupy* (Oxford: Oxford University Press, 2015).

[34] Curtin and Sanson, *Precarious Creativity*.

[35] Lorenza Antonucci, Myra Hamilton, and Steven Roberts, *Young People and Social Policy in Europe: Dealing with Risk, Inequality and Precarity in Times of Crisis* (Basingstoke: Palgrave Macmillan, 2014).

[36] Barbara Korte and Frédéric Regard, *Narrating Poverty and Precarity in Britain* (Berlin and Boston: de Gruyter, 2014), 9.

[37] Korte and Regard, *Narrating Poverty*, 11.

[38] Clemens Sedmak, *Dichte Beschreibungen: Erzählte Armut; Vom Wert der Literatur für die Armutsforschung* (Salzburg: Facing Poverty: Working Papers 02, 2003), 48.

[39] Thomas Melle, *3000 Euro* (Berlin: Rowohlt Berlin, 2014). Future references in brackets as (*3000 E*).

[40] Melle, *Die Welt im Rücken* (Berlin: Rowohlt Berlin, 2016), 333. Future references in brackets as (*WiR*).

[41] See Maurice Merleau-Ponty, *Phenomenology of Perception* [1959] (New York: Routledge, 2012).

[42] Julia Wolf, *Alles ist jetzt* (Frankfurt: Frankfurter Verlagsanstalt, 2013) further references in brackets as (*Aij*); Feridun Zaimoglu, *Isabel* (Cologne: Kiepenheuer & Witsch, 2014) further references in brackets as (*I*).

[43] See Roger Fowler, *Linguistics and the Novel* (London: Methuen, 1977), 103.

[44] Kurt Pinthus (ed.), *Menschheitsdämmerung. Ein Dokument des Expressionismus* [1920]. Revised edition (Reinbek: Rowohlt, 1993), 46, 51, 59.

[45] Jens Jessen, "Am Anfang war der Hass. Feridun Zaimoglu: *Isabel*," *Die Zeit* no. 12, March 13, 2014, http://www.zeit.de/2014/12/feridun-zaimoglu-isabel.

[46] Gottfried Benn, *Sämtliche Werke, Stuttgarter Ausgabe*, In Verb. mit Ilse Benn hg. v. Gerhard Schuster. Bd. I: Gedichte 1. (Stuttgart: Klett-Cotta, 1986), 14.

[47] Benn, *Sämtliche Werke* I, 15.

[48] David Herman, *Basic Elements of Narrative* (Chichester: John Wiley, 2009), 136; see also Monika Fludernik, *Towards a "Natural" Narratology* (London: Routledge, 1996); Marco Caracciolo, *The Experientiality of Narrative: An Enactivist Approach*, Narratologia, 43 (Berlin: de Gruyter, 2014).

[49] Erich Kästner, *Fabian* [1931] (Zurich: Atrium, 2006), 42.

[50] Kästner, *Fabian*, 63.

[51] Eibl, *Die Entstehung der Poesie*.

[52] See Niklas Luhmann, *Gesellschaftsstruktur und Semantik: Studien zur Wissenssoziologie der modernen Gesellschaft*, vol. 1 (Frankfurt am Main: Suhrkamp, 1980); *Love as Passion: The Codification of Intimacy,* trans. Jeremy Gaines and Doris L. Jones (Cambridge: Polity Press, 1986 [first published 1982]).

[53] Luhmann, *Love as Passion*, 16.

[54] Luhmann, *Love as Passion*, 15–16.

[55] Eva Illouz, *Why Love Hurts: A Sociological Explanation* (New York: Polity, 2012).

[56] Illouz, *Why Love Hurts*, 111.

Love as Anathema: Social Constraints and the Demise of Desire in Fatih Akin's *Gegen die Wand*

Sarra Kassem

A N IDEA OF LOVE as a power that conquers all prevails in cinematic narratives of romance. Such a representation taps into popular fantasies, yet it is utopian insofar as it overlooks the rigid social boundaries that constrain romantic desires. This article explores the representation of love in Fatih Akin's *Gegen die Wand* (Head On, 2004), which I argue reinforces the inescapable nature of certain norms that are set in place to regulate gender and sexuality, and thereby desire. Despite, or perhaps because of its pessimistic perspective regarding the possibility of transgressing boundaries, which ultimately reaffirms the moral imperatives that govern emotional lives, the film contests some of the most prevalent mythologies of love articulated by popular culture. Specifically, it lays bare how conforming to normative categories, compulsory as it may be, can be compromising and therefore not always conducive to happiness.

The meanings attached to the notion of love and the nature of intimacy have undergone a transformation in contemporary societies.[1] Notwithstanding the dramatic changes that have taken place in the structure of interpersonal relationships, cultural representations of love remain rather narrow, largely defined by classic notions of romance, as Stacey and Pearce point out.[2] Illouz demonstrates how social and cultural developments articulate a new utopia of romance, arguing that the prominence of love narratives in mass culture turned love into one of the most pervasive mythologies of contemporary life.[3] This idea is also asserted by Evans, who argues that "the expectations of romance and sexual pleasure within intimacy are the subject matter of various dream factories of the West which endlessly threaten the fragile possibilities of human happiness."[4] Because love is so widely narrativized through certain conventions, these conventions have come to shape how it is experienced. As Illouz puts it, "culture operates as a *frame* within which emotional experience is organized, labeled, classified and interpreted. Cultural frames name and define the emotion, set the limits of its intensity, specify the norms and values attached to it and provide symbols and cultural scenarios that make it socially communicative."[5] Her observation exemplifies that love is not just an emotion but in fact a cultural practice and, as Jackson too asserts, it is socially constructed.[6]

Acknowledging the constructedness of the notion of love means that its practice is conditioned by a set of norms that are socially and culturally enunciated and may vary across different cultures and different historical moments. Generally speaking, there is a tendency to associate Western cultures with a tolerance and openness in sharp contrast to Eastern ones, particularly Islamic cultures, which are perceived to safeguard more traditional, and even at times archaic, ways of practicing interpersonal relationships. Problematic as such binary divisions may be, it is true that cultural differences do exist. Unlike most Western societies for instance, where dating and sexual exploration prior to marriage are socially accepted, in some Islamic social contexts attitudes are less tolerant towards premarital sex. Likewise, in some Eastern cultures arranged marriages are normalized, whereas in most Western societies the convention is to marry out of love. While such differences reveal that the notion of love is not fixed, there is a set of ideas about love that dominates its cultural representation.

Popular culture contributes to normalizing certain modes of desiring and living out love, while marginalizing others. Because the norms that govern emotional lives are not universal, the respective narratives of love articulated through cultural production also vary across cultures. Studies on Turkish popular cinema, for example, note its fascination with remakes of Hollywood melodramas, which, however, were adapted in order to preserve Turkish cultural norms and values.[7] Notwithstanding such differences, monogamy and the ideal of the heterosexual couple have been systematically valorized relative to alternative relationship models, which even in recent years are locked in marginalized positions, though arguably to a lesser extent than in the past. As Jackson puts it, "it is in heterosexual relationships that romantic love has been institutionalized as the basis of marriage, and it is heterosexual love which dominates cultural representations of romance."[8] Because normative categories are seminal to the love narratives popular culture disseminates, Judith Butler's critique of regulatory regimes that render which modes of desiring and being desired are socially acceptable will be a key heuristic tool in the analysis that follows.[9] Recognizing love as an emotion that is lived out in ways delineated by norms that are culturally enunciated reveals its performative nature. "Part of our contemporary performance of gender is the performance of the lover or the loved, in appropriately gendered ways," observes Evans.[10] Along with asserting the performative nature of love, Evans's argument shows that love is inextricable from gender and sexual politics, and therefore, although the focus of this article is the representation of love, an enquiry into representations of gender and sexuality cannot be omitted from the discussion, not least because in *Gegen die Wand* the narrative of love is determined by the cultural norms about gender that underpin sexuality and desire.

Gegen die Wand

Gegen die Wand tells the story of Sibel and Cahit, two Turkish-Germans who meet at a psychiatric ward after failed suicide attempts. Cahit, an alcoholic drug addict in his mid-forties, is sunk in depression after the death of his German wife. Sibel, in her mid-twenties, was born and grew up in Germany, yet her family considers her to be Turkish, and as such she has to conform to the norms of a traditional Turkish femininity. Frantic to liberate herself from parental control so that she can experiment sexually with different partners, she asks Cahit to marry her. She believes that because Cahit is Turkish her family will accept him, and so she proposes to him a marriage of convenience that will help her to get out of the family home and gain her independence. After the wedding, she moves into his flat. The two of them live together, yet their relationship is platonic and she sleeps with other men. The marriage of convenience turns into a tragedy when Cahit, who ends up falling in love with her, accidentally kills his friend and Sibel's casual lover, Nico, during an argument sparked by an insulting comment Nico makes about her suggesting that Sibel is a prostitute and Cahit her pimp. Cahit is sent to prison and Sibel flees to Istanbul to escape her family's revenge for the offense her adultery brought to the family's honor. In search of salvation she turns to excessive alcohol and drug abuse. One night she gets raped by one of her acquaintances and then stabbed by three men on her way home. She is rescued by a taxi driver. Upon his release Cahit travels to Istanbul to look for her, only to find out that she is now a mother and has a new partner. Sibel visits him at his hotel and they consummate their relationship. He proposes that she leave her partner and follow him to Mersin. She initially agrees but then never shows up at the bus terminal. Cahit takes the bus to Mersin alone.

In *Gegen die Wand* the love story serves as a platform to engage with the social and cultural boundaries that constrain desire. Initially, love is absent from the relationship the two characters act out. It emerges with their separation and practically it remains unfulfilled, given that the two of them never become a real couple. The narrative draws upon several subjects that pervade discourses about love in ways that are worth exploring. Specifically, it engages with gendered power politics in romantic relationships, the tensions that emerge from the juxtaposition of ideals of freedom with the often impermeable, moral imperatives that constrain it, and the role of popular culture in shaping how emotional lives are lived out. Having sketched out the plot of the film, I will move on to explore the ways in which the film reconfigures the idea of male dominance, which according to feminist thought lies at the core of intimate (heterosexual) relationships, before analyzing how the film reinforces the tight set of normative boundaries it initially portrays as suffocating for its subjects. Then I will demonstrate that, pessimistic as the film may be regarding the possibility of transgressing such boundaries, it contributes to deconstructing some of the prominent mythologies upon which representations of love perpetually rest. In the last sections, I will explore the complex ways in which the film converges with representational patterns that demarcate cinematic narratives of love.

Reconfiguring the Rhetoric of Male Domination

According to feminist theorists, even in contemporary Western societies intimate relationships are structured by male dominance, and the practice of love is intertwined with the production of patriarchal power even when it appears to embrace equality.[11] Given that it addresses the cultural norms that constrain Sibel from pursuing her desires, *Gegen die Wand* acknowledges the different opportunities available to (Turkish) men and women to define the terms in which they desire, however, its construction of the heterosexual couple is not constitutive of gender positions that perpetuate the active male/passive female binary. Although it must be stressed that Sibel and Cahit are not a real couple, it is interesting how they both switch between dominant and subordinate positions within their relationship at different points in the film.

Strikingly, Cahit occupies more passive than active roles. He does not volunteer to rescue Sibel. She persuades him into a marriage of convenience and sets up the rules of their relationship. The depiction of his disempowered position marks a departure from dominant representations of gender roles within intimate relationships. And yet the emphasis the film puts on how his lack of control becomes a source of frustration for him, resulting in violent outbursts as he tries to assert his masculinity, illustrates how social norms regarding how a gendered subject should act generate tensions.[12] Sibel's character is also subversive to some degree. According to Giddens, "ideals of romantic love have long affected the aspirations of women more than those of men."[13] This idea is contested in *Gegen die Wand*, where Cahit is presented as aspiring to a more conventional relationship, whereas Sibel is impelled by her desire to live out her sexuality outside the romantic ideal. Her much-quoted statement at the beginning of the film, "Ich will leben, ich will tanzen, ich will ficken. Und nicht nur mit einem Typen," explodes the concept of a modest, veiled femininity commonly associated with representations of Muslim women.[14] This representation echoes Gidden's theoretical work, which argues that in contemporary societies women too claim their right to structure their sexual lives in ways that in the past were reserved for men.[15] Nevertheless, the film stresses that Sibel's sexual behavior is not socially acceptable in the traditional Turkish milieu that surrounds her. She is ostracized by her family when they discover her infidelity. Earlier in the film there is a scene in which her brother and his friends talk about their visits to prostitutes to satisfy sexual fantasies they think are not appropriate to practice with their wives, which shows that adultery is not prohibited for Turkish males. This contrast reveals the hypocrisy of cultural norms. In that sense, although the portrayal of Sibel's family's brutal response to her "promiscuity" adheres to the status quo, a critical point of view is also presented.

Stereotypes of masculinity are undermined in the film, given that Cahit does not fit the conventional profile of a hero. In fact, given his self-destructive behavior, he is portrayed as much more vulnerable and in need of rescue than Sibel is. However, much as the portrayal of the power dynamics that govern their relationship appears to resist representations of dominant males and disenfranchised women who live out their sexuality and thereby love lives in ways that are pre-modern, on closer inspection the film also propagates patriarchy, and herein lie some of its most apparent ambiguities. The sexuality Sibel desires is at odds with the norms of Turkish culture and therefore has to be tamed for the prevailing status quo to reassert itself. The threat she represents is neutralized by the end of the film, as she gradually conforms to a more traditional female role, that of a mother. Before conforming to this role, though, she is "punished" for her deviant sexuality, which does not accord with accepted standards. Upon her arrival in Istanbul Sibel's self-destructive behavior renders her the subject of violence. What makes her "punishment" particularly interesting is that the film represents it as self-inflicted, a result of her increasingly desperate attempts to challenge the sexual norms of patriarchal Turkish society, which causes her to seek out and provoke more and more dangerous situations. Her acts become increasingly self-destructive and this is brought out particularly during the scene of her assault, where she keeps on provoking the three men to beat her. Her rape and assault exposes her vulnerability and dissociates her representation from the notion of a powerful femininity she appeared to personify, revealing its illusionary nature.

Sibel's subordinate position is also asserted earlier in the film when she proposes to Cahit to marry her in order to liberate herself. The fact that she imposes her rescue upon him gives her a degree of agency, yet her marriage proposal also stresses the social boundaries that restrict her freedom. To gain her independence she has to get married, and although she is using Cahit to liberate herself, her "emancipation" depends on him. Most notably, her staging of a marriage is not a revolt against paternal control. It is a way out of that control without breaking her ties with her family, and this makes her reluctance to act against social norms manifest.

The ambiguities inscribed in her representation make it hard to discern to what extent she subverts the stereotype of a disenfranchised femininity.

The Impossibility of Transgression

In contemporary (Western) societies marriage and love have acquired new meanings. More specifically, during the second half of the twentieth century alternative models of kinship emerged and others that might have been deemed deviant in the past started to become normalized. A liberalization of love has occurred, and sexuality entered a realm of freedom that was inconceivable a few decades ago, as Giddens asserts. For Giddens, the emergence of what he calls "plastic sexuality," meaning a sexuality decentered from reproduction and thereby also from the male experience and the heterosexual couple, is key to the transformation that structures of intimacy have undergone.[16] Nevertheless, certain conditions are still relevant. As Evans observes, "we no longer assume that heterosexual relations have to be regulated and organized through marriage, but we do expect that marriage is constructed through love."[17] The marriage Sibel and Cahit act out is not grounded on mutual love, monogamy, and the prospect of reproduction. Sibel marries Cahit in order to gain the freedom to have multiple lovers, and in doing so she deviates not only from the norms of Turkish femininity but also from both Western and Islamic normative definitions of a wife. Such a marriage is fundamentally at odds with dominant ideologies and therefore threatening to the institutional arrangement of romance that society is intent on maintaining. The film is affirmative of the dominant model of marriage given that it reinforces that the relationship Sibel and Cahit have in the beginning is not sustainable. While in the beginning both have other sexual partners, this becomes a source of frustration for Cahit when he falls in love with her. Not only does he become jealous about her encounters with other men, but he also becomes frustrated about the boundaries she puts between them. For example, she resists sleeping with him because in her view this would truly make her his wife and therefore she would no longer be able to sleep with other men. Her argument exemplifies that her ideas about marriage adhere to the dominant model, too. The tragic developments that follow and the fact that a happy-ever-after ending is forever deferred as Sibel decides to forsake her desires and fulfill her maternal duty reinforce the prevailing social order.

The way the romance between the two characters evolves reveals the film's entrapment in rigid moral structures. Capturing the demise of their relationship, the film paints a bleak picture regarding the possibility of transgressing dominant models across both cultural contexts; Germany and Turkey are equally hostile to their relationship. Sibel's cousin Selma, an emancipated woman living in Turkey, does not approve of their sham marriage. She tells Sibel that she could identify alternative ways of claiming her freedom than getting married. Cahit's German friends, Maren and Nico, are also unable to comprehend the nature of Sibel and Cahit's relationship, that is, the fact that they are married but Sibel is sleeping with other men. This shows how both societies find the kind of relationship they are trying to live out incomprehensible and unacceptable. Strikingly, their relationship not only does not blend into the dominant social fabric, but it is even inconceivable within the subcultural milieu they inhabit.

Instead of representing romantic relationships in ways that suggest they can also be lived differently, the film would appear to uphold the authority of a narrow set of relationship models that have established themselves as normal, reproducing the ideal of the monogamous heterosexual couple. The alternatives embodied by Selma, who is a divorced, independent and professionally successful Turkish woman, and Maren, who maintains a casual sexual relationship with Cahit outside the dominant relationship model, are not celebrated by the film. Their representation underscores their loneliness, hence the alternatives they embody are presented as unfulfilling in the final instance; Selma lives alone and is implied that her existence is determined solely by her commitment to her job, and although there is little information in the film about Maren's life, she is mostly filmed drinking alone. As Leal and Rossade put it, "*Gegen die Wand* rejects the idea that independent women who choose not to define themselves through heterosexual relationships can achieve happiness."[18]

Because the film does not pin down the rupture of Sibel and Cahit's relationship to constraints imposed by others in their social environment, but to their own entrapment in normative understandings of what intimate relationships entail, it reinforces that certain norms are so deeply embedded that breaking free from them is far more difficult than it seems. Cahit maintains a no-strings-attached relationship with Maren, yet he is unable to break free from normative arrangements of marriage and live out his relationship with Sibel differently, presumably because he ultimately gets emotionally attached to Sibel. Sibel's perceptions of love, marriage, and sexuality are also imbued with contradictions that are worth underlining. Even though a conventional marriage is not what she desires, she appears to be assuming more traditional roles when she transforms Cahit's apartment into a mainstream site of courtship or when she cooks traditional Turkish meals for him. The scene where she prepares the traditional meal for him marks a pivotal shift in the representation of the two characters, and it is therefore worth exploring in more detail. There are two cooking sequences in *Gegen die Wand*. The first follows shortly after Sibel moves to Cahit's apartment. In this scene, Cahit prepares dinner and Sibel is dancing as they listen to the song "Temple of Love" by The Sisters of Mercy. On its own, the scene holds little significance with regard to the politics of intimacy negotiated in the film, yet its connotations become very significant when examined in relation to the second cooking scene, where the gendered division of domestic life is reversed. The second scene is sonically embellished by Sizen Aksu's pop song "Yine mi çiçek," which, as a Turkish song, contributes to creating a more "oriental" atmosphere and to underscoring a Turkishness that was absent from the earlier scene of Cahit preparing dinner for her. In this second scene, the camera follows Sibel doing the shopping in a small Turkish grocery store and preparing a traditional meal for Cahit. This time he sits back, gazing at her and sipping Raki. The very different composition of the two scenes underscores that from their start as an unconventional couple, Sibel and Cahit are gradually assuming more traditional gender roles (which are also aligned with Turkish cultural norms). This is particularly interesting in relation to Sibel, as in this scene she is represented in the role of a Turkish housewife, which is incompatible with her desire to not live out her interpersonal life in such terms. Herein lies the scene's complexity, as it lays bare that she has internalized certain norms much more than she would like to believe.

Her internalization of the moral principles that govern marriage is asserted when she resists sleeping with Cahit in order to preserve her sense of autonomy and independence. Getting sexually involved with him would affirm their marriage as real and therefore become an obstacle to the liberal sexuality she cherishes. Her perceptions regarding what a marriage entails (namely lifelong monogamy) underpin her resistance to a conventional marriage. This shows how Sibel's perceptions of relationships are highly circumscribed by the cultural norms she has inherited from her familial environment. Her decision to not leave her new partner should also be examined in relation to her rigid understanding of relationships. Given his alcohol and drug abuse, Cahit does not adhere to conventional definitions of a model husband and father, and this influences Sibel's decision not to leave her current partner; it is the laughter of her daughter playing with her father that makes her reconsider her decision to run away to be with Cahit. Ultimately, the film reinforces the social norms that determine the conditions of her existence. In doing so, it asserts the inescapability of certain kinds of culturally conditioned behaviors and therefore the impossibility of breaking out of normative categories. Underscoring that either cultural expectations or their own assumption of traditional roles will always bind Cahit and Sibel to certain modes of being, the film's critique of oppressive normative pressures to conform to certain roles is undone by its reluctance to let the two characters transgress social boundaries.

Happily-Ever-After: Deconstructing the Myth

The love narrative in *Gegen die Wand* eschews a happy ending. The relationship between them is portrayed as harmful to their well-being, and in this context, their separation is deemed essential to their survival. And yet, even though at the end of the film both lead lifestyles that are healthier, it is not suggested that they are happy. Cahit may no longer be permanently intoxicated but he is mostly filmed doing things on his own, which stresses his loneliness. The conventional relationship in which Sibel settles is socially acceptable, yet she never appears together with her new partner, which underscores that he is possibly emotionally insignificant to her. Her decision reflects a shift towards a more pragmatic set of choices, which, however, is represented as a compromise that runs counter to cultural models of romantic happiness. Conventional relationship models, compulsory as they may appear to be in the film, are not wholly valorized. *Gegen die Wand* questions their dominant construction as a source of fulfillment for the subject, making manifest how conforming to such relationships can also be bound with a failure to deliver happiness. This contributes to making a poignant critique of normative categories, but because no viable alternatives are portrayed, the narrative is less subversive than it may initially appear.

Another aspect that limits the film's subversive potential is the framework within which the characters' failure to reach romantic happiness is negotiated. Illouz proposes that it is essential to dissociate romantic misery and the failures of our emotional lives from weak psyches or dysfunctional personalities and focus instead on how institutional arrangements as well as the social and cultural tensions and contradictions that have come to structure modern selves and identities contribute to such failures.[19] *Gegen die Wand* illustrates how the juxtaposition of different norms regarding love, desire, and sexuality (which the film organizes into a binary division of traditional Turkish/modern German) becomes a source of tension. However, the film's critique of the social dimensions of the characters' unhappiness is disempowered by its emphasis on their dysfunctional personalities.

Fisher and Prager argue that in *Gegen die Wand* self-destruction is linked to the social isolation felt by the two characters, and that the film "is more concerned with their social wounds than their individual psychologies."[20] However, such an interpretation is difficult to sustain because even if social circumstances trigger their distress, the film ends up authorizing a dissociation of their struggle from social pathologies, given that their representation is defined by the mental disorders they suffer from. Both Sibel and Cahit are introduced in the narrative through their suicide attempts. Their recurring use of self-harm and violence along with their alcohol and drug abuse, which is presented not as a recreational behavior but as a means of coping with their distress and a form of escapism, suggest that they have identified very dysfunctional ways of dealing with their emotions.

Because of the multiple ambiguities inscribed in the film it is difficult to reach any firm conclusions regarding the ideological frameworks that inform its depiction of intimacy. On the one hand it appears to portray monogamous heterosexuality as compulsory, yet by revealing that love or marriage are not always entwined with happiness, the story the film tells runs counter to dominant representations of romance, which in most cases assert that love conquers all and is the ultimate source of happiness. Instead, it offers a set of images of intimacy that is multidimensional, informed by the apparent contradictions inherent in human nature and in the social structures that delineate romantic relationships in certain ways while excluding others.

Converging with Turkish Popular Culture

So far the analysis has focused on the representation of interpersonal relationships in the film. The second part of this essay looks at how these representations converge with narratives of love articulated by popular culture, more specifically Turkish popular cinema and Hollywood. In its construction of an ill-fated passionate love story, *Gegen die Wand* pays homage to Turkish popular culture. As Dönmez-Colin observes, *Gegen die Wand* "possesses the usual elements of Turkish melodrama from Kara Sevda (dark passion) and rape to honour."[21] This is made manifest in the Turkish songs of the soundtrack where the lyrics talk about the agony inflicted by passionate love, what in Turkish popular culture is described as *kara sevda*. The Turkish word "sevda" means love, and *kara sevda*, according to Suner, can be translated as "dark passion," referring to intense, passionate love.[22]

The East/West binary and the tensions engendered by the juxtaposition of Islamic traditions and Western norms that drive the narrative of *Gegen die Wand* are subjects commonly addressed by Turkish melodramas.[23] The film's representation of Sibel, for instance, adheres to Turkish cinematic constructions of "fallen women" whose depiction centers on their sexual desires, which are seen as "promiscuous." In Turkish films such women are portrayed as doomed to never find happiness, which is also true of Sibel, given that the film finishes with her in an unfulfilling relationship, alienated from her own self.

Parallels with Turkish melodrama can be drawn also with regard to the symbolic connotations attached to the different sites where the plot is set. As Gürata demonstrates, female roles in Turkish melodrama, especially films from the 1960s and 1970s, were associated with the domestic sphere, portrayed as a site sanctified by patriarchal laws. The home was represented as the opposite of the dance hall or the music club, which were the sites where "fallen women" were objects of the male gaze.[24] The different sites where *Gegen die Wand* is set reflect this paradigm. When Sibel goes out, her revealing clothing and sensual dancing instigates the male gaze, yet her behavior in the domestic sphere is much more aligned to patriarchal norms and adheres to traditional ways of being female and Turkish, as has been established earlier. Notably, the film pursues a very similar thematic agenda to that of the typical Turkish melodrama, reconfiguring it though, to provide a less dogmatic version of its motifs and iconography. Unlike most Turkish films, which, as Dönmez-Colin observes, endorse the conservative values of Turkish society, *Gegen die Wand* does not schematically reproduce the binary of the moral East and the corrupted West.[25] Instead, it stresses the failings of both West and East to offer a viable set of options to the two characters for determining their existence.

Gegen die Wand does not shy away from acknowledging the influences of popular culture upon the film itself and upon the characters in the film, exposing the process of imitation through which intimacy is performed. One of the most complex intertextual engagements with Turkish cinema can be evidenced in the use of "Ağla Sevdam," the song that Sibel listens to in the scene where she cuts her wrists, which is a reference to Mustafa Altioklar's *Ağir Roman* (Cholera Street, 1997). In *Ağir Roman* the song embellishes the scene of the main character Salih's suicide, a scene that shares contextual similarities with the respective suicide sequence from *Gegen die Wand*. Out of despair, Salih ends his life in response to his betrayal by Tina, whom he found in bed with another man. Tina takes revenge for Salih's death by killing the man and then punishes herself by committing suicide. Cahit's demise has analogies to the story of Salih. Salih's suicide is induced by Tina's infidelity, similarly to how Sibel's infidelity is liable for the killing of Nico that sends Cahit to prison.

The diegetic use of "Ağla Sevdam" in the scene of Sibel's suicide attempt and the fact that the camera actually captures the CD of the soundtrack of *Ağir Roman* make the citation of the earlier film obvious. The song does not simply cite *Ağir Roman* as a source of inspiration, as Göktürk points out.[26] It also underpins Sibel's identification with Tina, which is particularly interesting because such an identification is not compatible with the representation of Sibel's character and her desires. More specifically, up to that point, Sibel has not expressed any romantic interest in Cahit. It is suggested that she sees their marriage merely as one of convenience in order to pursue her desire of sleeping with other men. Therefore, the suffering she enacts when he is sent to prison appears hyperbolic and not particularly intelligible. This shift in her representation underscores the contradictions that underpin her desires and the complex ways that popular culture shapes how intimacy is lived out. It shows how Sibel is caught between her fantasy of sexual freedom and the romantic plots that popular culture offers even if these do not necessarily reflect her own aspirations of intimacy. Her re-enacting of Tina's tragedy illustrates that she is also drawn to the idea of romantic suffering familiar to her from cinematic love narratives, stressing in this way that these narratives forcefully shape how love is lived out. The spectacle of romantic suffering that the scene offers incorporates irony and pastiche. In this context, this scene shows that Akin is not trapped in the romantic narratives that (Turkish) popular culture disseminates but in fact is strategically using them to comment on their destructive potential and to expose their ambiguous nature.

Converging with Hollywood Melodrama

Melodrama as a genre is quite diverse. Its conventions have been appropriated in multiple ways across different moments in history and different cultural contexts, as Elsaesser points out.[27] Generally speaking, it is a genre defined by emotional hyperbole, meaning plots that involve extremes of polarized emotions: love and hate, joy and despair. These extremes, according to Neale, "mark and are marked by the vicissitudes of desire: its coming into existence, its realization (brief or lasting) or its failure, and in particular the blockages to its fulfilment."[28] In melodrama the quest for love requires the overcoming of obstacles. As Williams observes, the forces that beset the fulfillment of love are presented as more powerful than the protagonists, who are constructed as victims.[29] Depending on the kind of resolutions given in the end and whether there is a tragic ending where the narrative is built upon the protagonists suffering and the context of rupture, or a happy one where love triumphs, "melodrama would appear to function either subversively or as escapism—categories that are always relative to the given historical and social context," suggests Elsaesser.[30] While such a distinction may apply to Hollywood melodramas, it is not strictly the case in other cinemas; in Turkey for instance, the Yeşilçam melodramas of the 1960s largely incorporated tragic endings to assert the authority of traditional values, thereby affirming the status quo of a society that was perceived to be threatened by Westernization and modernization.

Although in terms of motifs *Gegen die Wand* shares startling similarities with Turkish melodramas, its interplay with classical Hollywood melodramas is also worth exploring. As Göktürk observes, music in *Gegen die Wand* "underscores the emotions of the characters and generates affective responses in the spectator, comparable to the ways music was used in classical Hollywood melodramas of the 1950s and 1960s."[31] However, the reality effect of the film is disrupted by the musical intervals that separate each section of the film. The intervals draw attention to the staging of the melodrama and invite the spectator "to step out of the illusionist enactment of the personalized story" and "to reflect on the dramatic action," argues Göktürk.[32] The effect of the interludes has been described as Brechtian, she observes, and this contributes to establish Akin as a successor to Fassbinder in reconfiguring melodrama.

Having said that, the film's reworking of the ideological impetus of the genre deserves unpacking. *Gegen die Wand* echoes the tradition of socially committed melodramas with which the films of Douglas Sirk, Nicholas Ray, or Vincente Minelli have been associated. Most Hollywood melodramas are produced within dominant patriarchal, Western, capitalist discourses and ideologies and reinforce the moral values existing in a given society, demonstrate Elsaesser and Williams, yet these filmmakers work within a genre typically perceived as an escapist form of mass entertainment, to express a critique, as Williams puts it, of the repressed normalcy of the societies in which their films are set.[33] Such films have been inspirational to European filmmakers, including Rainer Werner Fassbinder, who, inspired by the work of Douglas Sirk, also appropriated melodramatic conventions critically. In his BRD trilogy, which consists of *Die Ehe der Maria Braun, Lola,* and *Die Sehnsucht der Veronika Voss,* Fassbinder engages with social tensions in postwar Germany through the personal stories of three different women. In these films he makes use of the formal aspects of melodrama to construct the struggles of his heroines as a spectacle, yet without obscuring the social, political, and economic circumstances that underlie these struggles.

While Akin's ambition to appropriate melodramatic conventions critically cannot be dismissed, a degree of self-contradiction can also be identified. As Elsaesser observes, melodramas typically concentrate on the point of view of the victim, yet in the films of Sirk or Minelli all characters are constructed as victims and in this context the films are placing a critique at the societal level rather than at the level of individual pathologies.[34] *Gegen die Wand* challenges typical dichotomies between victims and villains that habitually underpin character development in melodrama and does not schematically associate victimhood with femininity. Yet, while it is true that both Sibel and Cahit are victims of social forces that dictate how relationships should be, the emphasis put on their dysfunctional personalities individualizes their struggles and undermines the critique of the social barriers that lead to their frustration and to the rupture of their relationship.

In *Gegen die Wand* it is the moral imperatives that govern interpersonal relationships that dictate the characters' separation. Their deviance, which unites them in the first place, ultimately forces them to go separate ways. Their reunion is only very brief because both societies are hostile to their deviant desires. The film criticizes the pressure to conform to socially and culturally defined modes of being and desiring. However, the heteronormative logic is not disrupted, because Sibel and Cahit cannot conceive of repudiating conventional models of courtship. The rupture of their relationship reaffirms the ideological frameworks that underpin the genre insofar as it reproduces the dominant moral structures that regulate romantic desires. Sibel forsakes the hedonistic lifestyle she cherished in favor of her maternal duty, conforming to a socially acceptable female role.

Much as Sibel's compromise reflects a reluctance to disrupt the prevailing status quo that popular culture is intent on maintaining, her domestication is negotiated as a sacrifice of personal happiness, reinforcing in this way that the social norms that regulate desire are inescapable. In view of its lack of a happy ending, the film repudiates the escapism that has largely defined Hollywood melodrama as a genre. The fact that both characters give up on what is presented as an ill-fated love and move on with their lives reflects a pragmatic decision, yet it is also a decision that reinforces their defeat. Pessimistic and grim as such a closure is in that it affirms that non-normative relationships are doomed to fail, it is also disruptive of melodramatic conventions. In *Gegen die Wand* there is no happy ending. But the ending is not exceedingly tragic either. It is left open whether Sibel and Cahit will ever find redemption and happiness or not. In fact, there are several moments of profound emotional intensity in the film, which echo melodramatic conventions, but these are often reworked in ways that run counter to generic expectations. Following Cahit's imprisonment, Sibel slices her wrists, but the following scene pictures her in a hospital having her wounds stitched. Upon her arrival in Istanbul she falls into a loophole of self-destructive behaviors that lead to her rape and assault, but ultimately she regains her strength to live, adopting a conventional lifestyle that is arguably imbued with less excitement in comparison to the hedonistic one she led in Germany, but which appears to be more viable. She does not resist meeting with Cahit when he comes to Istanbul, and briefly she even considers the possibility of running away with him, yet in the end she does not. These moments reflect how she indulges in romantic fantasy and pathos but she does not let them torment her. In a way, these moments tease the melodramatic formula upon which the narrative is built. The narrative revolves around melodramatic conventions, yet it provides resolutions that in the final instance are pragmatic and therefore subverts the melodramatic genre. Herein lies its complexity, which stems not only from its critical engagement with the social processes that regulate love and intimacy as well as the tensions and contradictions embedded in such processes, but also from its playful reworking of the generic platform upon which the film draws.

While *Gegen die Wand* fits within the tradition of critical melodrama, it is hard to evaluate whether its narrative can be regarded as subversive to social norms. More specifically, it is difficult to discern to what extent is it feasible to challenge or question the status quo when working within a genre that is habitually affirmative of prevailing social structures and dominant ideologies. Socially committed melodramas resist simplifying complex social processes and eschew resolutions that are utopian. Drama, however, derives from the impossibility of transcending social boundaries, a resolution that is in itself, at least to some degree, conformist.

Performing Intimacy

As established already, Sibel's representation displays behaviors that are not always compatible, and it could be argued that the contradictions that arise from her portrayal show how her gendered identity is multiply constructed and in flux. The hyperbole that characterizes her behavior exposes how it is performative, in the sense that Judith Butler set out in her study *Gender Trouble* and further elaborated in *Bodies that Matter*.[35] According to Butler, gender is in no way a fixed or stable identity. Rather it is "an identity tenuously constituted in time, instituted in an exterior space through a stylized repetition of acts."[36] Butler argues that although there are several ways of acting out a gendered identity, what one does or does not do is clearly not an individual matter, and certain gender norms are often more rigorously enforced than others. That Sibel's identity is performative is made manifest in the multiple transformations she undergoes in the course of the film. The modest femininity she plays out before her family at the start of the film gives way to a sensual one as soon as she liberates herself. Her obsession with embellishing her sexualized body is reflected in more radical modifications like tattooing her lower back and piercing her belly button. To externalize her until recently suppressed identity as a sexualized woman, Sibel transforms herself into a stylized object of desire, which demonstrates the extent to which femininity is a masquerade. Following Cahit's imprisonment, she discards her troublesome femininity and turns into an androgynous figure. Ultimately, the realization that she must perform her gender in more ordinary ways in order to survive leads to another transformation which more comfortably aligns her with a motherly figure; this time into a womanly but less sensual type of femininity. Sibel's recurring transformations reveal the artificiality of what is thought to be a natural performance. The hyperbole that characterizes some of her transformations however, also stresses her inability to identify more subtle ways of performing her gender.

Butler's use of the notion of performativity was originally developed in relation to gender and sexuality. However, it is a concept that can be extrapolated to theorizing the notion of love, not least because this is also largely interwoven with politics of gender and sexuality and as such is also subject to the same social and cultural norms that regulate how a gendered body should act. Recognizing love as being performative, tenuously constituted through a stylized repetition of acts, means that the ways it is lived out are not natural but re-enact narratives that prevail in each cultural context.

An understanding of love as a social construct and a matter of doing suggests that there are multiple ways that intimacy can be lived out, yet what one does or does not do is subject to tightly circumscribed social and cultural norms. Johnson argues that love "is enacted through a socially mediated set of beliefs and practices that reproduces a particular set of conditions—the conditions of heterosexuality" and "impels people to form monogamous relationships, have sex, and produce children."[37] Through its representation of the impact of cultural constructions of love, gender, and sexuality upon its subjects, the film stresses how certain norms, disseminated by popular culture, condition the way love is lived out. However, the film does not unsettle this normative order, since it ultimately deems alternative modes of doing to be unviable.

Conclusion

The narrative of love in *Gegen die Wand* draws upon generic conventions that echo both Turkish and Hollywood melodramas, adhering to representational patterns distinctive of how love is narrativized by popular culture. As the analysis has shown, its representation of love is also largely defined by the ideological frameworks popular culture produces, which are, in most cases, affirmative of the status quo. Specifically, the film tells a story that reiterates the monogamous ideal of the heterosexual couple. Given the changes that have taken place in the nature of romantic relationships and which have resulted in a pluralization of intimate relationships, the film's approach would appear reactionary, in that it does not portray alternative ways of living out love as viable. At the same time, though, revealing how the characters' perceptions are distorted by fictional constructions of love, *Gegen die Wand* undertakes a tangible critique of the narratives of love popular culture reinforces, although the film also reiterates these narratives. What makes it different from other cinematic texts is that it acknowledges that the characters' failure to live out a relationship that is viable could be down to their internalization not only of normative categories but also of notions of intimacy that are cinematic rather than real. In this way, the performative nature of intimacy is revealed, showing how this is based on a re-enactment of popular ideas of what constitutes being in love.

The binary of modernity versus tradition that informs the narrative is imbued with more complexity, reworked in ways that are less schematic in comparison to other cinematic texts that draw upon the trope of female oppression in Islamic cultures. The characters' perception of interpersonal relationships is shaped by both liberal and more traditional ideas, and the film shows how the juxtaposition of different and to a large extent conflicting norms becomes a source of tension for the characters. Showing how both Turkey and Germany are unable to accommodate their relationship with each other, it reaffirms that social norms across the ethnic divide are anathema to the modes of being the two characters desire. While this representation defies the binary of archaic East versus tolerant West, it is a representation ostensibly affirmative of normative modes of being and desiring, deeming alternative ways of performing intimacy inconceivable. The film shows that social norms can be oppressive and responsible for what Illouz names romantic misery, yet it would appear to propose that conforming to these norms is compulsory.[38] In that respect, the film is rather pessimistic in its perspective regarding the possibility of transgressing social boundaries. Much as the two characters appear to view the cultural norms that regulate desire as suffocating, ultimately the film suggests that both have been socialized in ways that make it impossible to break free from the norms that oppress them.

Rendering certain ways of experiencing intimacy impossible, the film subscribes to the limited repertoire of images of romance that popular culture disseminates. Despite its reluctance to challenge the hegemonic ideal of the monogamous heterosexual couple, the film unsettles popular narratives of love. Through a narrative where settling down in conventional relationships is not connected with happiness but in fact reflects a failure to transcend social boundaries, the film questions utopian representations of love that prevail in popular culture. Deconstructing the myth of "love conquers all," it offers a pragmatic representation that exposes how love might be constrained by the moral imperatives at work in both Western and Eastern social contexts.

Notes

[1] Anthony Giddens, *The Transformation of Intimacy: Sexuality, Love and Eroticism in Modern Societies* (Cambridge: Polity Press, 1993). Eva Illouz, *Why Love Hurts: A Sociological Explanation* (Cambridge: Polity Press, 2012).

[2] Lynne Stacey and Jackie Pearce, "The Heart of the Matter: Feminists Revisit Romance," in *Romance Revisited*, ed. Lynne Stacey and Jackie Pearce (London: Lawrence & Wishart, 1995), 11–45.

[3] Eva Illouz, *Consuming the Romantic Utopia: Love and the Cultural Contradictions of Capitalism* (Berkeley: University of California Press, 1997).

[4] Mary Evans, *Love: An Unromantic Discussion* (Cambridge: Polity Press, 2003), 5.

[5] Illouz, *Consuming the Romantic Utopia*, 3–4.

[6] Stevi Jackson, "Women and Heterosexual Love: Complicity, Resistance and Change," in *Romance Revisited*, ed. Stacey and Pearce, 49–62.

[7] Savaş Arslan, "Tootsie meets Yeşilçam: Narration in popular Turkish Cinema," in *Storytelling in World Cinemas, Volume 1–Forms*, ed. Lina Khatib (New York: Columbia University Press, 2012), 25–33.

[8] Jackson, "Women and Heterosexual Love: Complicity, Resistance and Change," 49.

[9] Judith Butler, *Gender Trouble: Feminism and the Subversion of Identity* (New York: Routledge, 1990); Judith Butler, *Bodies that Matter: On the Discursive Limits of "Sex"* (New York: Routledge, 1993).

[10] Evans, *Love: An Unromantic Discussion*, 15.

[11] Wendy Langford, *Revolutions of the Heart: Gender, Power and the Delusion of Love* (London: Routledge, 1999), 10–13.

[12] As Giddens too observes, even though the nature of intimate relationships has been subject to changes, for some men it is still difficult to come to terms with an increasingly democratized sphere of personal life. Giddens, *The Transformation of Intimacy*, 2.

[13] Giddens, *The Transformation of Intimacy*, 2.

[14] Moreover, her naked body features prominently in the film, contradicting the mystique with which images of the "oriental" woman are so often imbued.

[15] Giddens, *The Transformation of Intimacy*, 1.

[16] Giddens, *The Transformation of Intimacy*, 2.

[17] Evans, *Love: An Unromantic Discussion*, 21.

[18] Joanne Leal and Klaus-Dieter Rossade, "Negotiating Gender, Sexuality and Ethnicity in Fatih Akın's and Thomas Arslan's Urban Spaces," *German as a Foreign Language* 3 (2008): 59–87, here 75.

[19] Cf. Illouz, *Why Love Hurts*, 4.

[20] Jaimey Fisher and Brad Prager, *The Collapse of the Conventional: German Film and Its Politics at the Turn of the Twenty-First Century* (Detroit, Michigan: Wayne State University Press, 2010), 24.

[21] Gönül Dönmez-Colin, *Turkish Cinema: Identity, Distance and Belonging* (London: Reaktion, 2005), 75. See also Daniela Berghahn, "Seeing Everything with Different Eyes: The Diasporic Optic of Fatih Akin's *Head-On*," in *New Directions in German Cinema*, ed. Paul Cooke and Chris Homewood (London: I. B. Tauris, 2011), 235–51.

[22] See Asuman Suner, "Dark Passion: Fatih Akin's 'Head On,'" *Sight & Sound*, 15, no. 3 (2005): 18–21.

[23] *Sana Dönmeyecegim* (I Will Never Return to You, 1969), *Kinali Yapincak* (Golden Red Grape, 1969), *Kara Gözlüm* (My Dark-Eyed One, 1970), and *Dağdan Inme* (Came Down from the Mountains, 1973) are exemplary, according to Erdoğan, of Turkish cinema's fascination with the East/West binary, which was in most cases reworked in conjunction with class differences as well as other binary divisions such rural/urban or secular/Islamic. See Nezih Erdoğan, "Narratives of Resistance: National Identity and Ambivalence in the Turkish Melodrama between 1965 and 1975," *Screen* 39, no. 3 (1998): 259–71.

[24] Ahmet Gürata, "Translating Modernity: Remakes in Turkish Cinema," in *Asian Cinemas: A Reader and Guide*, ed. Dimitris Eleutheriotis and Gary Needham (Edinburgh: Edinburgh University Press, 2006), 242–54.

[25] Dönmez-Colin, *Turkish Cinema*, 143.

[26] Deniz Göktürk, "Sound Bridges: Transnational Mobility as Ironic Melodrama," in *European Cinema in Motion: Migrant and Diasporic Film in Contemporary Europe*, ed. Daniela Berghahn and Claudia Sternberg (Basingstoke: Palgrave Macmillan, 2010), 215–34, here 223–24.

[27] Thomas Elsaesser, "Tales of Sound and Fury: Observations on the Family Melodrama," in *Film Genre Reader III*, ed. Barry Keith Grant (Austin: University of Texas Press, 2003), 366–95, here 367.

[28] Steve Neale, "Melodrama and Tears," *Screen* 27 no. 6 (1986): 6–23, here 12.

[29] Linda Williams, "Melodrama Revised," in *Refiguring American Film Genres: Theory and History*, ed. Nick Browne (London: University of California Press, 1998), 42–88, here 42.

[30] Elsaesser, "Tales of Sound and Fury," 370.

[31] Göktürk, "Sound Bridges: Transnational Mobility as Ironic Melodrama," 221.

[32] Göktürk, "Sound Bridges," 221.

[33] Williams, "Melodrama Revised," 44. Elsaesser, "Tales of Sound and Fury," 390.

[34] Elsaesser, "Tales of Sound and Fury," 457.

[35] *Gender Trouble*, 140, and Butler, *Bodies that Matter*.

[36] Butler, *Gender Trouble*, 140.

[37] Paul Johnson, *Love, Heterosexuality and Society* (New York: Routledge, 2005), 1–2.

[38] Illouz, *Why Love Hurts*, 1–7.

Contributors

ESTHER K. BAUER is Associate Professor of German at Virginia Polytechnic Institute and State University. Her research specializes in German literature, art, and culture since the second half of the nineteenth century, particularly the interwar years and today. She is the author of *Bodily Desire, Desired Bodies: Gender and Desire in Early Twentieth-Century German and Austrian Novels and Paintings* (2014), and has published widely on subjectivity, gender, desire, sexuality, aging, and visualizations of bodies in works by Thomas Mann, Franz Kafka, Vicki Baum, Max Frisch, Judith Hermann, Alain Claude Sulzer, Egon Schiele, Otto Dix, and Christian Schad.

SVEN GLAWION is currently Post-Doctoral Fellow at the University of Brasília. He completed his PhD at the Humboldt University in Berlin in 2011, and from August–September 2016 was Professor Substituto at the University of Brasília. His research interests are German literature from the nineteenth and twentieth centuries, Gender Studies, and Queer Theory. He is the author of *Heterogenesis: Männlichkeit in deutschen Erzähltexten 1968–2000* (2012), and editor of *Erlöser: Figurationen männlicher Hegemonie* (with Jana Husmann-Kastein and Elahe Haschemi Yekani, 2007) and has published on constructions of masculinity in German literature.

SILKE HORSTKOTTE is Marie Skłodowska-Curie Research Fellow at the University of Warwick. She received her doctorate and her professorial qualification at the University of Leipzig, and held visiting professorships at Tübingen, Cologne, Leipzig, and the Memorial University of Newfoundland (Canada). Her work combines interests in contemporary German literature, narratology, religion and literature, and visual studies. She is the author of four monographs, on contemporary German literature (*Gegenwartsliteratur: Eine Einführung*, with Leonhard Herrmann, 2016), narratology in comics (*Focalization in Action*, with Nancy Pedri, currently under review), photography in fiction (*Nachbilder: Fotografie und Gedächtnis in der deutschen Gegenwartsliteratur*, 2009), and on the Romantic poet Clemens Brentano (*Androgyne Autorschaft: Poesie und Geschlecht im Prosawerk Clemens Brentanos*, 2004), and has published numerous articles as well as six edited collections.

SARRA KASSEM holds a PhD from Birkbeck, University of London (2015) on the representation of post-migrants in the films of Turkish-German filmmaker Fatih Akin. She took her undergraduate degree in Sociology at Panteion University, Athens, Greece and her MA in Criminology at Middlesex University, London. Dr. Kassem has been working as a researcher for Euromonitor International since 2006, and is also involved in curating film events. Her research interests involve German film, European cinema, migration studies, and social construction of deviance among others.

Maria Roca Lizarazu is an IAS Early Career Fellow in German Studies at the University of Warwick. She has recently completed her PhD on representations of Holocaust memory in contemporary German- and Austrian-Jewish literature at Warwick and has authored articles on figurations of postmemory in Katja Petrowskaja's *Vielleicht Esther* (*MLR*, forthcoming, 2018), and on renegotiations of trauma in the works of Eva Menasse and Benjamin Stein (*German Life and Letters*, forthcoming, 2019). A book chapter on the works of Gila Lustiger and Nicole Krauss for the collection *Translated Memories: Transgenerational Perspectives in Literature on the Holocaust*, to be published with Wayne State University Press, is in preparation.

Helmut Schmitz is Associate Professor of German at the University of Warwick. He is the author of a study of Hanns-Josef Ortheil's novels (1997) and of *On Their Own Terms. The Legacy of National Socialism in Post-1990 German Fiction* (2004) and has published widely on German cultural memory of National Socialism and the Second World War and on contemporary German literature. His most recent publications include the edited volumes *A Nation of Victims? Representations of German Wartime Suffering from 1945 to the Present* (2007), *Von der nationalen zur internationalen Literatur: Transkulturelle deutschsprachige Literatur im Zeitalter globaler Migration* (2009), *Autobiographie und historische Krisenerfahrung* (with Heinz-Peter Preußer, 2010) and *Narratives of Trauma: Discourses of German Wartime Suffering from 1945 to the Present* (with Annette Seidel-Arpacı, 2011).

Angelika Vybiral is ÖAD-Lektorin at the Department of German Studies at the Comenius University in Bratislava, Slovakia and lecturer at the Department of Romance Studies at the University of Vienna, Austria. Having studied French and German languages, literatures, and cultures in Vienna and the Sorbonne Nouvelle in Paris, France, she graduated in 2010 from Vienna University. She holds a doctoral fellowship of the Austrian Academy of Sciences and is currently finishing her PhD on the genderedness of medical-philosophical discourses in early-nineteenth-century France. She is the editor of *Wissen—Ordnung—Geschlecht* (2011, with Judith Hoffmann); a book chapter on "Weibliche Wachsfiguren" is forthcoming.

Lightning Source UK Ltd.
Milton Keynes UK
UKOW04n2029021217

313754UK00001B/155/P